# The Evolution of Psychological Theory

*A Critical History of Concepts and Presuppositions*

Second Edition
Richard Lowry

Aldine Publishing Company
New York

To Marsha and Heather
*Wie wahr, wie seiend.*

Editor: Kyle Wallace
Project Editor: Barry Katzen
Managing Editor: Robin Solinger
Book Designer: Roberta Landi
Compositor: Maple-Vail
Printer and Binder: The Maple-Vail Book Manufacturing Group

Aldine Publishing Company
200 Saw Mill River Road
Hawthorne, New York 10532

ISBN 0-202-25134-9 cloth; 0-202-25135-7 paper

Library of Congress Catalog Number 81-71339

Printed in the United States of America
10  9  8  7  6  5  4  3  2  1

The fundamental conceptions of psychology are practically very clear to us, but theoretically they are very confused, and one easily makes the obscurest assumptions in this science without realizing, until challenged, what internal difficulties they involve. When these assumptions have once established themselves (as they have a way of doing in our very descriptions of phenomenal facts) it is almost impossible to get rid of them afterwards or to make anyone see that they are not essential features of the subject. The only way to prevent this disaster is to scrutinize them beforehand and make them give an articulate account of themselves before letting them pass.

William James, *Principles of Psychology* (1890)

# Contents

## PART II.  THE NINETEENTH CENTURY

# Preface

Is there any point to studying the historical development of psychological theory, apart from the antiquarian interest of finding out "who said what, when"? This book is offered in the belief that there is. It is that such a study can provide valuable background for a critical, analytical, and—in the healthy, liberating sense of the term—*skeptical* understanding of the psychological conceptions and presuppositions of the present. This has been my aim throughout, and it has determined both the selection of materials and the manner in which they are presented. Although the book is not a textbook in the conventional sense of the term (i.e., "a comprehensive summary of everything a student needs to know"), it was written with students in mind, and I think it could be read with profit by students in a number of areas of psychological study. I must add, though, that it does presuppose a certain advanced familiarity with the standard undergraduate fare in psychology.

Many persons have helped me in the preparation of this book, most of them quite unknowingly. I cannot name them all; the list would be too long. The following, however, must be singled out for special appreciation: Frank Manuel, the late Abraham H. Maslow, Ricardo B. Morant, J. Ronald Munson, Ulric Neisser, the late L. Joseph Stone, and J. R. Strange (who once made me read all 1,377 pages of William James' *Principles of Psychology*). I am also grateful to those students who over the years have taught me that it is one thing to *know* something, and quite another to make it intelligible to others.

My greatest gratitude goes to my wife Marsha and my daughter Heather, to whom I have with great pleasure dedicated the book. Partly it is because of the patience and supportiveness that they have shown toward their resident scholar. But mainly it is for the way they have of reminding me, every day anew, that psychological theory has not yet caught up with psychological reality.

Special thanks are also due to John M. Wander of Aldine Publishing Company, who not only encouraged me to produce this second edition, but also offered useful suggestions about how it might best be done.

Some of the material in this book has been published elsewhere in an earlier form. I wish to acknowledge with gratitude the permission of the *Journal of the History of the Behavioral Sciences* to use portions of my work from "Psychoanalysis and the Philosophy of Physicalism," 1967, III, 2, and "The Reflex Model in Psychology: Origins and Evolution," 1970, VI, 1. Acknowledgment is also gratefully made to the following publishers for permission to quote works to which they hold copyright:

George Allen & Unwin, Ltd., for permission to quote from *The Interpretation of Dreams* by Sigmund Freud, translated and edited by James Strachey, London, 1953; Basic Books, Inc., for permission to quote from *The Interpretation of Dreams,* by Sigmund Freud, translated and edited by James Strachey, New York, 1955, and from *The Origins of Psychoanalysis: Letters to Wilhelm Fliess, Drafts and Notes: 1887–1902,* by Sigmund Freud, edited by Marie Bonaparte, Anna Freud, Ernst Kris, translated by Eric Mosbacher and James Strachey, New York, 1954; The Hogarth Press, Ltd., for permission to quote from *The Origins of Psychoanalysis: Letters to Wilhelm Fliess, Drafts and Notes: 1887–1902,* by Sigmund Freud, edited by Marie Bonaparte, Anna Freud, Ernst Kris, translated by Eric Mosbacher and James Strachey, London, 1954; Holt, Rinehart and Winston, Inc., for permission to quote from *Behavior: An Introduction to Comparative Psychology,* by J. B. Watson, 1914, and from *Elements of Psychophysics: Volume I,* by G. T. Fechner, edited by D. H. Howes and E. G. Boring, translated by H. E. Adler, New York, 1966.

# Introduction

This book is a critical history of the major psychological theories, conceptions, and points of view that have evolved over the past four centuries. Its aim, apart from the bare historical task of telling "who said what, when," is to provide a background for a critical, analytical understanding of the psychological conceptions and presuppositions of the present.

It will perhaps be evident from the modest size of the book that it is not an encyclopedic compendium of the subject. The focus here is on the *mainstream* of psychology's theoretical history; and once we get started we will be following a rather straight course down this mainstream, not often stopping to explore sidestreams along the way. This is certainly not to suggest that none of these sidestreams is worth exploring. Many will well repay whatever study is invested in them; that is especially true, I believe, of a number of twentieth-century sidestreams. A book, however, must have its limits, and such are the limits of this one. I hope that what it lacks in completeness will be compensated by conciseness, coherence, and clarity.

The history of the sciences in general can be divided into three large periods: the *ancient,* beginning with the flowering of Greek philosophical genius about 2500 years ago; the *medieval,* beginning around the year 400 AD; and the *modern,* which began phasing in during the fifteenth and sixteenth centuries, becoming unequivocally established by about the middle of the seventeenth century.

As indicated above, our focus here is on the last of these periods, the modern. In general, the focus will grow sharper and more detailed as we proceed from the earlier parts of this period up through the later. Thus, Part I gives a fairly coarse-grained overview of the psychological thought of the seventeenth and eighteenth centuries; Part II devotes about the same amount of space to a more fine-grained examination of the developments of the nineteenth century; and Part III, the largest of all, is directed to a quite detailed account of the three major theoretical movements of the twentieth century: Psychoanalysis, Gestalt, and Behaviorism. (Each of these parts will be introduced separately when we come to it.) At the end of the book there will then be a fairly brief concluding chapter, in which we stand back from details to consider some general questions concerning the values and pitfalls of psychological theorizing.

And here are a few guidelines that might prove helpful in reading this book. A large part of our interest will be in the *assumptions* by which psychological theories have been guided—their sources, connections, and involvements, and the illuminations and blind spots to which they contributed. For each of the theories that we will examine, therefore, the questions to ask are the following:

(1) What are its basic assumptions, where did they come from, and why were they made? (In this connection, we will be especially watchful of assumptions that stem from philosophical and ideological predilections.)

(2) Are they clearly recognized as assumptions, or just taken for granted as "the only reasonable hypothesis" or "the only view compatible with science"?

(3) What are the facts to which the theory refers? Does the theory take them as they come, or does it retailor them to fit its own pattern? Indeed, are they really *facts* at all, or only the reflections of the theory's prior assumptions?

(4) And overall, just how much of the theory comes from first making assumptions and then chasing them around in logical circles?

These are not the only questions, but they will get us started. They are all biased on the side of skepticism, and that is as it should be; for skepticism—not taking things for granted—is the first step in critical, analytical understanding. It will probably be easy to be skeptical of the theories that we will examine in the first two parts of the book. The difficult thing will be to maintain that attitude when we come to the theoretical movements of the twentieth century, since one or another of these is likely to fit fairly closely with one's own view of what the truth of things really is. Yet that is exactly where skepticism is most needed.

Part I

# The New Beginnings:
# 1650–1800

Some historical periods look back upon the past with a sense of kinship, respect, and sometimes even veneration. The period comprised by the seventeenth and eighteenth centuries was not one of these. On the whole, the intellectuals of these centuries saw the past—at least, the long medieval past—as benighted, superstitious, alien, and contemptible. This was especially true of the philosophers and philosopher-scientists of the period. They saw the medieval past as being so very wrong, so hopelessly muddled and misguided, that there was no alternative but to tear it all down and begin anew. One finds this sense of new beginnings in every sphere of Western intellectual life during the seventeenth and eighteenth centuries, including those where the questions asked were of a nature that we would nowadays call psychological. René Descartes, for example, began his major psychological treatise on "The Passions of the Soul" by saying that there was nothing so defective as what "the ancients" had delivered on this subject, and that he would therefore write as though he were "treating of a matter which no one had ever touched on before me." David Hume wrote that all previous writings might just as well be cast into the flames, as they contain nothing but "sophistry and illusion."

Although the psychological thinkers of this period were not always so free of "the ancients" as they supposed, they did labor mightily, and with some success, to pull down the theoretical structures of the past and raise new ones in their place. With subsequent enlargements and modifications, these new

3

structures proved serviceable well into the nineteenth century; and, indeed, much of the theoretical structure that we inhabit today is built on their surviving foundations.

A large part of these foundations had to do with the fact that the psychological thought of this period, along with just about every other realm of inquiry, was heavily under the influence of the broad philosophical movement known as mechanism. This was the view that the universe as a whole is one vast machine, a kind of cosmic clockwork, and that all its parts and processes are likewise governed by the inexorable laws of mechanical causation. The psychological extrapolation was that these parts and processes include those of mind and body. By the eighteenth century this extrapolation had spawned two distinct though often interwoven traditions, which we will be describing in Chapters 2 and 3 as "mental mechanism" and "physiological mechanism." Both, however, had their origins in the seventeenth century, mainly at the hands of Descartes, Hobbes, and Locke, with some indirect help from Galileo and Newton; and that is what we will examine first, in Chapter 1. These first three chapters will contain a fairly heavy dose of piecemeal theorizings about such things as perception, association, cognition, bodily movement, and the processes of the nervous system. In Chapter 4 we will stand back and take a large view, by examining the new image of human nature in which these and other theorizings culminated by the end of the eighteenth century.

# Chapter 1
# The Seventeenth Century

There is nothing in which the defective nature of the sciences
which we have received from the ancients appears more clearly
than in what they have written on the passions. . . . [What
they] have taught regarding them is both so slight, and for
the most part so far from credible, that I am unable to
entertain any hope of approximating to the truth excepting
by shunning the paths which they have followed. This is
why I shall be here obliged to write just as though I were
treating of a matter which no one had ever touched on before
me.

René Descartes, Les passions de l'âme (1649)

Harm I can do none, though I err no less than they [which
have written heretofore thereof]; for I shall leave men but as
they are, in doubt and dispute: but, intending not to take
any principle on trust, but only to put men in mind of what
they know already, or may know by their own experience, I
hope to err the less; and when I do, it must proceed from
too hasty concluding, which I will endeavour as much as I
can to avoid."

Thomas Hobbes, Human Nature (1650)

Throughout the long period of the Middle Ages (ca. 400–1400) it was scarcely
considered that there remained anything further to be learned about human
nature. There was, of course, still very much which was admitted to be
*unknown*—for of all the mysteries of creation, man was surely the greatest! But

the limits of mere mortal understanding on this important subject had, so it was thought, already been reached; accordingly, what was unknown was considered destined forever to remain so. This attitude endured well into the renaissance period of the fifteenth and sixteenth centuries; and then, with seeming abruptness, we find human nature beginning to be investigated with an optimism and systematic thoroughness unrivaled even by the ancient Greeks. Indeed, there was even talk that human nature might properly fall within the purview of "natural philosophy"—the ancestor of what we now call science— just as surely as might any other "natural" phenomenon.

Of course, it was not only in psychology that this vitalizing transformation occurred. Throughout the several centuries preceding the seventeenth, a quiet but momentous revolution had been taking place within the intellectual life of the West. The seventeenth century inherited the ferment of this revolution, added to it the catalyst of its own genius, and passed the result on to succeeding generations. Alfred North Whitehead has given what is perhaps the best brief characterization of the spirit and greatness of this important century. "It is the one century," he wrote,

> which consistently and throughout the whole range of human activities, provided intellectual genius adequate for the greatness of its occasions. The crowded stage of this hundred years is indicated by the coincidences which mark its literary annals. At its dawn Bacon's *Advancement of Learning* and Cervantes' *Don Quixote* were published in the same year (1605), as though the epoch would introduce itself with a forward and backward glance. The first quarto edition of *Hamlet* appeared in the preceding year, and a slightly variant edition in the same year. Finally Shakespeare and Cervantes died on the same day, April 23, 1616. In the spring of this same year Harvey is believed to have first expounded his theory of the circulation of the blood in a course of lectures before the College of Physicians in London. Newton was born in the year that Galileo died (1642), exactly one hundred years after the publication of Copernicus' *De Revolutionibus*. One year earlier Descartes published his *Meditationes* and two years later his *Principia Philosophiae*. There simply was not time for the century to space out nicely its notable events concerning men of genius.[1]

We cannot pause here to pursue the matter at length, so let it suffice to say just this: In all spheres of intellectual endeavor, from poetry and philosophy to physics and physiology, the historical importance of the seventeenth century can scarcely be exaggerated. For it was in this century that Western intellectual life first became recognizably *modern* in mood, temper, purpose, and presupposition.

Our task in this first chapter will be to space out, as "nicely" as may be possible, the seventeenth century's "notable events concerning men of genius" in the realm of psychology—specifically, of psychological theory.

## RENÉ DESCARTES

René Descartes' (1596–1650) niche in the history of psychology was secured chiefly through his treatment of that most ancient of psychological quandaries, the mind-body problem. For as far back into human history as we can penetrate, humankind seems to have drawn the distinction between *body* on the one hand, and *mind, soul,* or *spirit* on the other. And the mind-body problem, stripped down to its bare essentials, was simply this: What is the nature (or natures) of these two distinguishable components of a person, and what is the relationship between them? Are *body* and *mind* actually two different things, as they seem to be; or are they perhaps simply the same thing as seen from two different perspectives? To deny the first of these in favor of the second constitutes the position of psychophysical *monism.* Conversely, to deny the second and accept the first commits one to the position of psychophysical *dualism.*

Descartes' position on this issue is nowadays often misunderstood—in part, no doubt, because the issue itself has fallen into such undeserved disrepute and neglect. For this reason, we shall do well to begin by putting this misapprehension to rest. Descartes is often spoken of, rather contemptuously, as the father of mind-body dualism. In truth he was no such thing. Descartes did accept the doctrine of mind-body dualism; his psychology could scarcely have been the same without it. But to charge him with its paternity is both inaccurate and misleading. Mind-body dualism had long been a recognized doctrine, explicitly since Plato and implicitly far earlier even than that. Indeed, the whole structure of medieval theology had as one of its cornerstones the doctrine of the immortality of the soul, which was simply mind-body dualism in religious dress.

Hence, whatever else may be said about Descartes, it is by no means true that he invented the doctrine of mind-body dualism. What he *did* do was to take this long-extant doctrine and rework it into a form far better fitted to the times. And, in so doing, he unknowingly laid the foundations for much of what was to follow in psychology for at least the next few centuries. Specifically, what he did was to put forward the theory of mind-body *interactionism.* In its simplest form, the old dualism held only that man is composed of two distinct parts: a *body* and a *soul* or *mind.* Descartes' interactionism accepted this distinction, but it insisted on much else besides.

In pre-Cartesian dualism, the supposed relationship between body and mind always tended to be a little one-sided; for while the mind could easily affect the body, the body could exert only minimal effects upon the mind. During the Middle Ages especially, the body was considered to be a kind of husk, or vessel, which the soul entered at conception, inhabited during mortal life, and departed from at death. The body, indeed, was little more than an instrument (an *organon*) for the earthly pilgrimage of the soul. At times it was held (following the Aristotelian division of things) that there are three distinct souls in men ("nutritive," "sensitive," and "rational"), or at least three distinguishable aspects of a single soul; but in any case it was generally considered that the relationship between body and soul is rather like that between puppet and puppeteer.

As we have said, Descartes accepted the dualistic *distinction* between body and mind (in the seventeenth century there were really no compelling reasons not to); where he differed was in his understanding of the relationship between them. "It is not sufficient," he observed, "that the soul be lodged in the human body like a pilot in his ship, unless perhaps for the movement of its members." Rather, "it needs to be joined and united with it more closely, in order that, in addition to any such motor-function, it may have sensations and appetites and thus constitute a true man." [2] In short, Descartes was suggesting that the old dualism simply did not do justice to the observable facts of human nature. For it is quite clear, he argued, that the body is not merely a puppet of the mind. True, the mind pulls the body's strings; but the body pulls the strings of the mind at times, too. Descartes' interactionism, then, was not an attempt to *separate* body and mind, as is so often claimed, but rather to bring them more closely and intimately together.

This bringing together of body and mind was the major concern of Descartes' principal psychological work, *The Passions of the Soul* (1649). [3] His main argument in this work—that the causal relationship between mind and body is a mutual one—seems almost simple when stated outright. This, however, is only because we are by this time so accustomed to the idea. In the seventeenth century it was a wholly novel conception with wholly novel consequences: (a) One of the most obvious of these was that the soul, the mind, or what have you, now came to be seen in a radically new light. Previously it had been the supreme power behind the throne, the aloof inhabitant of the body which remained virtually unaffected by the conditions of its domicile. Now, on the contrary, it had to be seen as intimately "joined and united" with the body in mutual interaction. (b) A less obvious but at least equally important consequence was that the body, too, came to be seen in a new light. For one thing, the body now became an agent in its own right—a full partner, so to speak, instead of just a habitation. (c) Even more important, though, was this: In specifying the new relationship between body and mind, Descartes deprived the latter of certain functions which it was formerly thought to possess and attributed them instead to the body.

To understand this last point we must go back a bit. We noted earlier that, during the Middle Ages, the soul was usually regarded as comprising three distinct aspects; hence the designations "nutritive soul," "sensitive soul," and "rational soul" that figured so prominently in medieval psychology-theology. Each denoted a class of activities for which it was thought to be responsible. Thus, the nutritive or "vegetative" soul ensured the activities of assimilation and reproduction; its presence was to be found in all forms of life from the lowest (vegetables) to the highest (man). The sensitive or "animal" soul, on the other hand, was held to be responsible for the three powers of sense-perception, desire, and locomotion; it was to be found in animals and man, but not of course in plants. Finally there was the rational or human soul; its responsibilities included rational thought and deliberation, and its possession was the privilege of man alone.

For reasons we shall enter into in a later chapter, Descartes rejected this triparte distinction among souls, arguing instead that the only proper and exclusive function of the mind is thinking. In effect, then, he restricted the conception of the "soul" to what had formerly been regarded as only a single aspect, namely, the "rational soul."

But if thinking is the only proper function of the soul, what now becomes of those functions formerly attributed to the vegetative and animal "souls"? Clearly, they must be functions of the body. And here Descartes arrived at a conclusion staggering in its implications: that the "heat and movement" of the body are functions of the body itself—or, in a word, that the body possesses its own *inherent vitality!* In medieval dualism, it was the soul which gave life to the body and which, upon its departure, took life away again, thus leaving the body in the unfortunate condition known as "dead." To Descartes, on the contrary, this ancient version of vitalism was simply "a very considerable error":

> It arises from the fact that from observing that all dead bodies are devoid of heat and consequently of movement, it has been thought that it was the absence of the soul which caused these movements and this heat to cease; and thus, without any reason, it was thought that our natural heat and all the movements of our body depend on the soul: while in fact we ought on the contrary to believe that the soul quits us on death only because this heat ceases, and the organs which serve to move the body disintegrate.[4]

Thus, to recapitulate: Medieval dualism had held that the vitality of the body depends upon the behind-the-scenes activity of the nutritive and sensitive souls. Descartes, on the contrary, argued that the vitality of the body is an inherent function of the body itself.

At this point we must allow ourselves a moment's digression. The several centuries preceding the seventeenth had been a period of considerable progress in the sphere of mechanical technology. The fruits of this progress had been cumulative, and the inhabitants of the seventeenth century now rightly imagined themselves to be living in the most technologically advanced age that had yet existed. And yet, it was all really quite novel. The result was that seventeenth-century Man rarely failed to be fascinated and amazed by the wondrous workings of mechanical contrivances, while on a larger scale he stood in awe of what he vaguely imagined to be the as yet untapped potentials of the *Machine*.

Thus, to the seventeenth-century mind, Descartes' supposed inherent vitality of the body could mean only one thing: "The body of a living man differs from that of a dead man," he went on to observe,

> just as does a watch or other automaton (i.e., a machine that moves itself), when it is wound up and contains in itself the corporeal principle of those movements for which it is designed along with all that is requisite for its action, from the same watch or other machine when it is broken and when the principle of its movements ceases to act.[5]

The body, in a word, is an *automaton,* "a machine that moves of itself." And from this, two further conclusions also followed: (a) that the living human body is distinguished from all other automata only by the influence upon its actions of the rational soul (i.e., of thinking); and (b) that the living animal body, since it has no rational soul joined to it, is an automaton purely and simply.

In arguing that the animal body is a machine, Descartes put forward the most sophisticated physiological scheme that the world had yet seen. We say "physiological scheme," although in fact it was a scheme of animal behavior in general, for its concern was with "all the movements of the members" of the body, and this, in the last analysis, is what "behavior" is. Hence, though "psychophysiological" is clumsier, it is at the same time perhaps the more accurate term.

At the base of this scheme was a physiological conception that had been gaining steadily in momentum for several centuries. During the preceding two or three hundred years, anatomical observations upon human and animal bodies had been carried out on an unprecedented scale. And on the basis of these observations a number of relatively new anatomical facts had been firmly established. Among these was the conclusion that the organ of the body that is centrally involved in behavior is not the heart or the liver, as had been formerly thought, but rather the brain, for it is the brain that communicates directly with the terminal organs of behavior, the muscles, as well as with the terminal organs of perception, the sense organs, by means of certain fine structures known as nerves. And considering the tubelike character of these nerves, anatomists of the time had no difficulty in imagining them filled with a fluid substance, the "animal spirits," by means of which effects from sense organ to brain, and from brain to muscles, might be mechanically transmitted. Descartes' accomplishment was that he synthesized these various anatomical observations, along with the attendant conjecture about animal spirits, into a fairly coherent view of general bodily functioning. And for the seventeenth century this was a very considerable accomplishment indeed.

With the notion of animal spirits at its base, Descartes' psychophysiological scheme was in effect a theory of nerve-hydraulics. The movement of a limb, for example, occurs when a movement of animal spirits in the brain is transmitted by way of the nerves to a muscle. Perception, on the other hand, takes place when an external stimulus excites a movement of animal spirits in a sense organ, which movement is then transformed (again by way of the nerves) into a corresponding motion in the brain. In these conjectures there was nothing particularly novel about Descartes' psychophysiology; indeed, the notion of animal spirits had been put to such use for quite some while. What was novel was the conclusion he drew from them namely, that the excitation of a sense organ might be mediately communicated by the brain to a muscle, thus eventuating—automatically—in action. Thus his famous example of an involuntary, automatic response:

> If someone quickly thrusts his hand against our eyes as if to strike us, even though we know him to be our friend, that he only does it in fun, and that he will take great care not to hurt us, we have all the same trouble in preventing ourselves from closing them; and this shows that it is not by the intervention of our soul that they close, seeing that it is against our will, which is its only, or at least its principal activity; but it is because the machine of our body is so formed that the movement of his hand towards our eyes excites another movement in our brain, which conducts the animal spirits into the muscles which cause the eyelids to close.[6]

Although couched in terms of animal spirits and the like, Descartes' scheme of nerve-hydraulics is at this point clearly recognizable as an early version—indeed, the prototype—of reflex theory. This, however, is not to say that Descartes originated the notion of "reflex" itself. It had been known for a very long time that there were such things as reflexes. Galen, for example, had accurately described the pupillary reflex as early as the second century. (The term "reflex," on the other hand, does not seem to have been coined until about a century after Descartes.) Owing to their seemingly trivial status, however, they had been all but ignored. Descartes' singular departure was that he proposed such reflexive action as a *model* of behavior in general.

Like all who would view the "behaving organism" as a reflex mechanism, Descartes' immediate problem after stating the generalities of this theory was to account for specifics. Why, for example, does a given stimulus result in one action rather than another? Or conversely, why does a given stimulus sometimes terminate in one action, sometimes in another? Or finally, why does a given action sometimes result from one stimulus and sometimes from another? The problem, in brief, was to account for the regularities and irregularities of the supposed reflexive connections between sense organs and muscles, stimuli and responses.

In this attempt, it can only be said that Descartes failed utterly. The best he could do was to allude feebly to the "natural conformation of [the body's] parts," to the coarseness and mobility of the animal spirits, and to the distensibility of the "pores" through which they have to pass in their movement from sense-organ to muscle. Still, we do not fault Columbus just because he did not go on to discover Kansas; likewise we cannot blame Descartes for falling short on particulars. The important thing is that he posed and creditably defended a radically new idea: that "all the members [of the body] may be moved by the objects of the senses and by the animal spirits without the aid of the soul."[7]

So far we have been speaking only of the machine of the animal body; what now of the machine of the *human* body? As we have noted, the human body is to be distinguished from the animal body only in the fact that it is "joined and united" with a thinking, rational soul. But if the animal machine can get along so well without benefit of a thinking, rational soul, why not the human machine as well?

The truth is, it could. Without its rational soul, the machine of the human body would function just as well as the animal machine. But with it, Descartes argued, the human machine functions even better. For the effect of man's thinking, rational soul is nothing less than to organize and direct the otherwise mindless course of the animal spirits in their progression from stimulus to response. For reasons that we need not enter into just now, Descartes imagined the mechanism for this control to be "a certain very small gland" in the brain (usually identified with the pineal gland), whose slightest movements "may alter very greatly the course" of the animal spirits.[8] This "certain very small gland" served in Descartes' psychophysiological scheme as the locus of interaction between body and mind, for it was here that the body exerted its effects upon the mind, and here equally that the mind affected the body. In any case, suffice it to say that a man without his thinking, rational soul would be as much an automaton as a puppy or a panda; with it, he is a deliberate, rational being.

With this, we may terminate our consideration of Descartes, at least for a moment. In later chapters we shall refer to him frequently. It is true, of course, that his dualism-interactionism has been long and generally abandoned (explicitly at least); it is true also that his automaton theory has been worked and reworked until it is now scarcely recognizable. But the impetus provided by these two new theoretical beginnings can hardly be exaggerated.

### THOMAS HOBBES

An impetus of a different sort was provided by Descartes' English contemporary, Thomas Hobbes (1588–1679). "The minute and distinct anatomy of the powers of the body," Hobbes announced in the introduction to his *Human Nature* (1651),[9] "is nothing necessary to the present purpose." With this, of course, he avoided from the outset Descartes' lengthy entanglement with the mind-body problem. But at the same time he effectively cut himself off from the important conclusions to which this entanglement had led. Where he surpassed Descartes, in both depth and scope, was in his treatment of the "powers of the mind." Of these powers, he noted, "there be two sorts, [a] cognitive, imaginative, or conceptive and [b] motive." We may consider each in turn.

What exactly is involved in an act of perception? Philosophers had been troubling themselves over this question, in some form or another since the Greeks. Essentially, there are but two kinds of answers: the first, that we perceive things directly, or *objectively;* the second, that we perceive things only *subjectively* through the effects which they produce upon us. As is well known, Hobbes argued emphatically for the second of these alternatives.

> That the subject wherein colour and image are inherent, is *not* the object or thing seen.
>
> That there is nothing without us (really) which we call an image or colour.
>
> That the said image or colour is but an apparition unto us of the motion, agitation, or alternation, which the object worketh in the brain, or spirits, or some internal substance of the head.[10]

Now, as we noted with Descartes, the idea that perception amounts to some sort of effect which the perceived object "worketh in the brain, or spirits, or some internal substance of the head" was not a particularly new one. And when the process of perception is conceived of in just this manner, the doctrine of the subjectivity of perception follows inescapably. As might be expected, then, Descartes too had argued for the subjectivity of perception. It was Hobbes, however, who found in the doctrine suggestions of yet further consequences. If perception, for example, is "but an apparition unto us of the motion . . . which the object worketh in the brain," then does it now follow that all other mental occurrences are but these same motions, attenuated and variously combined? The answer, of course, is that it does so follow—providing we assume (a) that *all* mental activity is dependent upon motion in the brain and (b) that *all* such motion derives ultimately from external sources. Descartes had precluded both of these provisions with his assumption of a *res cogitans*— a thinking, rational soul. Hobbes, however, was able to take them entirely for granted, and thus it was that he arrived at the same well-worn doctrine of psychological empiricism that was later elevated by Locke and his followers to the level of a first principle.

Here, then, in general outline, is Hobbes' vision of the power "cognitive, imaginative, or conceptive." The prime movers in this scheme are external objects which cause motion "in the brain, spirits, or some internal substance of the head." When the motion is fresh and lively, it amounts to a perception (or "apparition") of the object that caused it. With time, though, the motion decays, so that it remains responsible only for such things as dreams, imaginings, remembrances, and the like.

It was at this point that there arose a problem with which Hobbes could cope only partially. Any general *scheme* of mental activity must eventually account for the *facts* of mental activity. And for centuries one of the most conspicuous of such facts was that mental activity is orderly and coherent. Some two millennia before Hobbes, Aristotle had remarked upon this coherence and even advanced three principles to account for it: (a) the temporal contiguity of the initial perceptions; (b) their similarity; and (c) their contrast. In point of fact, these three principles seemed to account for the general texture of mental coherence fairly well, and for this reason they survived and were still widely accepted even in the seventeenth century.

Hobbes' problem was that his motion-in-the-brain theory obliged him to reject all but the first of these principles. He could well imagine how motions in the brain might tend to "cohere" by virtue of their initial contiguity (for this required only that motions that begin together remain together), but it was not at all clear to him how such motions could be brought together by reason of their similarity or contrast. Thus, Hobbes' theory of the association of ideas (as it came to be called) was simply the Aristotelian scheme shorn of the principles of similarity and contrast. To put it in his own words:

> The cause of the coherence or consequence of one conception to another, is their first coherence or consequence at that time when they are produced by sense: as for example, from St. Andrew the mind runneth to St. Peter, because their names are read together; from St. Peter to a stone, for the same cause; from stone to foundation, because we see them together; and for the same cause, from foundation to church, and from church to people, and from people to tumult.[11]

Hobbes, of course, was quite convinced from this example that contiguity alone would allow the mind to "run almost from anything to anything." In fact, though, the issue went far deeper than this, and the problem of similarity and contrast troublesomely remained. As we shall see later, psychology was to be vexed by this problem for the better part of the next two centuries.

The second "power of the mind" to which Hobbes addressed himself included what we would today call "motivation." In this regard, it is often said that Hobbes did nothing more than revive the ancient motivational doctrine of hedonism—the theory that all human activity is directed to the achievement of pleasure and the avoidance of pain. Actually, though, Hobbes did far more than just revive the theory; he washed it, smoothed out its wrinkles, and put it into acceptable modern dress. And for Hobbes, acceptable modern dress entailed nothing less than subsuming hedonism under his theory of motions-in-the-brain.

His means for effecting this were grossly inaccurate, but the attempt was a noble one nonetheless. "Conceptions and apparitions," he argued,

> are nothing really, but motion in some internal substance of the head; which motion not stopping there, but proceeding to the heart, of necessity must there either help or hinder the motion which is called vital; when it helpeth, it is called delight, contentment, or pleasure, which is nothing but motion in the head: and the objects that cause it are called pleasant or delightful; . . . and the same delight, with reference to the object, is called love: but when such motion weakeneth or hindereth the vital motion, then it is called pain; and in relation to that which causeth it, hatred.[12]

Thus, motions in the brain may either help or hinder the vital motions around the heart, thereby giving rise to pleasure-love or pain-hate.

This, though, as Hobbes promptly recognized, is only emotion. Motivation is something else again. Hobbes attempted to bridge the gap between emotion and motivation by arguing that

> this motion, in which consisteth pleasure or pain, is also a solicitation or provocation either to draw near the thing that pleaseth, or to retire from the thing that displeaseth; and this solicitation is the endeavor or internal beginning of animal motion, which when the object delighteth, is called appetite; and when it displeaseth, it is called aversion.[13]

Thus, when the vital motions around the heart are enhanced by motions in the brain, there results not only the emotion of pleasure, but also an "appetite" for the object ultimately responsible for this motion; conversely, when the vital motions are hindered, there results an "aversion." From this, it was then only a small step to put forward in new dress the old hedonistic thesis that *all* behavior is motivated by such appetites and aversions.

As earlier with Descartes, we can scarcely avoid seeing in Hobbes' new hedonism a tendency toward behavioral automatism. For behavior, after all, was now simply a function of appetite and aversion; these, in turn, were produced by the effect of motions in the brain upon motions around the heart; and what were motions in the brain but the effects of external stimulation? Indeed, Hobbes' psychology had within it the seeds of an even more thoroughgoing automatism than did Descartes', for Hobbes had no recourse to the effects of a rational soul. The difference, though, was that Descartes argued for his automatism explicitly and in detail; Hobbes, on the other hand, did not. Had he done so, his place in the history of psychological thought would have been much greater.

## DESCARTES, HOBBES, AND THE MECHANICAL CONCEPTION OF NATURE

Descartes and Hobbes would both, no doubt, have resented being characterized as two peas out of the same psychological pod. And yet, their probable resentment notwithstanding, this is precisely what they were. For whatever their differences on specific points might have been, there was one important and far-reaching issue on which they both flatly agreed—namely, that the study of psychology is ultimately a study of *matter* ("animal spirits" or whatever) in *motion*.

It is now time to point out that this emphasis upon "matter in motion" was by no means the novel creation of Descartes, or Hobbes, or indeed of any other psychological thinker of the period. Every age has its vogue ideas, and the vogue idea of the early and middle seventeenth century was just this: that matter and motion constitute the warp and woof of the fabric of nature. Usually this idea is referred to as the "mechanical conception of nature," or, more simply, as "mechanism." For our own purposes, the important thing about mechanism is not whether Descartes or Hobbes originated it, but that they both accepted it and attempted to apply it where it had not been applied before—to psychology.

Granted, these first halting attempts at psychological mechanism were crude and naïve; they amounted, in fact, to little more than a few rough-hewn comparisons with mechanical timepieces, hydraulic systems, levers and pulleys, and the like. In truth, though, they could hardly have been otherwise, for the general conception of matter-in-motion then available was itself crude and naïve. Indeed, the whole of nature rather resembled a great game of billiards; matter was held to exist in the form of discrete corpuscles (literally, "little bodies") which could affect one another (i.e., affect one another's motion) only by coming into direct contact. This was simply an example of the limiting condition to which psychological mechanism is subject in any age, be it the seventeenth century, the nineteenth, or the twentieth: its success or failure depends upon the more general mechanistic conceptions available to it.

Although mechanism was eventually expanded into a philosophy of existence in general, its birthplace and permanent residence was in physics. Its appeal in physics was based upon two features. The first was its promise of systematic parsimony. Medieval physics had been a great tangle of form and substance, essence and attribute, and the like. In its own way, it explained just about everything—but so cumbrously that it eventually began to seem hardly worth the effort. Machanism, on the other hand, promised to account for physical phenomena by way of a single, unitary principle—matter in motion. The second feature was simply that mechanism seemed to do greater justice, and less violence, to the facts. In any case, by the middle of the seventeenth century the general character of the new, mechanical conception of nature had become fairly clear. The world was conceived to be, in the words of Galileo, "a multitude of minute particles having certain shapes and moving with certain velocities." Of this motion, there were considered to be (following Galileo's refurbishing of the old Aristotelian classification) only two kinds: (a) "natural," which was uniform and circular; and (b) "violent," which was accelerated and rectilinear. The second of these, violent motion, was so named because it referred to those cases in which motion was "forced," or transferred from one moving body to another; and this, as we have said, could occur only by way of direct contact.

## THE NEWTONIAN REVOLUTION

This essentially Galilean version of mechanism was, to be sure, a vast improvement upon the physics of the medieval world; nonetheless, it remained in many respects crude and naïve. In the ninth decade of the seventeenth century, however, the mechanical conception of nature, which had theretofore been but an infant, sprang suddenly into its full maturity. It became refined and sophisticated; and in consequence, as we shall see, the mechanistic trend within psychology also became refined and sophisticated.

This momentous development was effected, almost singlehandedly, by that most imposing genius of the seventeenth century, Isaac Newton. Although Newton's accomplishments in this regard were vast and complex, they may be summarized in a few words: In a single blow, he put forward a unified, coherent theory that accounted, with mathematical precision, for just about all the phenomena then of interest to physics—from planetary motions to oceanic tides. We cannot enter here into a detailed treatment of this theory, but two of its more novel and consequential features must not be allowed to escape our attention.

(1) In the earlier mechansim, the ultimate constitutents of matter were regarded as "minute particles having certain shapes." Newton, on the contrary, refined these crude little kernels of matter into infinitesimal, mathematical points. He dealt, that is, not with actual physical entities, but with *ideal constructions;* and in so doing he freed mechanism from the restrictions of dealing only with such things as could be held between thumb and forefinger.

(2) In the earlier mechanism, and indeed throughout the history of physical inquiry, it had been assumed that motion could be communicated from one body to another only by way of direct contact or through a series of such direct contacts. Newton, on the other hand, demonstrated that physical phenomena could be accounted for more fully and precisely if it were allowed that action could also be communicated from a distance, by way of attractive and repulsive *forces*.

Newton's revolutionary physical theory was presented to the world in the late 1680s under the title *Mathematical Principles of Natural Philosophy*. In the preface to this epoch-making work he ventured an opinion which was later expanded by others into a manifesto: "I wish," he wrote,

> [that] we could derive the rest of the phenomena of nature by this same kind of reasoning from mathematical principles; for I am induced by many reasons to suspect that they may all depend upon certain forces by which the particles of bodies, by some causes hitherto unknown, are either mutually impelled toward each other, and cohere in regular figures, or are repelled and recede from each other; which forces being unknown, philosophers have hitherto attempted the search of nature in vain.[14]

## JOHN LOCKE

Among those whose attention Newton's ideas very soon attracted was a countryman of his, John Locke (1632–1704). Already, Locke maintained an avid interest in the relatively new philosophy of mechanism, and he was quite conversant with the earlier mechanistic conceptions of such notables as Galileo and Robert Boyle. What he had heard of Newton's *Principles* intrigued him, but since he did not have (as Newton put it) "good mathematical learning," he had to seek assurance from others that the mathematics it contained could be relied upon. Receiving such assurance, he then proceeded to read the *Principles* for its more general ideas—which he adopted. Several years later, this same John Locke published a work that effected a minor Newtonian revolution within psychology.

Locke's interests in psychology lay chiefly in the sphere of cognitive functioning; hence the title of his principal psychological work, *An Essay Concerning Human Understanding* (1690).[15] At first glance, this work hardly seems to stand in the tradition of mechanism at all. Nowhere, for example, did Locke resort to physiological conjecture. (Actually, now and again he did mention "animal spirits," "motions," and the like, but he never seemed to take them too seriously.) As we shall see, though, this is at first glance only, for, in fact, Locke put forward a psychological mechanism of the most subtle kind—a mechanism, that is, purely of "ideas." Indeed, Locke's "ideas" were much the same sort of ideal constructions as Newton's "particles."

In introducing the *Essay,* Locke found it necessary "to beg pardon of my reader for the frequent use of the word *idea*." He averred, though, that he could not avoid so using it. In any case, he meant the term to be taken only in the neutral sense of "whatever it is that the mind can be employed about in thinking." "I presume it will be easily granted me," he continued, "that there are such ideas in men's minds: everyone is conscious of them in himself; and men's words and actions will satisfy him that they are in others."[16]

Since his concern was with ideas, the objects of thinking and understanding, Locke's first task was to determine whence they arise. And, to do this, he had first to determine whence they *do not* arise. Thus at the outset he undertook to do battle with the ancient doctrine of *innate ideas*. Hobbes had made a similar denial of innate mental contents some forty years earlier, but it was a denial and nothing more, a mere assertion-to-the-contrary hastily passed over in an initial paragraph. Locke, on the contrary, argued against the doctrine at greater length, and more persuasively, than anyone had ever done before.

What need concern us, though, is not that Locke took such great pains to deny the doctrine of innate ideas, but that he took even greater pains to erect an alternative doctrine in its place. This was the doctrine of *psychological empiricism*. Here, again, Hobbes had arrived at the doctrine earlier, but with Locke it received its fullest expression.

> Let us then suppose the mind to be, as we say, white paper, void of all characters, without any ideas: How comes it to be furnished? Whence comes it by that vast store which the busy and boundless fancy of man has painted on it with an endless variety? Whence has it all the materials of reason and knowledge? To this I answer, in one word, from *experience*. In that all our knowledge is founded, and from that it ultimately derives itself. Our observation employed either, about external sensible objects or about the internal operations of our minds perceived and reflected on by ourselves, is that which supplies our understanding with all the materials of thinking. These two are the fountains of knowledge, from whence all the ideas we have, or can naturally have do spring.[17]

Such, then, were the building blocks of Locke's psychology—ideas, which come only from experience. Of these ideas there were two sorts: "simple" and "complex." Of the experiences which give rise to them there were also two sorts: "primary" and "secondary." We shall consider the latter distinction first.

Locke's distinction between primary and secondary perceptual qualities is well known. Less well known is the fact that it derives rather directly from the mechanical conception of nature then fashionable. For the mechanical philosophy, we may recall, held that the *primary qualities* of nature are "matter" and "motion." Hence, any perception involving matter and motion must itself be "primary," while perceptions involving qualities other than matter and motion must be "secondary." Descartes and Hobbes had both argued for the *subjectivity* of perception, but they still failed to arrive at the primary-secondary distinction. It was made quite explicitly, however, by their near-contemporary, Galileo, who observed:

> To excite in us tastes, odors, and sounds, I believe that nothing is required
> in external bodies except shapes, numbers, and slow or rapid movements. I
> think that if ears, tongues, and noses were removed, shapes and numbers and
> motions would remain, but not odors nor tastes nor sounds. The latter, I
> believe, are nothing more than names when separated from living beings.[18]

Locke's statement of the primary-secondary distinction was perhaps less
blunt than Galileo's, but the meaning was quite the same. Those perceptions
involving "solidity, extension, figure, and mobility" are primary, and the
reason they are primary is simply that these qualities, and only these, are
inherent in "external sensible objects." All other perceptions, such as "colors,
sounds, tastes, etc.," are secondary, for they involve "nothing in the objects
themselves but powers to produce various sensations in us by their primary
qualities, i.e., by the bulk, figure, texture, and motion of their insensible
parts."[19]

Hence, as Locke himself recognized, this distinction between primary and
secondary perceptual qualities was not just a psychological distinction, but the
result as well of a "little excursion into natural philosophy."[20]

A second important distinction Locke drew was between simple and complex
ideas. In part, it was a systematic extension of his denial of innate ideas in
favor of psychological empiricism. Locke's psychological empiricism held that
all ideas derive from experience; yet, there were some ideas ("duration,"
"number," "infinity," "power," etc.) which seemed to be too "complex" to
derive from any specific experiences; hence, they must come from a *compounding*
of the "simple" ideas derived from *several* such experiences. Simple ideas, then,
are those ideas that derive *directly* from specific experiences; complex ideas are
those that derive *indirectly* from specific experiences by way of the compounding
of simple ideas.

To the question of how simple ideas come to be so compounded into
complex ones, Locke never offered any very explicit answer; he did, however,
offer an implicit one. In the fourth edition of his *Essay,* Locke added, rather
as an afterthought, a chapter entitled "Of the Association of Ideas." As we
have noted, others before Locke had written on the association of ideas (though
Locke was the first to call it by this name). Locke's treatment of the matter,
however, suggests that he was utterly ignorant of his predecessors. Indeed, he
did not even allude to Aristotle's principles of *similarity* and *contrast,* nor to
Aristotle's and Hobbes' *contiguity.* All he suggested was that "Some of our
ideas have a natural correspondence and connection one with another. . . .
Besides this, there is another connection of ideas wholly owing to *chance* or
*custom.*" In the first case, or so Locke would have it, ideas are truly and
properly associated because they are "allied by nature." Conversely, ideas
connected by "chance" or "custom" are wrongly associated; and it is precisely
such wrong association of ideas that makes for all that "is in itself really

extravagant, in the opinions, reasonings, and actions" of men.[21] Here again, though, Locke was regrettably inexplicit, for he omitted to state just what it was that was responsible for his supposed "natural correspondence and connection" between ideas.

As presented so far, Locke's psychology seems to contain two very important loose ends—namely, (a) how complex ideas come to be formed and (b) what accounts for the "natural correspondence and connection" that obtains between some ideas. The closest he came to tying these ends together was in a later chapter, "Knowledge in General." Knowledge, he wrote, "seems to me to be nothing but the perception of the connection and agreement, or disagreement and repugnancy of any of our ideas."[22] Though inexplicit, the intent of this pregnant little passage is fairly clear: Knowledge consists in the perception of some sort of relationship between ideas. And, of this relationship, there can be two and only two varieties: (a) connection and agreement, and (b) disagreement and repugnancy. It requires no great leap of the imagination to see these as analogous with, and almost certainly inspired by, Newton's *attractive* and *repulsive* forces.

Indeed, it is possible to see the whole of Locke's psychology as a kind of Newtonian cosmos in miniature. The particles or ultimate constituents of Locke's mental cosmos were, of course, the simple ideas. They in turn could, like their physical counterparts, cohere to form aggregate or complex ideas— at times, because of their "natural correspondence and connection one with another," at other times, for no better reason than "chance or custom." Knowledge, finally, was but the mind's perception of whether ideas *naturally,* and by some causes hitherto unknown, are either mutually impelled toward each other (Locke's "connection of and agreement"), and cohere in regular figures, or are repelled and recede from each other (Locke's "disagreement and repugnancy").

Was Locke consciously endeavoring to construct a psychology on the model of Newton's cosmos? To answer this question we should have to raise him from the dead, for while he lived he neither affirmed nor denied it. At any rate, this much is clear: (a) Locke was quite familiar with the Newtonian cosmology; (b) he accepted as true the refined scheme of mechanism that it embodied; and (c) in structure, though not of course in content, his psychology may be aligned almost point for point with the structure of the Newtonian cosmology.

The seventeenth century witnessed the birth or resurgence of a number of important, far-reaching, and distinctly modern psychological conceptions. In the approximate order of their appearance, these were (a) the theory of psychophysical interactionism, (b) the doctrine of the inherent vitality of the body; (c) the idea of behavioral automatism, (d) the argument for the subjectivity of perception, (e) the doctrine of psychological empiricism, (f) the distinction between "simple" and "complex" ideas, (g) the distinction between "primary" and "secondary" sensory qualities, and (h) the theory of the association of ideas.

## NOTES

1. A. N. Whitehead, *Science and the Modern World* (New York: Macmillan, 1925), p. 56.
2. N. K. Smith, ed. and trans., *Descartes' Philosophical Writings* (London: Macmillan, 1952), p. 149.
3. *The Philosophical Works of Descartes,* trans. E. S. Haldane and G. R. T. Ross, vol. 1 (Cambridge: University Press, 1931).
4. Ibid., p. 333.
5. Ibid.
6. Ibid., p. 338.
7. Ibid., p. 339.
8. Ibid., pp. 345–346.
9. *The English Works of Thomas Hobbes,* ed. W. Molesworth, vol. IV (London: John Bohn, 1840).
10. Ibid., p. 4.
11. Ibid., p. 15.
12. Ibid., p. 31.
13. Ibid.
14. I. Newton, *Mathematical Principles of Natural Philosophy,* trans. A. Motte, rev. F. Cajori (Berkeley: University of California Press, 1946), p. xvii.
15. J. Locke, *An Essay Concerning Human Understanding,* ed. A. C. Fraser (Oxford: Clarendon, 1894).
16. Ibid., vol. I, pp. 32–33.
17. Ibid., vol. I, 121–122.
18. M. Boas, *The Scientific Renaissance: 1450–1630* (London: Collins, 1962), p. 262.
19. Locke, *Essay,* vol. I, pp. 169–170.
20. Ibid., p. 177.
21. Ibid., p. 529.
22. Ibid., vol. II, p. 167.

## FOR FURTHER READING

Accounts of the development of psychological thought prior to the seventeenth century are to be found passim in any number of good works on the history of philosophy. Among the best of these, for this purpose, are the first volume of W. Windelband. *A History of Philosophy,* trans. J. H. Tufts (New York: Macmillan, 1901) and the first several volumes of F. Copleston, *A History of Philosophy* (Westminster, Md.: Newman, 1946). Of those accounts which are strictly psychological in scope, the best is still G. S. Brett, *History of Psychology,* 3 vols. (London: Allen and Unwin, 1912–1921), which is now also available in a one-volume abridgment by R. S. Peters (London: Allen and Unwin, 1962). Also to be recommended is R. I. Watson, *The Great*

*Psychologists from Aristotle to Freud* (Philadelphia: Lippincott, 1978). Well-chosen excerpts from pre-seventeenth century psychological writings are to be found in G. Murphy and L. B. Murphy, eds., *Western Psychology: From the Greeks to William James* (New York: Basic Books, 1969); B. Rand, ed., *The Classical Psychologists* (Boston: Houghton Mifflin, 1912); and W. S. Sahakian, ed., *History of Psychology: A Source Book in Systematic Psychology* (Itasca, Ill.: Peacock, 1968).

For an account of the "scientific revolution" that took place during the several centuries preceding the seventeenth, any one or several of the following volumes may be consulted with profit: M. Boas, *The Scientific Renaissance: 1450–1630* (London: Collins, 1962); H. Butterfield, *The Origins of Modern Science: 1300–1800* (New York: Macmillan, 1959); H. F. Kearney, ed., *Origins of the Scientific Revolution* (London: Longmans, 1964); and A. N. Whitehead, *Science and the Modern World* (New York: Macmillan, 1925). An interesting account of scientific revolutions in general, but one which is best studied after a certain background in the general history of science has been acquired, is T. S. Kuhn, *The Structure of Scientific Revolutions* (Chicago: University of Chicago Press, 1962).

Excerpts from the more important psychological writings of Descartes, Hobbes, and Locke may be found in the three above-mentioned "readers" by Murphy, Rand, and Sahakian.

Good accounts of Galilean and Newtonian mechanism, and of the history of physical inquiry in general during this period, are to be found in A. R. Hall, *From Galileo to Newton: 1630–1720* (London: Collins, 1963); and S. Toulmin and J. Goodfield, *The Architecture of Matter* (New York: Harper & Row, 1962).

# Chapter 2
# Mental Mechanism

> I shall not at present meddle with the physical consideration
> of the mind, or trouble myself to examine wherein its essence
> consists: or by what motions of our spirits, or alterations of
> our bodies, we come to have any sensations by our organs,
> or any ideas in our understandings; and whether those ideas
> do in their formation, any or all of them, depend on matter
> or no. These are speculations which, however curious or
> entertaining, I shall decline, as lying out of my way in the
> design I am now upon.
>
> John Locke, *An Essay Concerning*
> *Human Understanding* (1690)

This chapter and the one that follows deal with two aspects of a single theme. For this reason, particularly since they are both relatively brief, they might easily have been combined into a single chapter. The fact that they are presented as two separate chapters is intended to emphasize the separateness of the two courses of theoretical development to which they refer. The psychological thought of the eighteenth century was devoted chiefly to the elaboration and refinement of those mechanistic tendencies that emerged in the seventeenth century. From the very beginning, however, the pursuit of this task split off onto two paths which, though they led in the same general direction, remained throughout the century relatively isolated from one another. One of these approaches, the one that was already evident with Descartes and Hobbes, we shall consider in Chapter 3. In the present chapter we shall follow the path first embarked upon by Locke.

To explain behavior mechanically, Descartes and Hobbes had had to resort to the conjectured motions of animal spirits, in the brain and around the heart. Hence, their schemes of psychological mechanisms were from the outset weighed down with a lot of dubious physiological baggage. Locke, on the other hand, was able to choose another path, for in portraying the mind as kind of Newtonian cosmos in miniature, he freed psychological mechanism from this necessity of bolstering its explanations with physiological conjecture. He did not, of course, use the term "behavior," but it is clear what his statement on the matter might have been. He would have argued that a person's behavior is related to what goes on in his mind, that is, to thinking. Hence, if we can give a mechanical explanation to thinking, irrespective of its physiological accompaniments, we shall thereby provide a mechanical explanation of behavior as well. Locke's psychology, then, would not necessarily ignore physiology, but its foremost concern was with the mental, either experienced in oneself or inferred from the actions of others. It was, in short, a *mental mechanism.*

### GEORGE BERKELEY

In 1705, a society was formed at Trinity College, Dublin, for the purpose of discussing (among other things) "Mr. Locke's New Philosophy," as it was then called. The founder of this society was a certain George Berkeley (1685–1753). Several years later, this same George Berkeley took "Mr. Locke's New Philosophy," rid it of some of its cruder elements, and in so doing made of it a seemingly impregnable fortress.

Berkeley accepted Locke's psychological empiricism and his distinction between simple and complex ideas. What he did not accept was Locke's distinction between primary and secondary sensory qualities. In his *Principles of Human Knowledge* (1710) he wrote:

> They who assert that figure, motion, and the rest of the primary or original qualities, do exist without the mind, . . . do at the same time acknowledge that colors, sounds, heat, cold, and such like secondary qualities, do not, which they tell us are sensations existing *in the mind alone,* that depend on and are occasioned by the different size, texture, and motion of the minute particles of matter. . . . But I desire any one to reflect and try, whether he can, by any abstraction of thought, conceive the extension and motion of a body, without all other sensible qualities. For my own part, I see evidently that it is not in my power to frame an idea of a body extended and moved, but I must withal give it some color or other sensible quality. . . . In short, extension, figure, and motion, abstracted from all other qualities, are inconceivable.[1]

Berkeley's argument against the primary-secondary distinction was lengthy and at times abstruse. Eventually, it led him to the philosophical position of subjective idealism. For this reason, we shall do well to distinguish between its psychological component, which is important for our purposes, and its more general, philosophical overlay, with which we need not further concern ourselves. In the first of these, Berkeley simply pointed out the obvious: Locke's primary qualities have the same *psychological status* as his secondary ones; hence, there is no valid *psychological distinction* to be drawn between them. From this, he then went on to conclude that primary and secondary qualities have the same *ontological status* as well—that they exist "only in the mind."

As a psychological argument, Berkeley's denial of the primary-secondary distinction was simply making explicit what Descartes and Hobbes, before Locke, had already recognized—that sense-perception (and thus ideation) is an entirely *subjective* affair. Locke had argued that primary qualities *correspond directly* with certain features of the external world, while secondary qualities correspond only *indirectly*. Berkeley insisted that both kinds of qualities must be understood as corresponding only indirectly, if at all.

But if primary and secondary qualities are both equally subjective or secondary, then whence derive our notions of "external sensible objects"? So long as it is admitted that at least some perceptions are directly representative of the external world (as were Locke's primary qualities), the question does not arise. Berkeley, however, denied it, and thus the question became inescapable. The answer, according to Berkeley, is that our ideas of "external sensible objects" are complex *constructions,* of which the building blocks are Locke's simple ideas and the mortar Hobbes' contiguity "at the time when they are produced by the sense." Thus:

> Sitting in my study I hear a coach drive along the street; I walk out and enter into it; thus, common speech would incline one to think, I heard, saw, and touched the same thing, to wit, the coach. It is nevertheless certain, the ideas intromitted by each sense are widely different, and distinct from each other; but having been observed constantly to go together, they are spoken of as one and the same thing.[2]

Not only are "external objects" so constructed, but also the spatial relationships between them. Thus, in his *New Theory of Vision* (1709), Berkeley argued that the perception of distance is not a *perception* at all, but rather such a construction.

> Having a long time experienced certain ideas, perceivable by touch, as distance, tangible figure, and solidity, to have been connected with certain ideas of sight, I do, upon perceiving these ideas of sight, forthwith conclude what tangible ideas are, by the wonted ordinary course of nature, like to

follow. Looking at an object, I perceive a certain visible figure and color, with some degree of faintness and other circumstances, which from what I have formerly observed, determine me to think, that if I advanced forward so many paces or miles, I shall be affected with such and such ideas of touch.[3]

This notion that spatial relationships are not directly perceived, but only indirectly constructed, endured and became especially prominent in the second half of the nineteenth century. It has survived into the twentieth century, too, though its force has been tempered considerably by the counterclaims of Gestalt theory (Chapter 11). The more general idea, that our perception of reality-at-large is a construction, has also endured. For Berkeley, both notions were built around the association of ideas. Among the conditions of such association, we have already seen that he included contiguity. At times, he also spoke of "similarity" and "causality," but it was still contiguity that he made the most of.

### DAVID HUME

Berkeley's successor in the tradition of mental mechanism was David Hume (1711–1776). Hume's great contribution to this tradition was twofold. (a) In its general structure Hume's psychology went very little beyond those of Locke and Berkeley. With the exception of the primary-secondary distinction, which Berkeley had already put to flight, he accepted most of Locke's notions without great alteration. Unlike both Locke and Berkeley, however, Hume had the ability to express these notions explicitly and precisely. Thus, Hume contributed to the tradition of mental mechanism a *clarification* of some of its fundamental conceptions. (b) In addition, Hume rightly recognized that the whole effort of mental mechanism stood or fell upon the question of the association of ideas. Hence, he entered explicitly and at length into the issue of association itself. Up to this point, association had been considered only casually.

In his *Treatise of Human Nature* (1739), Hume summarized in a single paragraph what it had taken Locke and Berkeley a vast number of pages to say.

All the perceptions of the human mind resolve themselves into two distinct kinds, which I shall call *impressions* and *ideas.* The difference betwixt these consists in the degrees of force and liveliness with which they strike upon the mind, and make their way into our thought or consciousness. Those perceptions, which enter with most force and violence, we may name *impressions;* and under this name I comprehend our sensations, passions, and emotions. . . . By *images* I mean the faint images of these in thinking and reasoning;

such as, for instance, are all the perceptions excited by the present discourse, excepting only, those which arise from the sight and touch, and excepting the immediate pleasure or uneasiness it may occasion.[4]

Of course, the doctrine of psychological empiricism insists that "ideas" must in some fashion derive from "impressions." But Hume for the first time spelled out the assumption that mental mechanism made concerning the precise nature of this derivation—namely, that "ideas" differ from their generative "impressions" only in "force and liveliness."

A few paragraphs later, Hume's clarity of expression brought out another of mental mechanism's fundamental assumptions. He observed:

> There is another division of our perceptions, which it will be convenient to observe, and which extends itself both to our impressions and ideas. This division is into *simple* and *complex*. Simple perceptions or impressions and ideas are such as to admit of no distinction nor separation. The complex are the contrary to these, and may be distinguished into parts. Though a particular color, taste, and smell are qualities all united together in this apple, 'tis easy to perceive they are not the same, but are at least distinguishable from each other.[5]

To put the matter another way: with Berkeley, Hume recognized that impressions are rarely if ever "such as to admit of no distinction nor separation." Rather, they are complex, for they can "be distinguished into parts." The assumption of mental mechanism, which Hume readily accepted, was that such complex impressions can be analyzed into *psychologically discrete* sensory qualities. Thus, the complex impression of an apple was held to be a conglomeration of such simple impressions as red, round, firm, juicy, and the like. This conglomeration, in turn, had to resolve itself into its component parts before it could give rise to ideas. And since these component parts were *simple* impressions, it followed that the ideas to which they gave rise must also be simple. From these the *complex* idea of the apple would have to be reconstituted.

As we have noted, Hume clearly saw that the concept of association was crucial to the task of mental mechanism. Specifically, he observed that

> As all simple ideas may be separated by the imagination, and may be united again in what form it pleases, nothing would be more unaccountable than the operations of that faculty, were it not guided by some universal principles, which render it, in some measure, uniform with itself in all times and places. Were ideas entirely loose and unconnected, chance alone would join them; and 'tis impossible that some simple ideas should fall regularly into complex ones (as they commonly do) without some bond of union among them, some associating quality, by which one idea naturally introduces another.[6]

In describing the inner nature of this associating quality, Hume showed even more clearly than Locke had done that the concept of the association of ideas was altogether congenial with the Newtonian cosmology. It is, he wrote, a "gentle force," indeed, "a kind of *attraction,* which in the mental world will be found to have as extraordinary effects as in the natural, and to show itself in as many and as varied forms."[7]

In a word, Hume was here recognizing explicitly what we have suggested was implicit with Locke—that the concept of the association of ideas was altogether congenial with the Newtonian cosmology. Of the conditions or laws governing the operation of this "gentle force," Hume posited three: "resemblance," "contiguity in time or place," and "cause and effect." These he later reduced to two by regarding "cause and effect" as simply a special case of "contiguity in time or place."

With Berkeley, Hume agreed that complex ideas of "external objects" are, in reality, constructions. His reasons for doing so, however, were more explicit than Berkeley's. As we have seen, Hume's formulation of mental mechanism assumed that all ideas initially derive from simple impressions; hence, they themselves must be initially simple. And since the idea of an external object is a complex one, it must have been *constructed* out of these simple ideas. In this it must be noted that the "construction of reality" was not so much a discovery by Berkeley and Hume as it was a conclusion drawn from their initial assumptions.

Assumptions, once made, have a way of gathering momentum and, thereby, leading to all manner of curious conclusions. To illustrate this, let us consider for a moment that celebrated passage, dear to all who style themselves "tough-minded," in which Hume denies that there is an idea "of what we call our self."

> For my part, when I enter most intimately into what I call *myself,* I always stumble on some particular perception or other, of heat or cold, light or shade, love or hatred, pain or pleasure. I never can catch myself at any time without a perception, and never can observe anything but the perception.[8]

Whether there is or is not a "self," or an idea of a "self," we need not here presume to determine. We may, however, inquire into the reasons that led Hume to deny it. As we have seen, Hume insisted that all ideas must derive from *simple* impressions, which is to say that all ideas must exist *initially* in the form of uncompounded simple ideas. Hence, the idea of a "self" would have to be either a simple idea or a conglomeration of a number of simple ideas. Now the latter possibility clearly holds little promise, for the complex idea compounded out of such simple ideas as, say, "red," "round," "firm," and "juicy" would be the idea not of a "self," but of an "apple." So we are left with only the first possibility—namely, that the idea of a "self" would have to be a simple idea deriving from some simple impression.

Now once the question of "a self" is phrased in just this manner, we should hardly be surprised to discover that it cannot be answered "without a manifest contradiction and absurdity."

> For from what [simple] impression could this idea be derived? . . . Pain and pleasure, grief and joy, passions and sensations succeed each other, and never all exist at the same time. It cannot, therefore, be from any of these impressions, or from any other, that the idea of self is derived; and consequently there is no such idea.[9]

In short, Hume's denial of the idea of a "self" was a denial of its possibility *ex hypothesi*.


## DAVID HARTLEY

Like Descartes and Hobbes before them. Locke, Berkeley, and Hume were psychologists only incidentally. Their primary concern was with the philosophy of knowledge. Accordingly, their interest in specifically psychological issues extended only as far as the epistemological implications that might be drawn from them. The case was quite otherwise with their countryman David Hartley (1705–1757). Hartley, a physician by training, concerned himself with the psychology of mental mechanism *qua* psychology. (In this regard, it may be noted that Hartley was the first to describe his psychology as a variety of "mechanism.") To him, mental mechanism, the association of ideas, and psychological empiricism were all distinctly psychological issues. His design, accordingly, was to cast these issues into distinctly psychological terms. This he did in his *Observations on Man* (1749), which was later esteemed by his successor, James Mill, as the "really master-production in the philosophy of mind."

Hartley's contributions to mental mechanism were two in number: (a) Like Hobbes before him, Hartley thought it necessary to rely upon one, and only one, principle of association: *contiguity*. As we shall see later, his reasons for doing so were much the same as Hobbes'. In this, though, he went a few paces beyond Hobbes in distinguishing between two possible kinds of contiguity: "simultaneous" and "successive." This distinction was, of course, implicit in Locke and Berkeley, and especially in Hume's "contiguity in time or place." But Hartley for the first time clearly drew it out. (b) In addition, Hartley gave the first really clear and psychologically meaningful *definition* of "association"; that is, he specified the conditions under which association might be expected to occur. These two contributions were presented together in Hartley's "Proposition 10":

> Any sensations *A, B, C,* etc., by being associated with one another a sufficient number of times, get such a power over the corresponding ideas *a, b, c,* etc., that any one of the sensations *A,* when impressed alone, shall be able to excite in the mind *b, c,* etc., the ideas of the rest. Sensations may be said to be associated together, when their impressions are either made precisely at the same instant of time, or in the contiguous successive instants. We may therefore distinguish association into two sorts, the synchronous, and the successive.[10]

There is more to be said about Hartley, but it will have to be saved for the next chapter, on physiological mechanism, where it fits more comfortably.

## *JAMES MILL*

This chapter and the two that follow it are concerned primarily with the course of psychological thought during the eighteenth century. James Mill (1773–1836), however, did not publish his psychological work until well into the nineteenth century. It would have been much tidier if he had published it no later than 1799; but as he did not, we must now jump ahead of the chronological course that we have set for ourselves. This is unavoidable, for it was Mill who afforded the Lockean theory of mental mechanism its fullest possible expression.

Mill's great contribution to the tradition of mental mechanism was that he brought its major concern and underlying assumption for the first time clearly out into the open. "Inquires into the human mind," he wrote, "have for their main, and ultimate object, the exposition of its more *complex* phenomena." But in this, he continued it is necessary

> that the simple phenomena should be premised; because they are the elements of which the complex are formed; and because a distinct knowledge of the elements is indispensable to an accurate conception of that which is compounded of them.[11]

Thus at the outset Mill set forth explicitly what had always been the implicit task and final goal of mental mechanism: to *analyze* the mind into its distinct, uncompounded, fundamental components. Hence the title of his principal psychological work, *Analysis of the Phenomena of the Human Mind* (1829).

This analysis of the mind's "more complex phenomena" must clearly begin, Mill considered, with an analysis of the sensations from which they are ultimately derived. Thus, his first task in the *Analysis* was to determine the

simple, uncompounded components in which any sensation may be understood
to consist. These, he concluded along with his predecessors, are *distinct sensory
qualities*—the smell of a rose, the color blue, the visible form of a circle, and
so forth. Thus:

> When we smell a rose, there is a particular feeling, a particular consciousness,
> distinct from all others, which we mean to denote. In like manner we speak
> of the smell of hay, the smell of turpentine, and the smell of a fox.

"In all these cases," he concluded, "what we speak of is a point of
consciousness."[12] The significance of Mill's use of the phrase "point of
consciousness" should by this time be fairly clear: it suggested that such a
distinct sensory quality could be regarded as a kind of Newtonian particle of
the mind—a kind of mental atom from which, along with other such atoms,
all the "more complex phenomena" of the mind could be constructed.

Mill's general term for these mental atoms was "feelings," of which he
considered that there were two and only two varieties: (a) "sensations" (Hume's
"impressions") and (b) "ideas," which like Hume he considered to be the
"copies, images, or representatives" of sensations. These, then, and these alone
were the fundamental constituents, or particles, into which the mind's "more
complex phenomena" were to be analyzed. In this regard we need only repeat
that Mill was simply making explicit what mental mechanism had been tacitly
advocating all along.

In making the point explicit, however, Mill at the same time brought to
light that important but unspoken assumption on which the whole thrust of
mental mechanism had been based. And that assumption was just this: that
sensory qualities—red, round, firm, juicy, and the like—are not just *distinguishable,* but psychologically *distinct.* As we have seen, David Hume had
already made this assumption fairly explicit. But he had done so only in
passing. Mill, on the other hand, made of it such an integral and explicit
part of his psychology that it could not fail to be noticed. Repeatedly
throughout his *Analysis* there occurred such statements as the following:

> From a stone I have had, synchronically, the sensation of color, the sensation
> of hardness, the sensation of shape, and size, the sensation of weight. When
> the idea of one of these sensations occurs, the ideas of all of them occur.
> They exist in my mind synchronically; and their synchronical existence is
> called the idea of the stone; which, it is thus plain, is not a single idea, but
> a number of ideas in a particular state of combination.[13]

Locke, Berkeley, Hume, and Hartley had been saying the same thing all
along, but none had been quite so blunt about it.

Let us pause for a moment to examine the logic underlying this assumption.

As Berkeley and Hume had noted, sensations in the rough are rarely if ever simple and uncompounded. The sensation of a stone, for example, consists in a variety of distinguishable sensory qualities. In this respect, most if not all actual sensations may be said to be "complex." Now, the mental mechanists went further than this and asserted that such sensations could not give rise to ideas unless they were first *de*composed into their constituent "simple sensations." In this state, they could then give rise to "simple ideas," which could in turn be *re*composed into a "complex idea" corresponding to the initial complex sensation. Such, then, was the mental mechanists' paradigm: complex sensations→simple sensations→simple ideas→complex ideas.

But how much less cumbersome it might have been had they only allowed that complex sensations could give rise to complex ideas at the outset, without the mediation of simple sensations and ideas. And the question that importunately arises is—why didn't they? The answer is not difficult to find. Had mental mechanism allowed the existence of complex ideas that were not composed of simple ideas, it would have found itself right back where it started, without points, without particles, without everything else so dear to its theoretical heart. In short, the machine of the mind would thereby have lost its structural similitude with the machine of Newton's cosmos. We shall pursue this point further in a moment.

Let us grant for the present that the first task of psychology is to analyze the "more complex phenomena" of the mind into their simplest components. Of necessity, the second task would be to specify the operations whereby these simple components recombine to form the "more complex phenomena" with which we started. With Hume, Mill rightly perceived that at the heart of this second task lay the matter of the association of ideas. We need not here describe the whole of Mill's associationism; suffice it to say that for the most part it incorporated what his predecessors had delivered on the matter. There was, however, one important departure that we shall do well to look into.

With Hobbes and Hartley, Mill considered that *contiguity* alone (whether synchronous or successive) was sufficient to account for the phenomena of association. Now, as we have seen, Locke, Berkeley, and Hume had made a place for *resemblance* as well. Hartley, on the other hand, had not included resemblance, but neither did he explicitly exclude it. Mill's great departure was that he explicitly denied resemblance as an effective principle of association.

On this point we must be very clear. Mill did not deny that similar ideas are sometimes associated with one another; what he did deny was that this similarity is the *cause* or *condition* of their association. "I believe it will be found," he observed,

> that we are accustomed to see like things together. When we see a tree, we generally see more trees than one; when we see an ox, we generally see more oxen than one; a sheep, more sheep than one; a man, more men than one.

"From this observation," he concluded, "I think, we may refer resemblance to the law of frequency [contiguity], of which it seems to form only a particular case."[14]

If prizes were given for flimsy explanations, Mill's explanation of resemblance as a special case of contiguity would surely receive one. For it was, as his son John Stuart Mill later put it, "perhaps the least successful attempt . . . to be found in the work."[15] And, this being so, we are confronted by yet another importunate question: If Mill was willing to accept resemblance as a *fact* of association, why was he *un*willing to accept it as a *principle* of association? We cannot, of course, know Mill's actual motives, but this much is in any case clear. He and his mental-mechanist predecessors rightly perceived that the stimultaneous or successive contiguity of sensations, and thus of ideas, could be comfortably contained within the Newtonian scheme of things. For these were precisely the orders in which *objects* were regarded as existing in the external, sensible world. Thus, Mill was simply being a good Newtonian when he wrote:

> Of the order established among the objects of nature, by which we mean the objects of our senses, two remarkable cases are all which here we are called upon to notice; the *synchronous order,* and the *successive order.* The synchronous order, or order of simultaneous existence, is the order in space; the successive order, or order of antecedent and consequent existence, is the order in time. Thus the various objects in my room, the chairs, the tables, the books, have the synchronous order, or order in space. The falling of the spark, and the explosion of the gunpowder, have the successive order, or order in time.[16]

In brief, Mill subscribed to the then universally accepted view that spatial ("synchronous") and temporal ("successive") relationships between objects are real, objective features of the external world. And from this he rightly concluded that the association of ideas through *contiguity* could readily be traced to the order of the sensations from which they arose, and thence to the order of the objects by which these sensations were initially excited.

But what of association through *resemblance?* We have all as children puzzled over the question, If a tree fell in an uninhabited forest, would there be any sound? The question that the mental mechanist had to ask himself about resemblance was of a similar sort. If objects existed in an uninhabited universe, would there be any resemblance? Of necessity, his answer would be in the negative: Objects can bear spatial and temporal relationships to one another, irrespective of there being anyone to observe them, but resemblance, like beauty, exists only in the eyes of the beholder, if at all.

Here, then, is the dilemma in which Mill perhaps found himself. Resemblance could be *referred* to external objects, but it could not be *traced* to them, for it was held not to exist in the external world at all. Thus, to admit resemblance as an effective principle of association would be to compromise the subsidiary doctrine of psychological empiricism. And yet, to deny resemblance altogether would be to fly in the face of a brute fact—that similar ideas are sometimes associated. His path of escape from this dilemma was, one might say, between the horns: he admitted resemblance as a fact of association but attempted to explain it as simply a special case of association through contiguity.

We noted earlier that Locke might have preserved a place for resemblance and contrast by regarding them as the mental analogues of Newton's "attraction" and "repulsion." Hume seems actually to have done so, although he considered that contrast-repulsion was but a special case of resemblance-attraction. We may now observe that this too would have seriously compromised the doctrine of psychological empiricism. Specifically, it would have been patent nonsense to maintain that two *ideas* attract or repel one another (resemble or contrast with one another) according as their corresponding *objects* attract or repel one another in the external world. Rather, if ideas indeed do "attract" or "repel" one another, they do so altogether independently of the attractive and repulsive forces existing between their respective objects. So again, resemblance and contrast could be *referred* to external objects, but they could not be seen as inhering in the objects themselves. Hume ignored the problem; Locke passed it off by regarding the "correspondence and connection" of similar and contrasting ideas as "natural."

The conclusions to which Locke's mental mechanism inescapably lead are nowhere better seen than in Mill's attempt to *reconstruct* the "more complex phenomena" of the mind. As we have seen, the only elements that could enter into this process were simple ideas, the copies or representatives of discrete sensory qualities. They in turn (by virtue of the recurrent contiguity of the sensations from which they derived) could unite to form complex ideas. Such complex ideas could then unite (again, by virtue of recurrent contiguity) to form even more complex (or "duplex") ideas, and so on. Thus:

> Brick is one complex idea, mortar is another complex idea; these ideas, with ideas of position and quantity, compose my idea of a wall. My idea of a plank is a complex idea, my idea of a rafter is a complex idea, my idea of a nail is a complex idea. These, united with the same ideas of position and quantity, compose my duplex idea of a floor. In the same manner, my complex idea of glass, and wood, and others, compose my duplex idea of a window; and these duplex ideas, united together, compose my idea of a house, which is made up of various duplex ideas.

"How many complex, or duplex ideas," he continued with almost rustic wonderment, "are united in the idea of furniture? How many more in the idea of merchandise? How many more in the idea called Everything?"[17]

After James Mill's *Analysis*, there was simply nothing that Lockean mental mechanism could do for an encore. Its accounts with reality were now closed, and there was nothing further that could be said on the matter. Every possible question had been answered; every possible loose end had been tied off. Given any complex mental phenomenon, the theory could—in principle—resolve it into its component parts.

Whether it did so well or ill was, of course, quite another matter. So long as a theory remains a vague and ill-defined doctrine, it is able to go relatively unchallenged. As soon, however, as it begins to make definite and explicit assertions, it begins to display its weaknesses, its limitations, its absurdities. Here, then, is one of the great cardinal rules of psychological theorizing: If you would preserve your theory safe from all attack, be sure to keep it as vague and inexplicit as possible. Locke, of course, had carried this principle out to the letter. Berkeley, Hume, and Hartley, however, had each in his own way violated it: they had taken the trouble to render some of the implications of mental mechanism definite and explicit. Their efforts in this direction, though, were as nothing compared with those of their later countryman, James Mill. With James Mill, the Lockean doctrine of mental mechanism received its fullest, its most brilliant expression; with him also it died.

As we have noted, however, all this did not take place until well into the nineteenth century. In the eighteenth century, Locke's mental mechanism still carried the day. And how, indeed, could it have been otherwise? For as we have seen repeatedly, the theory was entirely compatible and even congenial with that other grand enthusiasm of the age, the Newtonian cosmology. In addition, it seemed altogether capable of performing its assigned task, which was to account for "the phenomena of the human mind." Taken together, these two factors seemed to ensure for mental mechanism a long life and undarkened future.

## NOTES

1. *The Works of George Berkeley*, vol. VII (London: Thomas Nelson, 1949), p. 45.
2. Ibid., vol. VI, p. 188.
3. Ibid.
4. D. Hume, *A Treatise of Human Nature* (Oxford: Clarendon, 1888), p. 1.
5. Ibid., p. 2.
6. Ibid., p. 10.
7. Ibid., pp. 12–13.
8. Ibid., p. 252.
9. Ibid., pp. 251–252.
10. D. Hartley, *Observations on Man: His Frame, His Duty, and His Expectations* (Gainesville, Fla.: Scholars' Facsimiles and Reprints, 1966), p. 65.

11.  J. Mill, *Analysis of the Phenomena of the Human Mind* (London: Baldwin and Cradock, 1829), vol. I, p. 1.

12.  Ibid., p. 7.

13.  Ibid., p. 57.

14.  Ibid., pp. 78–80.

15.  J. S. Mill, ed., *Analysis of the Phenomena of the Human Mind* (London: Longmans, 1869), vol. I, p. 111.

16.  J. Mill, *Analysis,* pp. 53–54.

17.  Ibid., pp. 81–82.

## FOR FURTHER READING

A good survey of the history of the concept of "association," from classical antiquity up through about 1920, is H. C. Warren, *A History of Association Psychology* (New York: Scribner, 1921).

Excerpts from the more important psychological writings of Berkeley, Hume, Hartley, J. Mill, and other persons falling within or alongside the tradition of mental mechanism are to be found in the following collections: W. Dennis, ed., *Readings in the History of Psychology* (New York: Appleton-Century-Crofts, 1948); R. J. Herrnstein and E. G. Boring, eds., *A Source Book in the History of Psychology* (Cambridge, Mass.: Harvard University Press, 1966); G. Murphy and L. B. Murphy, eds., *Western Psychology: From the Greeks to William James* (New York: Basic Books, 1969); B. Rand, ed., *The Classical Psychologists* (Boston: Houghton Mifflin, 1912); and W. S. Sahakian, *History of Psychology: A Source Book in Systematic Psychology* (Itasca, Ill.: Peacock, 1968).

# Chapter 3
# Physiological Mechanism

The metaphysicians who have hinted that matter may well be endowed with the faculty of thought have perhaps not reasoned ill.

—Julien Offray de la Mettrie,
*L'Homme Machine* (1748)

As a program for psychological inquiry, mental mechanism had one great methodological advantage: it could undertake to grapple with psychological phenomena without recourse to premature physiological speculation. And as we have seen, in the seventeenth century when mental mechanism was born, physiological speculation was indeed premature. In this respect, Locke's resolution "not at present [to] meddle with the physical consideration of the mind, or trouble myself to examine wherein its essence consists" may be seen as an attempt to liberate psychology from a system of physiological conjectures that could only stultify it.

As a program of *mechanistic* explanation, however, mental mechanism had one very grave shortcoming. The central aim of mechanism was to explain all things in terms of "matter in motion." Descartes and Hobbes, with their "animal spirits" and "motion-in-the-brain," had faithfully adhered to this purpose. Locke's mental mechanism, on the other hand, had made a significant departure. It retained "motion" of a sort, and thus "mechanism" of a sort, but it had refused to specify the physical, or material, status of its fundamental particles, the "simple ideas."

This refusal, of course, left open the possibility (explicitly seized upon by Berkeley) that "ideas" were not material at all, but rather immaterial. But even if mental mechanism's "ideas" were *not* regarded as immaterial, its failure to specify the fashion in which they might be material must have placed a considerable strain upon the general mechanistic imagination. Were ideas material in their own right? If so, then they must be regarded as little chunks of "mental matter" spatially arranged "in the mind." Clearly this would have been an unattractive possibility, for it was simply a corporeal soul dressed in modern garb.

And yet, the only apparent alternative was the one which Locke had sought to avoid from the outset: namely, to explain mental activities in terms of conjectured bodily activities. Thus, toward the middle of the eighteenth century we find another psychological enthusiasm beginning to gain momentum. Since its emphasis was upon the activities of the body, and since these activities were regarded solely as the result of "matter in motion," this new enthusiasm is best described as *physiological mechanism.*

## THE SOURCES OF PHYSIOLOGICAL MECHANISM

Physiological mechanism was based upon two quite distinct assumptions: (a) that the activities of the body can be exhaustively accounted for in terms of familiar mechanical principles and (b) that mental phenomena ("ideas," "thoughts," and the like) are nothing more than the *products* of these activities of the body.

(1) The former of these assumptions was first clearly stated by Descartes. The animal body, he had argued, is purely and simply an automaton, "a machine that moves of itself." As we have seen, Descartes arrived at this conclusion by attributing the functions of the old Aristotelian nutritive and sensitive souls to the body itself; in consequence, he was able to regard the body as being possessed of its own *inherent vitality.* With this, though, we shall now do well to pause and consider two questions: (a) why, before Descartes, did vitality seem to require the behind-the-scenes activity of nutritive and sensitive souls, and (b) why did Descartes see fit to attribute vitality to the body in its own right?

(a) The answer to the first question is not difficult to find. With certain exceptions (e.g., Greek hylozoism), matter had been traditionally regarded as *intrinsically* inert, lifeless, and insensible. And, since the body was composed of matter, it too had to be regarded as intrinsically inert, lifeless, and insensible. Accordingly, the vitality of the body could only be seen as *extrinsic*—as depending, that is, upon some external agency. Hence, the nutritive and sensitive souls.

This view of the problem, we must grant, is not so simple-minded as it might seem. If matter were intrinsically *alive,* how then would we explain the fact that the great majority of material things are *not* alive? If, on the other hand, matter is intrinsically not alive, how else (except by way of an external vital agent) could we account for the fact that some material things *are* alive? But we need not argue here for the existence of nutritive and sensitive souls; suffice it to say that, if the doctrine was false, it was not conspicuously so.

(b) Why, then, did Descartes abandon the sensitive and nutritive souls in favor of inherent bodily vitality? We might like to imagine that it was the result of a shrewd scientific insight, a century or two ahead of its time. In truth, though, it was nothing of the sort. Indeed, Descartes would probably never have arrived at the idea, had he possessed a fuller knowledge of actual physiological phenomena. In keeping with the rather crudely mechanistic physiology of his time, Descartes considered that bodily vitality consisted in nothing more than "the heat and movement of the members." The implication was inescapable:

> Because we do not doubt there being inanimate bodies which can move in as many as or in more diverse modes than can ours, and which have as much heat or more (experience demonstrates this to us in flame, which of itself has much more heat and movement than any of our members), we must believe that all the heat and all the movements which are in us pertain only to the body.[1]

In effect, then, what Descartes did was to whittle down the concept of "vitality" to a point where it could be comfortably digested by the concept of "matter." (It apparently did not occur to him that his conception of vitality made it necessary to regard a flame as being more "alive" than an animal body.)

So far as he went, though, Descartes was quite correct: *if* heat and movement are part and parcel of vitality, then the animal body *does* display a certain inherent vital activity. Observations that would support this view were numerous. Some were simply commonsensical, as, for example, that a chicken abruptly decapitated continues for a while to move about. Others were the result of active physiological investigation, such as the continued beating of muscle fibers dissected out of the heart. In the mid-eighteenth century, these and many other observations were brought together by the physiologist Albrecht von Haller, who concluded:

> Therefore . . . the muscular fiber are by their very nature irritable; they are able to function by themselves alone without any influence reaching them from outside. Some writers are inclined to call this the "vital force," but such a term does not seem justified in my view, since it is possible to

demonstrate effects caused by it even after life has departed. I prefer to call this the "inherent or intrinsic force" of the muscles.[2]

Here, then, is where the twin questions of inherent bodily activity and physiological automatism stood toward the middle of the eighteenth century.

(2) In putting forward his theory of physiological automatism, Descartes (and those who followed his lead, including von Haller himself) stopped just short of a precipice. The *human* body, he considered, may be distinguished from other animal automata by the fact that its behavior is organized and directed by the activities of the rational soul. The precipice, of course, was this: Apart from prior theological commitments (in which Descartes was not lacking), from just what considerations is the presence of this rational soul to be inferred? Descartes' answer was twofold: (a) we cannot doubt that we think (for the very act of doubting would be an admission of it); (b) nor can we doubt that it is of the nature of rational souls to think and of the nature of mere animal bodies, mere matter, not to think. Now the first part of this answer might hold back the tide of doubt for a while, but sooner or later someone was bound to consider another possibility—namely, that thinking, too, is a natural function of the body, and thus that Man, like his brute animal neighbors, is purely and simply an automaton.

### JULIEN OFFRAY DE LA METTRIE

These wider possibilities of physiological automatism were first seized upon, elaborated, and popularized by the French physician Julien Offray de la Mettrie (1709–1751). With Descartes and von Haller, de la Mettrie agreed that the animal body is possessed of its own inherent vital activity and, thus, "that animals are pure machines."[3] From here, though, he pushed the issue far beyond where his predecessors had been content to let it rest. Physiological automatism stops just short of man, he recognized, for no better reason than that man *thinks;* and this, in turn, rests upon the dogmatic assumption that thinking is *alien* to matter. De la Mettrie, on the contrary, was roundly convinced

> that thought is so little incompatible with organized matter, that it seems to be one of its properties on a par with electricity, the faculty of motion, impenetrability, extension, etc.[4]

And if this be true, he argued, then man, like puppies and pandas, is nothing more nor less than—a *machine*. Hence the almost aggressive title of de la Mettrie's principal psychological work, *L'Homme Machine* (*Man a Machine,* 1748).

At first glance, *L'Homme Machine* seems not so much a sober psychophysiological treatise as a cynical and embittered polemic. There occur throughout, for example, such roguish and rebellious assaults as the following:

> Although [Descartes] extols the distinctness of the two substances ["body" and "mind"], this is plainly but a trick of skill, a ruse of style, to make theologians swallow a poison, hidden in the shade of an analogy which strikes everybody else and which they alone fail to notice. For it is this, this strong analogy, which forces all scholars and wise judges to confess that these proud and vain beings, more distinguished by their pride than by the name of men, however much they may wish to exalt themselves, are at bottom only animals and machines which, though upright, go on all fours.[5]

We may admire the plucky, straightforward way in which de la Mettrie expressed his views, but we must at the same time take great care to separate the wheat from the chaff. De la Mettrie's great contribution to the development of psychological thought lay not in his vituperative attacks against theologians, pedants, and human vanity in general, but rather in his explicit statement of the powerful concept of *organization*.

Without this conception, those who would regard thinking as a natural function of matter would have to admit that a chair, a tree, or a stone could think just as readily as a man. With it, on the other hand, they were saved from this embarrassing version of hylozoism. For it could now be argued that thinking is *not* a natural function of just any collection of matter, but rather only of matter which has a certain *complexity of structure*. Thus:

> Grant only that [living] matter is endowed with a principle of motion, which alone differentiates it from the inorganic . . . and that among animals . . . everything depends upon the diversity of this organization: these admissions suffice for guessing the riddle of substances and of man. It [thus] appears that there is but one [type of organization] in the universe, and that man is the most perfect [example]. He is to the ape, and to the most intelligent of animals, as the planetary pendulum of Huyghens is to a watch of Julien Leroy. More instruments, more wheels and more springs were necessary to mark the movements of the planets than to strike the hours; and Vulcanson [a craftsman noted for his mechanical statues], who needed more skill for making his flute player than for making his duck, would have needed still more to make a talking man, a mechanism no longer regarded as impossible, especially in the hands of another Prometheus.[6]

Such, then, was the basis for de la Mettrie's potent and highly novel treatment of the problem of thinking (in which matter he considered that "Locke had the bad luck to make shipwreck," while Descartes was simply "much deceived"). Thinking was to be regarded simply as a function of the complex structure of the body. It comes as naturally to an organ with the structure of the brain as contraction to the muscles, breathing to the lungs, and secretion to the glands. Accordingly, man differs from other animal automata only in the complexity of his bodily structure. And this is a difference not of kind, but of degree. Or as de la Mettrie put it:

> Man is not molded from a costlier clay; nature has used but one dough, and has merely varied the leaven.[7]

From this, the further conclusion was virtually inescapable. "Is more needed," he asked,

> to prove that man is but an animal, or a collection of springs which wind each other up? . . . If these springs differ among themselves, these differences consist only in their position and in their degrees of strength, and never in their nature.[8]

One of the most prominent features of *L'Homme Machine* is that the specific psychological hypotheses that it contains are often more crude and naïve than anything ever put forward by de la Mettrie's psychological predecessors or contemporaries. In one place, for example, he observed that

> Raw meat makes animals fierce, and it would have the same effect on men. This is so true that the English who eat meat red and bloody, and not as well done as ours, seem to share more or less in the savagery due to this kind of food. . . . This savagery creates in the soul, pride, hatred, scorn of other nations, indocility and other sentiments which degrade the character, just as heavy food makes a dull and heavy mind whose usual traits are laziness and indolence.[9]

With a psychology based upon such observations as this, and concluding in the assertion that "man is but . . . a collection of springs which wind each other up," it is small wonder that de la Mettrie was (as his royal patron, Frederick the Great, put it) "imposed upon by the pious insults of the theologians."[10] In some respects, he richly deserved their insults.

What must be remembered, though, is that de la Mettrie was not attempting to put forward a detailed psychological or psychophysiological theory. His concern was rather to present a *programmatic outline* for such a theory, based upon the concept of complexity of organization, and with the ultimate aim of propagating a kind of neo-Epicurean attitude toward life. His effect, then, upon the subsequent history of psychological thought must be seen chiefly as a stimulus and as a challenge. For this reason, we may conclude our consideration of de la Mettrie with his closing words in *L'Homme Machine:*

Let us then conclude boldly that man is a machine, and that in the whole universe there is but a single substance differently modified. . . . Such is my system, or rather the truth, unless I am much deceived. It is short and simple. Dispute it now who will.[11]


## DAVID HARTLEY

De la Mettrie had addressed himself only to the general question, How can mere matter produce mental phenomena? His answer, accordingly, was only a general one: Matter can produce sensation, thought, imagination, and the like by virtue of the complexity of its organization. So conceived, this fundamental tenet of physiological mechanism was thereby rendered more plausible, but it was still by no means compelling. For it is one thing to draw the general outlines of a theory, and quite another to pursue the matter systematically and in detail.

It is in this latter task that David Hartley (1705–1757), de la Mettrie's English contemporary, must again attract our attention. Like de la Mettrie, Hartley considered mental activity to be the product of bodily activity. Quite unlike de la Mettrie, however, Hartley's chief concern was not with the grinding of antitheological axes, but rather with the construction of a sober and detailed psychophysiological theory.

As we have seen, Hartley belonged also within the tradition of mental mechanism. Like Locke before him, he attempted to construct a psychology on the Newtonian model. Unlike Locke, though, he made his intentions clear and explicit. Unlike Locke also, Hartley had a sound appreciation for the implications and details of the Newtonian model, *qua* physical theory, as well as a thorough familiarity with what was then known of the physiology of the nervous system. Hartley was indeed a mental mechanist, but he also went well beyond mental mechanism.

Hartley described the background of his *Observations on Man* (1749) rather modestly as follows:

About eighteen years ago I was informed, that the Rev. Mr. Gay, then living, asserted the possibility of deducing all our intellectual [activities] from association. . . . [And] from inquiring into the power of association I was led to examine both its consequences, in respect of morality and religion, and its physical cause.[12]

Like de la Mettrie, then, Hartley considered that the matter under consideration had rather direct consequences "in respect of morality and religion" (in the eighteenth century just about everything did), and about half of his book was taken up with an elaboration and, at times, rationalization of them. In the present account, however, we need consider only his treatment of the two matters having direct psychological import: "the power of association" and "its physical cause."

We have already seen Hartley's treatment of "the power of association" in its purely mental aspect. It was very brief and to the point:

> Any sensations *A, B, C,* etc., by being associated [through either "synchronous" or "successive" contiguity] with one another a sufficient number of times, get such a power over the corresponding ideas *a, b, c,* etc., that any one of the sensations *A,* when impressed alone, shall be able to excite in the mind *b, c,* etc., the ideas of the rest.[13]

In order to explain the "physical cause" which Hartley imagined to underlie this power of association, we must go back a bit. Newton's theory of action at a distance had given the general doctrine of mechanism a kind of intellectual cramp, for it seemed to suggest that two distant bodies could affect each other without any physical medium existing between them to communicate the effect. Indeed, the whole idea smacked of the mysterious and appeared, if anything, to be a frontal assault *against* mechanism. To save the appearances, then, Newton discovered—rather, invented—the "ether," a subtle, elastic, fluid-like physical medium which was imagined to fill up the spaces between physical bodies and particles and to communicate effects between them. This latter task of the ether, the communication of effects, was held to be accomplished by way of "vibrations."

Without entering in detail into the reasons why the ether was considered to propagate effects through vibrations, suffice it to say here that Hartley saw in this doctrine a powerful instrument for the forging of a thoroughly mechanistic psychology. The older mechanism, as exemplified by Descartes and Hobbes, had been forced to rely for its physical basis upon some rather crude "motions in the brain." Hartley, writing on the other hand about a century later, knew full well that the brain is not just a jug with "animal spirits" sloshing around in it. On the contrary, it is composed of some rather substantial tissue whose particles are clearly incapable of dashing about from pillar to post, or sense organ to muscle. Psychological mechanism, then, was faced with a minor dilemma: it was committed to framing its explanations in terms of matter-in-motion, yet, the matter of the brain was apparently incapable of motion.

To this problem the doctrine of vibrations held out a ready-made solution, for, in its terms, a body could vibrate and yet not move about. Or, to put it another way, the matter of the brain could now be in motion and yet remain stationary. It was not only a handy solution—it was ideal!

According to Hartley, then, sensations may be regarded as entering into the nervous system in the form of vibrations, which eventually give rise to *localized* vibrations in "the white medullary substance of the brain."[14] These vibrations in the brain substance tend to persist for a while after the sensible object is removed, and, if repeated often enough, they tend (through a kind of summation of effect) to create relatively enduring "vibratiuncles [literally, little vibrations] and miniatures, corresponding to themselves respectively."[15] These vibratiuncles, it need hardly be said, are the physical counterparts of ideas.

From these conjectures about the physical bases of sensations and ideas, Hartley was then able to go further and speculate on the physical bases of the *association* of ideas. As might be expected, his initial statement in this regard was simply a translation of his earlier proposition into physical terms. Thus:

> Any vibrations $A$, $B$, $C$, etc., by being associated together a sufficient number of times, get such a power over $a$, $b$, $c$, etc., the corresponding miniature vibrations, that any of the vibrations $A$, when impressed alone, shall be able to excite $b$, $c$, etc., the miniatures of the rest.[16]

From this, though, he then went on to consider what might be the underlying *reason* for the association of ideas. It is to be found, he suggested, in the tendency of spatially contiguous vibrations to fuse and mingle:

> Since the vibrations $A$ and $B$ are impressed together, they must, from the diffusion necessary to vibratory motions, run into one vibration; and consequently, after a number of impressions sufficiently repeated, will leave a trace, or miniature of themselves, as one vibration, which will recur every now-and-then, from slight causes. Much rather, therefore, may the part $b$ of the compound miniature $a + b$ recur, when the part $A$ of the compound original vibration $A + B$ is impressed.[17]

Let us now attempt a brief summary of Hartley's theory of "the power of association" and "its physical cause." (a) To each sensation there corresponds a localized vibration in "the white medullary substance of the brain." This tends to persist so long as the stimulus in question is present, but to decay once the stimulus is removed. If, however, the stimulus (and thus the corresponding vibration) is sufficiently repeated, there arises a relatively enduring miniature vibration, or vibratiuncle. This may be regarded as the physical correlate of an "idea." (b) Since vibratory motions tend to diffuse outward from their center, it follows that spatially contiguous vibrations in the brain will eventually "run into one vibration." And thus it is that "the part $b$ of the compound miniature $a + b$ [may] recur, when the part $A$ of the compound original vibration $A + B$ is impressed [alone]." Or, in short, thus it is that ideas may become associated by virtue of the contiguity of their generative sensations. (c) Underlying this theory was one very large assumption of which Hartley seems to have remained unaware. In basing association upon the fusion of vibrations in the brain, Hartley necessarily assumed that *temporally contiguous stimuli* (i.e., "synchronous" or "successive") give rise to *spatially contiguous vibrations* in the brain. Hartley was not the last psychological theorist to make this assumption.

Another question to which Hartley addressed himself was that of motivation. Here, through the fairly simple device of positing "motory vibrations and vibratiuncles," he was able to frame a theory of motivation (or "muscular motion") that was simplicity itself:

> The motory vibratiuncles will also cohere to ideal ones by association. Common ideas may therefore excite motory vibratiuncles, and consequently be able to contract the muscles.[18]

Nor was Hartley unaware of the problem in which such a theory necessarily terminates. Muscular movements can occur only if they are preceded by an associated sensation or idea, but they cannot become so associated except through having *previously* occurred *contiguously* with that sensation or idea. What, then, is responsible for the occurrence of the movement while it is in the process of becoming associated with a sensation or idea? Essentially, there are two possible answers: (a) that the movement in question is initially "emitted" randomly, or (b) that it is initially produced by some other sensation or idea with which it has a "natural and original connection." Since the former alternative would scarcely have been intelligible in the mid-eighteenth century, Hartley quite naturally selected the latter. From this he was led to the view (although he did not put it in quite these words) that all behavior, however complex, is but elaborated reflexive activity. (Thus his apologetic description of the theory as a variety of "mechanism.")

In considering motivation, Hartley spoke often of pleasure and pain, and for this reason he has often been described, like Hobbes, as an advocate of psychological hedonism. It must be noted, though, that Hartley's concern with pleasure and pain was only incidental; his chief interest was to account for the "facts" of hedonism (seeking pleasure and avoiding pain) in terms of vibrations and association. Thus, on the assumption that pain is "nothing more than pleasure itself, carried beyond a due limit,"[19] he reasoned that pleasure is more easily obtained that pain and, therefore, more *frequent*. This, conjoined with the principle of frequency as a factor in the formation of associations, led him to the conclusion "that a power of obtaining pleasure, and removing pain, will be generated early in children, and increase afterwards every day."[20]

Both varieties of psychological mechanism—mental and physiological—had their modern origins in the writings of Descartes and Hobbes. Owing, however, to the dearth of secure and relevant physiological knowledge, physiological mechanism languished for the hundred or so years following Descartes and Hobbes, while mental mechanism (of the Lockean variety) carried the day.

Thus, by the time physiological mechanism began to gather momentum, toward the middle of the eighteenth century, mental mechanism already had a sixty-years head start. Eventually, physiological mechanism caught up with and even surpassed mental mechanism, but this we shall postpone until a later chapter.

## NOTES

1. *The Philosophical Works of Descartes,* trans. E. S. Haldane and G. R. T. Ross, vol. I (Cambridge: University Press, 1931), p. 332.
2. S. Toulmin and J. Goodfield, *The Architecture of Matter* (New York: Harper & Row, 1962), p. 313.
3. J. de la Mettrie, *Man a Machine,* trans. M. W. Calkins (Chicago: Open Court, 1912), p. 142.
4. Ibid., pp. 143–144.
5. Ibid., p. 143.
6. Ibid., pp. 140–141.
7. Ibid., p. 117.
8. Ibid., p. 135.
9. Ibid., p. 94.
10. Ibid., p. 9.
11. Ibid., pp. 148–149.
12. D. Hartley, *Observations on Man: His Frame, His Duty, and His Expectations* (Gainesville, Fla.: Scholars' Facsimiles and Reprints, 1966), p. v.
13. Ibid., p. 65.
14. Ibid., p. 8.
15. Ibid., p. 58.
16. Ibid., p. 67.
17. Ibid., p. 70.
18. Ibid., p. 102.
19. Ibid., p. 35.
20. Ibid., p. 112.

## FOR FURTHER READING

A good background account of the matters considered in this chapter is to be found in S. Toulmin and J. Goodfield, *The Architecture of Matter* (New York: Harper & Row, 1962).

Excerpts from the more important psychophysiological writings of Descartes, de la Mettrie, and Hartley may be found in the following collections: R. J. Herrnstein and E. G. Boring, eds., *A Source Book in the History of Psychology* (Cambridge, Mass.: Harvard University Press, 1966), and W. S. Sahakian, *History of Psychology: A Source Book in Systematic Psychology* (Itasca, Ill.: Peacock, 1968).

# Chapter 4
## The New Image
## of Human Nature

And how admirably calculated is this view of the human
race, emancipated from its chains, released alike from the
dominion of chance, as well as from the enemies of its
progress, and advancing with a firm and inedviate step in
the paths of truth, to console the philosopher lamenting the
errors, the flagrant acts of injustice, the crimes with which
the earth is still polluted!

Marquis de Condorcet, *Outlines
of an Historical View of the
Progress of the Human Mind* (1795)

In large measure, the psychological and philosophical thought of the seventeenth
and eighteenth centuries can be seen as a groping toward a new image of
human nature. By the end of the period—specifically, by the middle and later
years of the eighteenth century—this new image had been fairly well achieved.
At its center stood three distinct but usually intertwined assumptions which,
by the end of the period, had come to seem all but self-evident: (a) that man
is an *animal,* differing from other animals only in degree; (b) that human
nature is the product of *experience;* and (c) that human nature is essentially
*simple.* We may consider each of these in turn.

51

## MEN AND ANIMALS

In the medieval world, man was considered to be a member of the genus "animal" by virtue of his possession of a "sensitive soul" (which, as we have seen, was responsible for such "animal functions" as sense perception, desire, and locomotion). He differed radically, however, from other members of this genus (e.g., cats, dogs, cows, chickens, and the like) by virtue of possessing also an imperishable "rational soul" (whose function, of course, was "thinking"). Here then, in brief, was the medieval view of the relationship between animals and men: animals do not have a rational soul, wherefore they do not think, wherefore men and animals are in all *important* respects distinct from one another.

In contrast to this ancient human arrogation, the eighteenth-century conception of human nature was roundly impressed by the fundamental similarity and even kinship between men and animals. This was not achieved by raising animals up, but rather by taking mankind *down* a peg or two. As de la Mettrie had put it: "Man is not molded of a costlier clay; nature has used but one dough, and has merely varied the leaven." Indeed, the whole of nature was conceived, in the words of Denis Diderot, to be one great, unbroken "chain of beings," extending "from the inert molecule . . . to the living molecule, to the microscopic animal, to the plant-animal, to the animal, to man."[1] Granted, then, that men and brute animals are different; the great insight of the eighteenth century was that they are not *radically* different. We may speak of man as being *more* complex or *more* highly organized—but that is all, for it is only a difference of degree, not of kind.

Listen now to the words of Jean-Jacques Rousseau as he gives full expression to this new, eighteenth-century view of the relationship between man and animals:

> If we strip this being [man], thus constituted, of all the supernatural gifts he may have received, and all the artificial faculties he can have acquired only by a long process; if we consider him, in a word, just as he must have come from the hands of nature, we behold in him an animal weaker than some and less agile than others; but, taking him all round, the most advantageously organized of any. I see him satisfying his hunger at the first oak, and slaking his thirst at the first brook; finding his bed at the foot of the tree which afforded him a repast; and, with that, all his wants satisfied.[2]

This realization, of course, did not prevent the intellectuals of the time from eating their newly discovered animal kin, nor from hitching them up to carriages and plows, but it was still a far cry from the chasm which had traditionally been posed between man and his animal neighbors. As we shall see later, this chasm was even further diminished in the late nineteenth century.


## THE IMPORTANCE OF EXPERIENCE

To anyone familiar with the intellectual currents of the eighteenth century, one thing at least is quite clear. The *sine qua non* of "enlightened" psychological thinking during the period was adherence to Locke's doctrine of psychological empiricism. Indeed, by the middle and later years of the century, this doctrine (and with it a good deal of the conceptual apparatus of mental mechanism) was widely accepted as one of nature's most fundamental truths; accordingly, it came to be regarded as the touchstone of all other assertions about human nature.

Ostensibly, psychological empiricism amounted only to a denial of the doctrine of innate ideas—the theory that some ideas are innate, implanted in us by God, or whatever. In truth, though, it was but an expression, an offshoot, of a far deeper issue—the perennial question of nature versus nurture. Is human nature chiefly the result of "innate characteristics," or is it rather the product of "experience"? In one form or another, the question had been asked since the Greeks.

The medieval conception of human nature was for the most part based upon the preeminent importance of "nature" or "innate characteristics." Man, it held, has an "essence" or "inner nature" which remains unaffected by the vicissitudes of sensory experience. True, these vicissitudes impose certain alterations upon him, but these are only "accidents"—throughout it all, his inner nature remains entirely the same. Thus, the medieval conception of human nature tended toward a rather thoroughgoing *nativism*.

The eighteenth century, on the other hand, accepted in a rather wholesale manner the preeminent importance of "nurture." Man, it held, is wholly a product of his surroundings. His only contact with these surroundings is through his sensations; hence, man is wholly a product of his sensations, or otherwise said, of his experience. By contrast, then, the new image of human nature tended toward the opposite extreme of thoroughgoing *environmentalism*.

There were, of course, some quite notable exceptions to this tendency toward wholesale environmentalism. Still it is true to say that environmentalism, as thus formulated, carried the day. Both varieties of psychological mechanism— mental and physiological—took it entirely for granted. So also did the theory of human nature held by the average literate and enlightened person of the age.

With wholesale environmentalism taken thus for granted, three conclusions quite naturally followed—conclusions which would scarcely have been dreamed of during the Middle Ages, and certainly never agreed to, but which by the end of the eighteenth century seemed altogether obvious. The first was of a very general sort: if man is wholly a product of his environment, then to understand a particular man we need only understand the environmental forces which act upon him. The second was simply the first translated into the language of social-political philosophy: if human nature is wholly the result of environment, then *individual differences* in human nature are likewise wholly the result of environment. The third, in turn, was but the second translated into the language of social-political *activism:* if you would improve the man, you must first improve the environment; or conversely, if you improve the environment, you thereby necessarily improve the man.

Each of these conclusions had important and far-reaching practical consequences, and we may now pause briefly to inquire into some of these.


### Insanity

It is not the purpose of this volume to present a detailed account of the history of psychiatric thought and practice. Still, some general observations do seem in order at this point, for it is inevitable that an age's conception of human nature will have a bearing on its attitude toward the problem of insanity.

From the Greeks down to the eighteenth century, there had been essentially only two ways of viewing the problem of insanity:

(1) The older of the two was the theory of *demonic possession,* so called, which held that the insane person is possessed, or controlled, by some malevolent, alien intelligence. Usually, this possession was held to be beyond the deliberate control of the afflicted person, and in this case he was regarded only as the unwilling *victim* of insanity. At other times, though, and particularly during the late Middle Ages, the person's insanity was considered to be the result of a contract between himself and the possessing demonic agency, into which he had freely entered in return for certain supernatural powers and concessions. Here, of course, the insane person's role in his insanity was seen to be that of a *conspirator.*

In either case, the treatment of insanity when viewed as demonic possession was apt to be rather severe, for it was well known that demons are a tenacious lot. There is a certain grim irony to the fact that the most drastic form of such treatment—burning at the stake—came to be known by the lofty Inquisitional phrase, *auto da fé* (act of faith). Less drastic forms of treatment included a variety of tortures, some relatively crude, some highly imaginative. All of these treatments, from mere breaking on the rack to burning at the stake, were based upon one simple therapeutic principle: if the body were made a sufficiently uncomfortable habitation for the possessing demon, it would forthwith pack up and leave.

(2) The second such view of insanity was comprised by what we might speak of as the theory of *organic etiology*. It too was of ancient origin, going back at least as far as the Greeks. As its name would suggest, the theory held insanity to be a consequence of some sort of bodily disturbance or defect. Thus, beginning with the Greeks and extending up at least through the fifteenth and sixteenth centuries, insanity was often considered to be the result of an imbalance among the several bodily "humors." (This theory of bodily humors is usually traced to the Greek physician Hippocrates [ca. fourth century BC], from whom also derived the classification "blood," "phlegm," "black bile," and "yellow bile" which remained fairly standard right up through the close of the medieval period.) By the eighteenth century, this ancient and venerable notion of humoral imbalance had for the most part given way to the rather more sophisticated (though, in most cases, no less conjectural) theory that insanity is the result of a pathological state of the brain.

Although the treatments prescribed by the theory of organic etiology tended to be somewhat more humane than those inspired by the theory of demonic possession, they were by no means all pleasant and salubrious. At times they involved nothing more harmful than changes in diet, climate, and locale; equally often, though, they amounted to a kind of medical *auto da fé*, consisting in numerous bloodlettings, cold baths, and violent and repeated showers. Worse than any of its treatments, however, was the general *attitude* toward insanity fostered by the organic theory, for it suggested, especially in its brain-pathology form, that insanity could be arrested and perhaps even mitigated somewhat, but that it could not be cured.

These, then, were the two principal headings under which the problem of insanity had been traditionally viewed. By the time the eighteenth century rolled around, the actual care and treatment of the insane seems to have been based upon a kind of eclectic blending of the two views. The great psychiatric reformer of the age, Phillipe Pinel (1745–1826), described it thus:

> Derangement of the understanding is generally regarded as the result of an organic lesion of the brain and therefore as incurable. . . . Thus public mental asylums have been considered places of confinement and isolation for dangerous patients and pariahs. Therefore their custodians, who in most cases are inhuman and unenlightened, have taken the liberty of treating these mentally sick in a most despotic, cruel, and violent manner.[3]

In this respect, Pinel may be seen as the eighteenth century's foremost psychiatric spokesman for the new image of human nature, for it was he who first recognized and put into practice the great psychiatric implication of this new image—that if you would effectively treat the insane, you must first improve their immediate surroundings. Thus, his famous reply to Couthon, the president of the Paris Commune: "Citizen, it is my conviction that these mentally ill are intractable only because they are deprived of fresh air and of their liberty."[4] Thus, also, his many famous asylum reforms, including the removal of the chains and fetters by which the insane had been customarily bound.

It was Pinel also who recognized and attempted to put into practice the even broader implications of the new conception of human nature: (a) that insanity is at least in part the product of "moral causes" (these being what we would today distinguish as "psychological causes"), and (b) that it could accordingly be treated and perhaps even cured through "moral treatments." To be sure, psychotherapy had been practiced in some form or another since the dawn of time, but here in the late eighteenth century it was for the first time recognized and practiced *as such,* without recourse to demons, humoral imbalances, or conjectured brain lesions. We may note, in fact, that Pinel's psychotherapeutic principles were not very different from those often subscribed to today: experience, he observed, "continually shows the happy results of a conciliating attitude, of a kind and compassionate firmness."[5]

### Social and Political Philosophy

Certainly the most resounding consequence of the new image of human nature was the effect it had upon social and political philosophy. This effect, of course, was complex and many-sided, but we shall pause here to mention only two underlying themes.

(1) If human nature is chiefly a product of environmental influences, then it clearly follows that *individual differences* in human nature are also chiefly the results of environmental influences. Thus, the differences between peasants, philosophers, and kings are not intrinsic, but derive rather from the differences between their respective circumstances. In short, the manifest differences between men are only *extrinsic;* intrinsically, men are *equal.*

(2) And yet, if men are intrinsically equal, how does it come about that some men are rulers and others subjects? How, in a word, do we account for the phenomenon of *government?* In former times, the question had been answered on the basis of the doctrine of "divine right," which in effect asserted that men are not equal at all, extrinsically *or* intrinsically. The ruler, it held, is serving as God's temporal agent. Thus, not only was the government of the ruler justified, but revolt against it was tantamount to a revolt against God himself. The effect of the new image of human nature, especially of its assertion of intrinsic human equality, was naturally to throw this doctrine out of court.

The question of government, then, resolved itself into two possibilities: men are governed either by force or by their own consent. In the former case, it was apparent that a government could survive only so long as it was strong enough to *compel* obedience. For as Rousseau wrote in 1762:

> As long as a people is compelled to obey, and obeys, it does well, [but] as soon as it can shake off the yoke, and shakes it off, it does better still; for, regaining its liberty by the same right as took it away, either it is justified in resuming it, or there was no justification for those who took it away [in the first place].[6]

The alternative to this answer—that men are governed by their own consent—was not so much a description of existing political systems as a guiding principle. In fact, it was a kind of historical myth, but it was nonetheless the novel contribution and crowning gem of eighteenth-century political thought. It was a myth, moveover, by which the two great political revolutions of the period, the American of 1776 and the French of 1789, were profoundly influenced. This, namely, was the myth of the "social contract"—the theory that human society is a *contractual relationship* designed to serve the mutual interests of those who are party to it. Indeed, if men are intrinsically equal, how could it be otherwise? A particular government is justified only so long, and insofar, as it expresses the general will of the governed; conversely, when this government ceases to express the general will of the governed, it is then the privilege of the governed to dissolve the contract on which it was based. The American Declaration of Independence of 1776 put the whole argument quite succinctly:

> We hold these truths to be self-evident; that all men are created equal; that they are endowed by their creator with certain unalienable rights; that among these are life, liberty, and the pursuit of happiness; that to secure these rights, governments are instituted among men, deriving their just powers from the consent of the governed; that whenever any government becomes destructive to these ends, it is the right of the people to alter or to abolish it, and to institute new government, laying its foundation on such principles, and organizing its powers in such form, as to them shall seem most likely to effect their safety and happiness.

### THE GREAT SIMPLIFICATION

The following passage is taken from the preface of the Baron d'Holbach's *Common Sense, or Natural Ideas Opposed to Supernatural* (1772). We quote it here because it is so characteristic of the age and because it gives expression to yet another tenet—the last that we shall consider—of the age's conception of human nature.

> Truth is simple; error is complex, uncertain in its progress, and full of windings. The voice of nature is intelligible; that of falsehood is ambiguous, enigmatical, mysterious; the way of truth is straight; that of imposture is crooked and dark. Truth, forever necessary to man, must necessarily be felt by all upright minds; the lessons of reason are made to be followed by all honest men. Men are unhappy only because they are ignorant; they are ignorant only because everything conspires to prevent their being enlightened; they are so wicked only because their reason is not yet sufficiently unfolded.[7]

Whatever else might be said about human nature in the eighteenth century, one thing seemed quite clear: like nature itself, human nature was simple, uncomplicated, harmonious, and readily intelligible. Indeed, human nature was so simple and clear that it could be summarized (and often was) in a couple of paragraphs. Usually such a summary would run like this:

Man is born with the ability to receive sensations, to derive simple ideas from them, and to combine these simple ideas into complex ideas. In the natural course of things, these complex ideas mirror the external reality from which they were at length derived, and it is to this natural process of forming true ideas that we give the name "reason." At other times, though, ideas are formed unnaturally (as Locke had noted) by chance or custom, the result, of course, being ignorance and unreasonable superstition.

Now to some of these sensations is attached pleasure, to others pain. This is so because nature has wisely provided that we should seek those things which enhance our self-preservation and avoid those which endanger it. And since self-preservation is the *only* goal that nature could have imparted to us, it is therefore clear (as the Italian penal reformer Cesare Beccaria put it) that "pleasure and pain are the only springs of action in beings endowed with sensibility."[8] In this regard, it is evident that the man with a sufficiently developed reason will be relatively happy, for he has clearer ideas of the external world and is therefore better able to secure its pleasures and avoid its pains. Conversely, the man of ignorance and superstition will be relatively unhappy.

The eighteenth century had a way of making strange bedfellows, and certainly two of the strangest are to be found in this marriage of Locke's psychological empiricism with the motivational doctrine of hedonism. Eventually it gave rise to what is perhaps the grossest psychological simplification of all— the notion that happiness and unhappiness are but the effects of one's *immediate* external situation. Or as the great Voltaire put it, as though it were a truth so obvious as to need no defense: "That man is at present happy who is experiencing pleasure, and that pleasure can only come from outside."[9]

In part, this great eighteenth-century simplification of human nature was a corollary of its wholesale environmentalism. In part, also, it was an elaboration of the thesis that man is an animal (for it was well known that animals are simple, uncomplicated creatures). For the most part, though, it was a straightforward denial of the rather gloomy (or so it seemed at the time) medieval image of human nature. In the Middle Ages, man was regarded as a creature of conflicts, contradictions, and contrarieties. He had been formed in the image of his Creator, and yet he was tainted by Original Sin. He had a spiritual nature and a carnal nature, and so long as the spirit inhabited the flesh, the two were constantly at odds. The happiness of the spirit was to be found in the love of God; the happiness of the flesh in love of self. In short, human nature was held to be the scene of a constantly raging battle between the forces of light and the forces of darkness, between the demands of the spirit and the demands of the flesh.

The claim of the great eighteenth-century simplification, on the other hand, was that man's only nature is his animal nature, that his only happiness or unhappiness is his immediate sensory pleasure or unpleasure. How utterly simple and clear it all seemed, how utterly true and unquestionable. Man is an animal with simple animal needs; let these needs be satisfied, intelligently and in accordance with the light of reason, and all is well. Thus, as the Baron d'Holbach further observed, in what was perhaps the epitome of eighteenth-century reflections upon human nature:

> To learn the true principles of morality, men have no need of theology, of revelation, or gods: They have need only of reason. They have only to enter into themselves, to reflect upon their own nature, consult their sensible interests, consider the object of society, and of the individuals, who comprise it; and they will easily perceive that virtue is the interest and vice the unhappiness of beings of their kind.[10]

In seeking to understand these first two centuries of psychology's modern era, one point must be made very clear: At the heart of most seventeenth- and eighteenth-century intellectual activity was the deep and abiding conviction that the past, particularly the long medieval past, had been all wrong, and that "we" on the contrary stood at the dawn of a new age. The past, then, was considered to have been but one vast darkness; the mission of the new age was to dispel that darkness. Thus, the period was variously (and at times arrogantly) described by its inhabitants as the age of "enlightenment," of *illuminismo,* of *Aufklärung,* or as the *siècle des lumières.*

This mood of "enlightenment" and "new beginnings" was not, of course, the prerogative of psychology alone; rather, it was characteristic of the age in general. But we could hardly hope to understand the psychology of the period without first understanding how very dependent it was upon this one initial affirmation. In large measure, the psychology of the seventeenth and eighteenth centuries was a deliberate reaction against, and denial of, the tenets of medieval psychology. Medieval psychology accepted innate ideas; the new psychology (with the exception of Descartes) denied them, arguing instead that all ideas derive from experience. Medieval psychology took the existence of a soul as a first principle; by the end of the eighteenth century, the new psychology took the *non*existence (or, at least, nonimportance) of a soul as a first principle. More generally, medieval psychology regarded man as a tainted but still partially divine performer in a purposeful cosmic drama; by contrast, the new psychology considered him to be a mere animal—albeit "the most advantageously organized of any"—inhabiting a blindly mechanical universe.

## NOTES

1.  J. Kemp, ed., *Diderot: Interpreter of Nature,* trans. J. Stewart and J. Kemp (New York: International Publishers, 1963), p. 134.
2.  J. J. Rousseau, *The Social Contract and Discourses,* trans. G. D. H. Cole (New York: Dutton, 1950), p. 200.
3.  G. Zilboorg, *A History of Medical Psychology* (New York: Norton, 1941), p. 337.
4.  Ibid., p. 332.
5.  Ibid., p. 337.
6.  Rousseau, *Social Contract and Discourses,* p. 4.
7.  F. E. Manuel, ed., *The Enlightenment* (Englewood Cliffs, N.J.: Prentice-Hall, 1965), p. 62.
8.  Ibid., p. 143.
9.  F. Voltaire, *Philosophical Letters,* trans. E. Dilworth (Indianapolis, Ind.: Bobbs-Merrill, 1961), p. 137.
10. Manuel, *Enlightenment,* pp. 61–62.

## FOR FURTHER READING

Excellent background accounts of the matters considered in this chapter are to be found in the following works: C. L. Becker, *The Heavenly City of the Eighteenth-Century Philosophers* (New Haven, Conn.: Yale University Press, 1932), and F. E. Manuel, *The Age of Reason* (Ithaca, N.Y.: Cornell University Press, 1951).

Several well-chosen excerpts from the psychological writings of the eighteenth-century *philosophes* are to be found in F. E. Manuel, ed., *The Enlightenment* (Englewood Cliffs, N.J.: Prentice-Hall, 1965).

The student who might wish to inquire into the "new image of human nature" in greater depth would be well advised to begin with the following, readily available volumes: C. Beccaria, *On Crimes and Punishments,* trans. H. Paolucci (Indianapolis, Ind.: Bobbs-Merrill, 1963); A. N. Condorcet, *Sketch for a Historical Picture of the Progress of the Human Mind,* trans. J. Barräclough (London: Weidenfeld and Nicolson, 1955); J. Kemp, ed., *Diderot: Interpreter of Nature* (New York: International Publishers, 1963); J. J. Rousseau, *The Social Contract and Discourses,* trans. G. D. H. Cole (New York: Dutton, 1950); and F. Voltaire, *Philosophical Letters,* trans. E. Dilworth (Indianapolis, Ind.: Bobbs-Merrill, 1961). Then, by way of contrast, he would be advised to read the whole of B. Pascal, *Pensées,* trans. W. F. Trotter (New York: Dutton, 1958).

# Part II

# The Nineteenth Century

There were three extremely important differences between the psychological thought of the nineteenth century and that of the two preceding centuries. The first was that, whereas the psychological thinkers of the seventeenth and eighteenth centuries considered themselves to be tending the vineyards of philosophy, those of the nineteenth century saw themselves as part of the newly triumphant enterprise known as natural science. Of course, this new attitude did not arrive full-born on January 1, 1800, but it was certainly strongly present by the middle of the century, and by the 1880s firmly established.

The second difference was that the psychology of the seventeenth and eighteenth centuries had been almost exclusively the province of British and French thinkers. That of the nineteenth century, on the other hand, was strongly infused by the Germanic *Geist*, with all its tendencies toward thoroughness, depth, subtlety, and (sometimes) ponderosity. The student of modern history will know that psychology was not the only realm in which the Germanic spirit showed its genius during the nineteenth century.

The third difference was that the psychology of the late nineteenth century had the benefit of Charles Darwin's theory of organic evolution. Up until that time, the chief focus of psychology had been the perceptual and cognitive processes of human adults. Now it became (not quite overnight, but shortly) the study of much else besides: children, animal behavior, instinct, emotion, motivation, varieties, differences, comparisons, and continuities. More than that, it now had some powerful new weapons in its conceptual arsenal: environmental exigency, functional utility, adaptation, and survival.

The result of it all was that by the end of the nineteenth century psychological inquiry had gathered enormous momentum, and it had moreover blazed many of the theoretical trails that we are still following. Our opening excursion into this important century will be in Chapters 5 and 6, where we examine what became of the traditions of mental and physiological mechanism under the new Germanic influence. It is here, too, that we will see the first efforts to turn psychology into a *Naturwissenschaft,* a natural science. We will then devote the whole of Chapter 7 to examining the impact of Darwinian evolutionary theory, and conclude in Chapter 8 with a sketch of one of the most endearing figures in the whole history of psychology, William James. This chapter on James will serve a purpose similar to that served by the last chapter of Part I, in that it will provide an overview of the "enlightened" (or "scientific") vision of human nature that predominated toward the end of the nineteenth century. It will also convey a sense of the existential tension generated by this vision in those who, like James, saw clearly that the search for psychological truth has momentous issues hanging in the balance.

## Chapter 5

# The New German Mechanism

That the course of our thoughts is often so inconsequent, abrupt, and apparently irregular . . . deceives in the same way as the wandering of the planets. The conformity to law in the human mind resembles exactly that in the firmament.

Johann Friedrich Herbart, *Lehrbuch zur Psychologie* (1816)

No other forces than the common physical-chemical ones are active within the organism. In those cases which cannot at the time be explained by these forces, one has either to find the specific way or form of their action by means of the physical-mathematical method or to assume new forces, equal in dignity to the chemical-physical forces inherent in matter, reducible to the force of attraction and repulsion.

Emil du Bois-Reymond, letter to Karl Ludwig (1842)

The seventeenth and eighteenth centuries were English and French centuries almost exclusively. With only a few exceptions, the great and novel ideas of the period originated with English thinkers. These, in turn, were taken over by the French *philosophes* who reworked them into easily digestible literary form, popularized them, and spread them abroad. In other countries, by contrast, there was precious little in the way of intellectual achievement during the period, save for the fashionable activity of translating English and French ideas into the idiom of the homeland. In Germany this aping of foreign manners and thought became so acute that French was widely adopted as the literary and courtly language, with the German tongue itself being left to the masses and the marketplace. Throughout the whole of the seventeenth century, for example, the Germanic nations could lay claim to only one great philosophical genius. This man was Gottfried Wilhelm Leibniz—who published his major works in French. In the eighteenth century, the principal German court was that of Frederick the Great in Berlin; its language was French, and its intellectual darlings included Julien Offray de la Mettrie.

By the early years of the nineteenth century, on the other hand, German intellectual life had begun to have an identity of its own. So also German psychology. In this chapter and the next, we shall consider the earlier stages of this newly born German psychology. We may begin, in the present chapter, by recounting the changes that were undergone by those two great traditions of psychological thought, mental and physiological mechanism, as they passed through German hands.


## MENTAL MECHANISM

The tradition of mental mechanism that began with Locke and ended with James Mill was inspired by and modeled upon the Newtonian physical theory; we have made this observation so often that it has by this time perhaps become tiresome. Let us, however, steel ourselves to it for just a moment longer to consider just what were the actual points of correspondence between mental mechanism and Newtonian physical theory. As we have noted, the explanatory strength of Newtonian physical theory depended principally upon two features: the first, that physical phenomena could be resolved (conceptually, at least) into complexes of infinitesimal points; the second, that effects between distant bodies could be communicated by way of attractive and repulsive forces. Now the first of these notions clearly stayed with mental mechanism throughout, as is evidenced by its unremitting preoccupation with the analysis of complex mental phenomena into distinct, uncompounded, elementary components. But what of the second? Locke, we may recall, suggested that ideas might have a natural "connection and agreement" or "disagreement and repugnancy." Hume, somewhat later, regarded the association of ideas as "a kind of attraction, which in the mental world will be found to have as extraordinary effects as in the natural, and to show itself in as many and as varied forms." Following Locke and Hume, though, the notions of attraction and repulsion seem to have been abandoned entirely. James Mill, who gave mental mechanism its most thoroughgoing and explicit statement, said nothing of them whatever.

Consider now what the English mental mechanism lost in its reluctance to take attraction and repulsion seriously. The physical universe portrayed by

Newton was a *dynamic* one, full of forces, motion, and change. The world of the English mental mechanism, on the other hand, was unmistakably *static*. There was change of a sort, and thus "motion" of a sort, but it was at best dull, plodding, passive motion. This dull, plodding passivity was grounded, as we have seen, in the subsidiary doctrine of psychological empiricism, and in this we find the principal distinction between the English mental mechanism and its later German counterpart.

The English doctrine of psychological empiricism never seems to have sat very well on the German imagination. It was David Hume's elaboration of this doctrine, for example, that awoke the great Prussian philosopher Immanuel Kant (1724–1804) from his well-known "dogmatic slumbers." Although Kant does not properly lie within the tradition of German mental mechanism, his rejection of psychological empiricism contriubted to its development nonetheless. For. this reason, we shall do well to pause briefly to consider him. Recall for a moment that familiar assertion of English mental mechanism: All knowledge derives from experience. Prior to Kant, the ambiguity concealed within this seemingly simple statement had never been clearly recognized. Not until his influential masterwork, the *Critique of Pure Reason* (1781–1787), was it brought out into the open. "There can be no doubt," Kant began,

> that all our knowledge begins with experience. For [how otherwise] should our faculty of knowledge be awakened into action? . . . In the order of time, therefore, we have no knowledge antecedent to experience, and with experience all our knowledge begins.

Up to this point, then, Kant saw no reason to take issue with the assertion. Beyond it, though, he quickly drew the line, for while it is quite true that "all our knowledge begins with experience," he continued,

> it does not follow that it all arises out of experience. [On the contrary] it may well be that even our empirical knowledge is made up of what we receive through impressions and of what our own faculty of knowledge (sensible impressions serving merely as the occasion) supplies from itself.[1]

The distinction intended by this passage is entirely valid. The assertion that all knowledge derives from experience may be taken in one or the other of two quite distinct senses. (a) The first amounts only to a denial of innate or *a priori* ideas. It holds simply that experience is a *necessary condition* for knowledge, or as Kant put it, that "in the order of time . . . we have no knowledge antecedent to experience." Thus, no experience, no knowledge. (b) The second sense is a much stronger one; it argues that experience is not only a necessary condition for knowledge, but a *sufficient* one as well. Further, if experience is a sufficient condition of knowledge, then knowledge is the *necessary consequent* of experience. This of course is simply psychological empiricism stated in its most extreme terms: knowledge *is* experience, experience *is* knowledge. Thus the familiar tendency of mental mechanism to portray "the mind" (Kant's "faculty of knowledge") as a kind of blank tablet, the mere passive recipient of external impressions.

As we have just seen, Kant accepted the first sense of the assertion but rejected the second. Experience is indeed a *necessary* condition of knowledge, he considered, but it is by no means *sufficient*. For knowledge consists not only in what we passively receive through experience, but also in what "our own faculty of knowledge" actively "supplies from itself." Thus we must distinguish between the *contents of experience,* which are the raw materials of the mind, and the *operations of the mind* by which these contents are worked up into "knowledge." And from this distinction one very important question inevitably follows: Do these "operations of the mind" derive from experience, or are they not perhaps *innate?* As James Mill apparently recognized some years later, there is one and only one operation of the mind that is compatible with the doctrine of psychological empiricism, and that is association by contiguity. Any other operations of the mind could readily be seen as native endowments.

In short, Kant had found a chink in the doctrine's armor; and he did not hesitate to thrust his blade through to the hilt. Beyond this point, though, we need not attempt to follow his alternative to psychological empiricism, for it lies well outside the course on which we are set. Suffice it to say that Kant opened a way back to the conception of native, or innate, psychological endowment, without recourse to the doctrine of innate ideas. As we shall see later, his influence upon subsequent German psychological thought was deep and far-reaching.

With Kant's distinction before them, later German psychologists could then speak of inherent operations of the mind without compunction. And if they were mechanistically inclined, as many continued to be, they would have no difficulty whatever in seeing in these inherent operations of the mind a reflection of the inherent operations of the Newtonian cosmos. For the moment, we may consider the two earliest of these mechanistically inclined German psychologists: Johann Friedrich Herbart (1776–1841) and Moritz Wilhelm Drobisch (1802–1896).

### J. F. Herbart

In his *Lehrbuch zur Psychologie (Textbook in Psychology,* 1816),[2] Herbart grafted the Newtonian conception of attractive and repulsive forces onto psychology almost without alteration. The basic notions from which he extracted the most novel consequences were (a) that a "concept" is *attracted* "by its own effort" into consciousness, and (b) that "opposed concepts" exert a *repulsive* force upon one another. Unfortunately, Herbart did not state precisely what he meant by "consciousness," "concepts," and "opposed concepts," but this need not prevent us from understanding his general argument.

Imagine two concepts, $a$ and $b$. If they are not opposed, then they will have no effect upon each other and may accordingly exist in consciousness simultaneously. If, however, they are opposed, they will exert a repulsive force upon each other, and the stronger of the two will repel the weaker out of consciousness. The suppressed concept will then be, in effect, *unconscious*.

At this point we must pause for a brief backward glance. What becomes of a "mental content" (or "concept") when one is no longer conscious of it? The earlier psychology, English mental mechanism in particular, had drawn no distinction between "consciousness" and "mind." Thus, it would have been obliged—had the question ever confronted it—to phrase its answer as follows: A mental content of which one is no longer conscious is a mental content that no longer exists. Now, on the face of things, this answer would seem to make a certain amount of sense, for how can one speak of a "mental content" that is no longer contained "in the mind"? This, however, is based on the assumption that "mind" and "consciousness" are identical. If, on the other hand, one may assume that there is *more* to the "mind" than meets the eye of "consciousness," then one finds no difficulty at all in speaking of "unconscious mental contents." For reasons that we shall consider in a moment, Herbart found this assumption not only legitimate but unavoidable.

According to Herbart, a mental content that has been repelled from consciousness does not thereby cease to exist. It is still "in the mind"; The only difference is that it has been suppressed below the *threshold* of consciousness. And even here it does not lie dormant, for all the while it is being *attracted* "by its own effort" back into consciousness, that is, back above the threshold of consciousness. So long as the "opposed concept" exerts its stronger repulsive force the suppressed mental content will be in a state of dynamic *equilibrium*. When the opposition is removed, however, it will gravitate back into consciousness.

Consider now the case of two "opposed" mental contents, $a$ and $b$, in which the stronger, $a$, has repelled the weaker, $b$, below the threshold of consciousness. If there now occurs a third mental content, $c$, which is "opposed" to $a$ and also stronger than $a$, this occurrence will have the effect of suppressing $a$ below the threshold of consciousness, thus removing the hindrance from $b$. Thus $b$, whose gravitation toward consciousness is now unimpeded, will rise above the threshold of consciousness. In a word, $b$ will now be *recalled* as the result of the occurrence of $c$. It could be said that $b$ and $c$ are "associated," but what has really happened is that $c$ has suppressed the "opposed" mental content which formerly held $b$ in equilibrium. In any case, this is what Herbart imagined to be the process by which an unconscious mental content finds reentry into consciousness.

In addition to a "threshold of consciousness" (or "statical threshold"),

Herbart also spoke of a "mechanical threshold." His notion here was that, even though a mental content might be held in equilibrium *outside* of consciousness, it could still exert effects *upon* consciousness. This, of course, was but a direct consequence of Herbart's two earlier assumptions: the first, that "opposed concepts" mutually repel one another; the second, that a suppressed mental content is attracted back toward consciousness. All of which involved Herbart straightaway with what would today be spoken of as a "dynamic unconscious."

Herbart's reasoning at this point ran somewhat as follows: so long as a suppressed mental content remains above the mechanical threshold, it will contribute to what goes on inside consciousness, even though it is itself *un*conscious. This conclusion is demanded not only by the logic of attractive and repulsive forces, but by the phenomena of the human mind as well. For how otherwise could we even begin to explain the fact that "the course of our thoughts is often so inconsequent, abrupt, and apparently irregular"? Clearly, the course of conscious thought must be acted upon by events outside it. Thus, he concluded, this inconsequent, abrupt, and irregular appearance of the stream of conscious thought "deceives in the same way as the wandering of the planets. The conformity to law in the human mind resembles exactly that in the firmament." [3]

Herbart's psychology was, of course, a thoroughly Newtonian affair. It was a psychology of attractive forces and repulsive forces, of equilibrium, motion, and change. Herbart even went so far as to provide his reader with mathematical formulae by which the comings and goings of "concepts" could be (in principle, if not in fact) calculated. We need not consider the more specific features of Herbart's new and distinctly German variety of mental mechanism, for most of these soon became lost in the wash of history. As we shall see presently, though, several of its more general features have endured—albeit in disguised form—right up to the present.

## M. W. Drobisch

Herbart's most immediate successor in the German tradition of mental mechanism was Moritz Wilhelm Drobisch. Drobisch did not go out of his way to give credit to Herbart for his ideas, but the debt is plainly visible nonetheless. Thus, in his *Empirische Psychologie nach naturwissenschaftlicher Methode* (*Empirical Psychology According to the Methods of Natural Science,* 1842), Drobisch spoke of attractive and repulsive forces among mental contents as though they were facts beyond dispute:

> The fact, that only a few ideas can enter our consciousness at once, shows to be sure at first glance, that they displace, suppress, therefore, as it were, expel one another; but also on the other hand, that they are not able to

avoid one another, but are held together by an attractive force. The same thing likewise appears in associations, those quite involuntary and artless combinations of simultaneous ideas. It is, therefore, possible to attribute similar attractive and repellant forces to ideas, after the analogy of the physical-chemical hypothesis of attractions and repulsions of elements.[4]

In brief, it may be said that Drobisch accepted Herbart's psychology of attractive and repulsive forces almost point for point. There was one respect, though, in which Drobisch went beyond Herbart.

When we discussed Herbart earlier, we noted his assertion that opposed concepts eventually enter into a state of equilibrium with one antoher, that is, they reach a point at which the forces of their separate tendencies to gravitate toward the center of consciousness are balanced off against the forces of their mutual repulsion. Now according to this theory, so long as the number of concepts in the mind remains constant, the equilibrium between them will endure indefinitely. As soon, however, as some new concept enters the picture, the equilibrium will be upset, at least temporarily, until a new equilibrium is achieved.

Now, inasmuch as new concepts are continually introduced by way of perception, it follows that the Herbartian apparatus of the mind will always be *vacillating* between equilibrium and disequilibrium. Herbart had made all of this quite explicit, but it was Drobisch who saw that it might be worked up into a kind of Newtonian theory of emotion and motivation. His argument ran as follows: If the mind has no contents, then there is nothing to be in motion, and it is consequently at rest. If the mind has a constant number of contents, then a state of equilibrium is eventually reached, and it is consequently at rest again. If, as in reality, the mind is always receiving new contents, then it is continually striving to be at rest. In short, the mind is always either at rest or striving to be at rest. Accordingly, we may say that equilibrium (or rest) is the goal to which all mental processes tend, and that disequilibrium is the frequent but untoward deviation from that state.

The implications that Drobisch drew from this line of reasoning may impress us as vaguely familiar. If equilibrium, or rest, is the natural state of the mind, then its absence (disequilibrium) must be felt as unpleasant; and in this we find the source of "feelings" and "desires." Thus:

> If I have a feeling of . . . equilibrium, a change in it will be a feeling of disturbance. [In this respect] the feeling of psychical equilibrium is precisely similar to that of bodily health: of both there exists no positive feeling. The body as well as the mind is in a state of equilibrium when one has no feeling of its activities, just as a machine in which there is the least possible friction makes but little noise. Desires and feelings are, therefore, the indices of the deviation from the state of equilibrium of ideas.[5]

When Drobisch wrote in the early 1840s, there was really no way in which this nascent theory of emotion and motivation could have been taken further. As we shall see later, its development had to await the contribution of Darwin. For the moment, we may simply observe that Drobisch's allusion to "a machine in which there is the least possible friction" was not entirely accidental.

## PHYSIOLOGICAL MECHANISM

Let us now turn to consider the events that were taking place within physiological mechanism during these same early decades of the nineteenth century. We may begin by briefly recalling what physiological mechanism, up to this time, was all about. As a strictly physiological theory, physiological mechanism rested upon two assumptions, or hypotheses, that had originated with Descartes: (a) that the vital activities (Descartes' "heat" and "movement") of the body are inherent functions of the body itself, rather than of some external vital agency, and (b) that the operations by which the body produces these vital activities are essentially "mechanical" in nature. In order to have significant psychological implications, the theory of physiological mechanism required still another hypothesis, which will be discussed in a later chapter. For the moment, let it suffice to point out that physiological mechanism, *qua* physiological theory, was a systematic denial of the ancient doctrine of vitalism.

Up through the end of the eighteenth century, the burden of proof in this contest between vitalism and mechanism still rested heavily with the mechanists. Thus, around 1770 the English anatomist John Hunter could still confidently assert that mere matter, however complex its organization, could not be the sole author of vital phenomena:

> Animal and vegetable substance differ from common matter in having a power superadded totally different from any other known property of matter, out of which arise various new properties; it cannot arise out of any peculiar modification of matter, but appears to be something superadded. . . . Organization may arise out of living parts, and produce action; but life can never arise out of, and depend on, organization. . . . . Organization and life are two different things.[6]

Hunter's confidence, however, was not to be shared by his vitalistic successors. By the beginning of the nineteenth century, the balance between vitalism and mechanism began to shift. Within a few decades more, vitalism was in conspicuous retreat. By the middle of the century it had been banished from the realm of respectable physiology almost entirely.

This demise of physiological vitalism was based principally upon two developments. First of all, the period between, say, 1780 and 1850 was one of great physiological discovery. This in itself would not have been enough to send vitalism into retreat, save that most of the physiological discoveries made during the period seemed to speak rather strongly in favor of the mechanistic interpretation. The second development was of a theoretical sort: toward the middle of the century, physiological mechanism gathered around it a coterie of brilliant men who spoke forcefully and convincingly in its behalf. We may begin by considering some of the more important physiological discoveries that were made during this period, along with their attendant implications.

### Physiological Discovery

As a result of the work of such luminaries as Lavoisier (around 1775) and Dalton (around 1810), the science of chemistry had by the early years of the nineteenth century been transformed into a thoroughly Newtonian science.

*The Chemistry of the Body.* The mechanistically inclined physiologist could allow himself to take considerable comfort from this transformation of inorganic chemistry, for it was at this same time that physiologists were coming to appreciate just how much the vitality of the body depended upon the chemical events that take place within it. The reasoning here is easy to follow: If vitality is a function of chemical processes, and if, in turn, these chemical processes may be understood to take place in accordance with established physical theory, then vitality, too, may be understood in terms of established (that is to say, Newtonian) physical theory. Thus the chemist Justus Liebig, who presented the first thorough analysis of the chemistry of digestion, wrote in 1842 of the "vital force" that resides in living animal tissue:

> The vital force causes a decomposition of the constituents of food, and destroys the force of attraction which is continually exerted between their molecules; it alters the direction of the chemical forces in such wise, that the elements of the constituents of food arrange themselves in another form. . . . It causes the new compounds to assume forms altogether different from those which are the result of the attraction of cohesion when acting freely, that is, without resistance. . . . The phenomenon of growth, or increase in the mass, presupposes that the acting vital force is more powerful than the resistance which the chemical force opposes to the decomposition or transformation of the elements of the food.

In Liebig's view, as in the view of many of his contemporaries, a "vital force" of this sort was not only in accord with the facts of animal chemistry, but entirely consistent with the principles of Newtonian physics. For "there is nothing to prevent us," he concluded, "from considering the vital force as a peculiar property, which is possessed by certain material bodies, and becomes sensible when their elementary particles are combined in a certain arrangement or form."[7]

*The Nervous System.* It was one thing to understand the chemistry of digestion, but quite another to extend this understanding to the phenomena of vitality in general. Thus, what the chemist J. J. Berzelius wrote in 1813 could still have been justifiably written in the 1830s or 1840s:

> The unknown cause of the phenomena of life is principally lodged in . . . the nervous system, the very operation of which it constitutes. Nothing of which chemistry has taught us hitherto has the smallest analogy to its operation, or affords us the least hint toward a knowledge of its hidden nature.[8]

This, however, is not to say that the nervous system remained a mystery entirely. True, the chemistry of the nervous system—which at that time would have been the most direct link with Newtonian physical theory—was still elusive, but on other fronts knowledge was advancing at a considerable rate. A full account of the advances in our knowledge of the nervous system and sense organs that took place during this period would require more time and space than is presently at our disposal; we shall consider, therefore, only those discoveries that played a significant role in the later development of physiological mechanism.

*The Electrical Nature of Nervous Activity.* Up through the middle of the eighteenth century, there had been only two mechanical theories of nervous activity. The first was the theory of animal spirits passing through tube-like nervous structures; the model of the nervous system to which it gave rise was that of a rather clumsy hydraulic apparatus. The second was David Hartley's theory of vibrations; it too was rather clumsy, though not so much so as the animal-spirits model. Their differing degrees of clumsiness aside, however, both of these theories suffered from one quite considerable shortcoming, which was that they were both wrong. For, in point of fact, the nature of nervous activity was not hydraulic or vibratory at all—at least, not in the senses intended by these early theories. In the fullness of time, it was discovered to be—electrical. As early as 1780, the Italian physicist Galvani had observed that a frog's leg would twitch when the surface and interior of its muscle were connected in series with two different metals. By the time that Emil Du Bois-Reymond (whom we shall meet later) published his classical researches in electrophysiology in the 1840s, the electrical nature of nervous activity in general had been long since recognized as fact.

The importance of this discovery will not become entirely clear until later. We may, however, point in its general direction. If nervous activity is essentially electrical in nature, and if electrical phenomena can be understood in terms of Newtonian principles, then it is clear that nervous activity too can be understood in terms of Newtonian principles. Up through the 1830s and 1840s, it was quite firmly believed that electrical phenomena could in fact be explained by Newtonian principles, but it had not as yet been demonstrated. The required demonstration, however, was not long in coming. Later in the chapter, we shall look into this matter more thoroughly.

*The Unidirectionality of the Nervous System.* According to the animal-spirits model of nervous activity, motion within the nervous system could proceed in either direction. In the usual case, of course, the passage was from sense organ to brain to muscle. But, given the proper conditions, it could equally well proceed in the opposite direction, from muscle to brain to sense organ. Hartley's vibratory theory had not accepted this bidirectionality of the nervous system quite so explicitly, but it still tacitly assumed it, particularly when it tried to account for the association between "ideal" and "motory" vibrations.

Here again, these two early theories suffered from the same shortcoming, which was that they were wrong. By the 1820s or 1830s, the unidirectionality of nervous activity had been fairly firmly established, both anatomically and functionally. The sensory nerves, it had been discovered, are essentially afferent, whereas the motor nerves are essentially efferent. Thus, peripheral nervous activity was now known to proceed (except in extraordinary cases) only in the "forward" direction, that is, from the periphery toward the center along sensory nerves, and from the center toward the periphery along motor nerves.

*The Nervous System as a Conductor.* This unidirectionality of the nervous system later came to be known as the "law of forward direction in the nervous system." Ostensibly, the phrase "forward direction" is simply a label for an empirical generalization. If we examine it closely, however, we shall see that it conceals an extra empirical assumption of considerable proportions. The assumption derived in part from the observation of peripheral nervous activity, in part from an increased knowledge of the histology of the central nervous system, and in part from the compelling analogy of nonbiological electrical circuitry. If one studies a peripheral motor or sensory nerve, it soon becomes clear that the principal function of this nerve is to *conduct*. Thus, it receives the nervous impulse at one end, conducts it to the other end, and there discharges it (usually to another nerve, sometimes to an effector). Indeed, since this same thing is observed to occur in all peripheral sensory and motor nerves, it may be said that the principal function of the peripheral nervous system *as a whole* is to conduct.

But what of the central nervous system? Improved microscopic techniques had led in the 1830s to the discovery that the gray matter of the brain is cellular in structure, and that the white matter is fibrous. Thus, the central nervous system too was now known to be composed of individual neural units. And from this it was only a short step to the further consideration that the principal function of these central neural units is precisely the same as that of the peripheral units—namely, to receive, to conduct, and to discharge.

All in all, the nervous system was seen as a kind of biological electrical system, and the analogy that it ostensibly afforded to nonbiological electrical systems was quite naturally an atttractive one. Now, in any of the electrical circuitry then known, what was involved was the simple passage of a current from one end of a conductor (or series of conductors) to the other. This, so it was imagined, is what happens throughout the nervous system as well: the nervous impulse passes from one end of a nerve (or series of nerves) to the other, just as in a Galvanic circuit current passes along a conductor from one pole of a battery to another. It was of course recognized that the nervous system must contain many such paths of conduction in parallel, but there was no doubt that the entire apparatus could be understood in terms of the principles of simple electrical circuitry.

Thus, each individual unit of the nervous system (central as well as peripheral) was regarded as a conductor, and from this it seemed to follow that the nervous system *as a whole* is a conductor. Following the analogy provided by man-made electrical systems, the sensory and motor peripheral nervous systems were taken to be conductors purely and simply, while the central nervous system was conceived of as a very complicated electrical switchboard. Here, then, was the model of neural activity that evolved during the first half of the nineteenth century and endured fairly intact until quite recently: the excitation of a sense organ produces an electrical impulse which is conducted along afferent peripheral pathways into the central nervous system; here it is switched onto an efferent pathway, along which it is conducted until it reaches an effector.

The overarching implication of this model was one which we shall meet again and again as we proceed. If the nervous system as a whole is simply a *conductor* of electrical impulses, and if the central nervous system is simply a *switching station* between afferent and efferent pathways, it then follows that any excitation of a sense organ will eventually find its way to an effector, thus terminating in action of some sort. In its details, this model of nervous activity was of course a far cry from the animal-spirits model of Descartes, but in its general appearance it was much the same. For both models began with peripheral excitation and ended—inevitably—with peripheral action. Or to put it another way, both models were essentially *reflexive* in character. The older model was based upon the view of the nervous system as a partially closed hydraulic apparatus; the newer model achieved the same effect by regarding the nervous system as an electrical conductor. We may refer to the line of reasoning upon which the newer theory was based as the neurological fallacy of composition—that is, the fallacy of attributing to the nervous system as a whole the properties of its individual parts.

## The Field of Interpretation

Throughout the first several decades of the nineteenth century, the contest between physiological vitalism and physiological mechanism remained undecided. Vitalism, as we have said, was on the retreat, but it was still by no means vanquished. The superlative physiological treatise of the 1830s and 1840s, for example, was the two-volume *Handbook of Human Physiology* (1833–1840); its author, Johannes Müller, was a thoroughgoing vitalist. The reason why vitalism still survived, of course, was simply this: it was not obviously false, and its alternative, mechanism, was not obviously true. It is true that many of the newly discovered facts of physiology seemed to lend themselves to a mechanistic interpretation, but battles of this magnitude are never decided by facts alone. Facts naturally play a significant role in the contest, but it is on the field of interpretation that the really decisive movements are made.

It is in this connection that we must now turn to witness the birth of a new and distinctly German variety of physiological mechanism—a variety which carried the day by dint of its interpretative brillance.

In the year 1845 a group of men, most of them former students of Johannes Müller, joined together to form what they called the *Berliner Physikalische Gesellschaft* (Berlin Physical Society). At the heart of this society, and animating its actions throughout, was the consuming faith that *all* phenomena—including the phenomena appropriate to "living matter"—could be exhaustively accounted for in terms of established physical principles. This conviction, of course, was nothing new; it had been in the air now for the better part of two centuries. But, at the hands of the *Physikalische Gesellschaft*, it was very soon transformed from a mere conviction into a plausible, detailed hypothesis.

The mood and temper of the new German physiological mechanism may be best conveyed by recounting a pledge made in 1842 by two of the most active fomenters of the *Physikalische Gesellschaft*, Ernst Brücke and Emil Du Bois-Reymond. In a letter to Karl Ludwig, a German physiologist of similar leanings, Du Bois-Reymond wrote that he and Brücke had made

> a solemn oath to put into effect this truth: "no other forces than the common physical-chemical ones are active within the organism. In those cases which cannot at the time be explained by these forces, one has either to find the specific way or form of their action by means of the physical-mathematical method or to assume new forces, equal in dignity to the chemical-physical forces inherent in matter, reducible to the force of attraction and repulsion."[9]

The pledge was physicalistic to the core, and so also were the ambitions of the *Physikalische Gesellschaft*, for which it served as a kind of manifesto. In this connection, though, one point must be made very clear. These German physiological mechanists were not simply physiologists who happened to be infatuated with the lofty sounds of physical jargon. They were dedicated and competent men who knew their physics at least as well as their physiology. As we shall see in a moment, the eminent success of the movement stemmed in no small measure from the fact that its authors had a physicist's understanding of physical theory.

It was through the genius of Hermann von Helmholtz (1821–1894), after whom the German physicalistic movement came later to be named, that the ambitions of the *Physikalische Gesellschaft* received their most critical support. In his now famous paper "On the Conservation of Force" (1847), Helmholtz put forward his principle of "constancy," thus bringing physiology within the theoretical scope of Newtonian physics, so it seemed, much as Lavoisier and Dalton had done for chemistry. Helmholtz' constancy principle held that the various forms of physical energy can be converted into one another with neither a gain nor a loss in the process. Or to put it another way: that the energy within any closed physical system remains *quantitatively* constant, although it may undergo various *qualitative* transformations. By means of this principle, physicalistically minded physiologists could then seek, all the more convincingly, to explain the internal processes and thus the actions of living organisms in terms of those two conceptual bulwarks of established physical theory, attraction and repulsion.

To appreciate the impact of Helmholtz' constancy principle upon physiology, and later upon psychology, we shall do well to consider the matter in some detail. We may begin by recounting what were then regarded as the most inviolable of all established physical principles, Newton's three laws of motion. The first is often spoken of as the law of inertia: Every body continues in its state of rest or of uniform motion in a straight line, except as it is compelled by force to change that state. Before passing on to the remaining two laws of motion, it should be pointed out that this law actually pertains to two different kinds of inertia. The first is the familiar inertia of rest; the second is the "inertia" of uniform rectilinear motion. Thus, the broader implication of the law is that the mechanical state of a body will be "conserved," whether it be at rest *or* in motion.

The second Newtonian law of motion had to do with *changes* in the mechanical state of a body: Change of motion takes place in the direction of the straight line in which an applied force acts and is directly proportional to the amount of that force. For our present purposes, the important implication of this second law is contained in the phrase "directly proportional."

The third law was a corollary of the first two: Every action has an equal and contrary reaction, that is, the mutual actions of two bodies on each other are always forces equal in amount and opposite in direction. Here, for our purposes, the important implication is contained in the phrase "equal in amount."

As they stood, Newton's three laws of motion taken together implied a conservation of "mechanical force," that is, they implied that the combined total of potential and kinetic energy within any isolated physical system would remain a constant quantity, even though their respective proportions might vary. From this point, the line of reasoning proceeded somewhat as follows: If mechanical energy is conserved, might it not be that energy-in-general is conserved? Thus, in an isolated physical system, might it not be that the combined total of *all* forms of energy remains at a constant level, even though their respective proportions vary? The answer, of course, is *yes*—provided that the various forms of energy (mechanical, chemical, heat, "vital," and the like) may be converted into one another.

In the 1840s, several different investigators took this final step and argued that the principle of the conservation of energy holds good not just for mechanical energy, but for physical processes in general. The most comprehensive of these treatments was that of Helmholtz. We cannot here enter into the details of Helmholtz' argument; suffice it to say simply that he rendered the general conservation of energy plausible by showing it to be compatible with Newtonian theory. Thus, once again, the general principle of "constancy": the amount of energy within any closed physical system remains *quantitatively* constant, although it may undergo various *qualitative* transformations.

Helmholtz' "Conservation of Force" is usually remembered as a contribution to physical theory—as, indeed, it was. What is often forgotten, however, is that Helmholtz' principal interest in physical theory lay in its application to physiology (in the broader sense of the term). He was a physician and physiologist by training, and, though it goes without saying that he was competent in physics as well, he was first and foremost a biologist. (He himself might have preferred the designation "biophysicist.") Let us, then, briefly consider the implications that Helmholtz' constancy principle seemed to hold for physiology or, more generally, for organic functioning.

The most general of such implications was this: If the various forms of physical energy are interconvertible, then the Newtonian laws of "mechanical force" could be extended (so it was imagined) to embrace energy in general. A numerical correspondence had already been found between mechanical energy and heat, and it seemed only natural to expect that the various other forms of energy would also be found to correspond. In any case, it was quite firmly believed that all forms of energy could *in principle* be explained by the Newtonian mechanics and, thus, that they were all essentially mechanical in nature. Pursuing this same line of reasoning into the realm of biology, organic functioning could now be seen as a complex but nonetheless mechanical process of energy exchange and transformation. Thus, in the living organism as in the universe at large, the various forms of energy are converted into one another with neither a loss nor a gain of the overall quantity of energy. The difference between the two is this: The universe is an isolated physical system, by definition; thus, it receives no energy from other systems, nor does it lose any energy to them. The organism, on the other hand, is only relatively isolated; it receives energy from, and expends energy upon, the environment. Still, both the organism and the universe are physical systems, and both may be understood (it was imagined) in purely mechanical terms.

Consider, now, what might be some of the more specific implications of this line of thought. The living organism, we may say, receives energy from the environment through two means: first, through the metabolism of ingested materials; second, through the stimulation of a sense organ. For the moment, we need pursue only the second of these. The external energy that is responsible for the stimulation of a sense organ may be light, in the case of vision; chemical, in the case of taste; mechanical, in the case of hearing; and so on. But, no matter what form of energy it is that excites a sense organ, it will in any case be converted into electrical energy. In this form, it will then be conducted through the peripheral-sensory nervous system, the central nervous system, and on out into the peripheral-motor nervous system. Eventually, this impulse of electrical energy will be conducted to an effector, where it will again be qualitatively transformed (e.g., into mechanical energy). Now, according to the principle of constancy, the quantity of energy will remain unaltered throughout all of these qualitative transformations. Thus we may expect the quantities of energy at the sensory and motor ends of the circuit to be, if not identical, then at least proportional.

The line of reasoning put forward in the above paragraph can be summarized as follows: the greater the stimulus, the greater its consequences, its effects, within the nervous system. If the nervous system is simply a conductor, and if energy is neither gained nor lost in transformation, then how, indeed, could it be otherwise? In the next chapter, we shall see how this particular implication of German physiological mechanism helped to give birth to psychophysics and to the "New [German] Psychology" in general. In later chapters, we shall see how it helped to spawn yet other psychological movements. For the moment, though, we may content ourselves with observing only the most immediate psychological consequences of the new, German, physiological mechanism.

## THE THEORY OF PUNCTIFORM SENSATIONS

As we have noted, the nervous system was now to be regarded as a biological electrical apparatus. It was, however, a quite specific kind of electrical apparatus. It was *complex* insofar as it was composed of many individual circuits, and yet each of these individual circuits was taken to be essentially *simple*. Thus, each of the individual receptor units in a given sense organ was held to be connected, in a fairly direct and uncomplicated fashion, with some specific "projection area" in the brain. Imagine, for example, that light, reflected from an apple falls upon the retina of the eye. Now the retina, as it happens, is composed of a very great number of individual receptor units. All of these upon which the image of the apple falls with sufficient intensity will be excited—but they will be excited only as discrete individual units! These excitations will then be conducted through the nervous system along discrete, individual paths of connection. Finally, they will each terminate at discrete, individual projection areas. These projection areas, of course, may be variously interconnected with one another within the brain itself; nonetheless, up to this point the various excitations engendered by the image of the apple have been discrete, or *punctiform*.

With this we come to a curious turn of events. The image of the apple gets projected into the brain in the form of a mosaic of punctiform excitations. And yet, the *perception* of the apple is not punctiform at all. Here, then, was the theoretical question encountered by the new, German model of the nervous system: How can punctiform sensations (or projections) be transformed into unified perceptions? As we shall see in later chapters, much of the subsequent development of German psychology turned upon this very question.

During the 1850s and 1860s there were several attempts to frame a plausible answer to the question. Some of these were spoken of as "nativistic," others as "empiristic"; in point of fact, though, their similarities were far greater than their differences. We may consider them in chronological order.

The first was the theory of Rudolf Hermann Lotze (1817–1881), usually spoken of as the theory of *local signs*. Lotze was concerned, in particular, with the perception of spatial relationships. How does it happen, he asked (though not in just these words), that the various parts of the apple are perceived as being spatially related to one another? Clearly, the various parts of the apple excite retinal receptors which are themselves spatially related. It is true also that the projection areas with which these receptors are connected are spatially related. These two facts, however, in no way tell us about the *perception* of spatial relationships, for perceptions come from sensations, and sensations come from receptor excitations alone. There is no receptor excitation corresponding to a spatial relationship; accordingly, there is no sensation. How, then, is there perception?

Lotze's answer to the question may be briefly summarized as follows: The excitation of any given receptor gives rise to not just one sensation, but *two*. The first of these is the thing that we ordinarily recognize as a sensation; it would correspond to some particular part of the apple. The second sensation, on the other hand, pertains not to the apple, but rather to the receptor itself.

It is, in effect, a "local sign" (or "sign of location"), a sensation pertaining to that receptor and it alone, which tells the mind precisely which receptor has just been excited. Given these local signs, the mind can then go about the task of reconstructing the spatial relationships of the external world. Imagine, for example, two retinal receptors that are always excited simultaneously; on the basis of this recurrent temporal togetherness, the mind will conclude that sensations arising from these two receptors derive from the same location in the external world. On this same basis, it is also plain to see how other kinds of recurrent temporal relationships would lead the mind to reconstruct other kinds of spatial relationships. The necessity of the concept of "local sign," of course, is given by the term "recurrent," for the mind cannot make use of a receptor's recurrent temporal relationships unless there is some mark, or sign, by which that receptor can be recognized on each occasion.

Lotze's theory was "empiristic" insofar as it held that recurrent experiences are required for the construction of spatial relationships. And yet, it was entirely consistent with the Germanic tendency toward Kantian "nativism" insofar as it supposed an innate mental operation. This operation, of course, was that of reconstructing spatial relationships from recurrent temporal relationships.

We may note also that Lotze was led, in much the same way as was Herbart, to the conception of *unconscious* mental contents and processes. We are not conscious of local signs, he observed, and yet we know they must exist, for otherwise the perception of spatial relationships would be impossible. Similarly, we are not conscious of the process whereby spatial relationships are constructed, and yet we know that it too must exist. *Ergo,* there are mental contents and events that remain unconscious to us.

Lotze put forward his theory of local signs in 1852. A somewhat similar theory, concerned also with the perception of spatial relationships, was proposed about a decade later by Ewald Hering (1834–1918). The principal defect of Lotze's theory, Hering argued, was that it required the mind to keep track of as many local signs as there are individual receptors. And so, Hering proposed instead that each individual receptor be conceived of as giving rise not to a unique local sign but rather to three separate "spatial feelings." Thus, for example, a given receptor in the retina would give rise, when excited, to one spatial feeling corresponding to its horizontal position, to another corresponding to its vertical position, and to yet another corresponding to its depth. Each receptor's combination of spatial feelings would then be distinct from that of any other, and yet the individual spatial feelings themselves would differ only in degree. From this point on, perceived spatial relationships would be constructed in much the same fashion as proposed by Lotze. Hering's theory has been rightly considered to be more "nativistic" than Lotze's, inasmuch as it presupposed a certain spatial ordering of sensations from the outset.

These speculations of Lotze and Hering culminated, in the 1850s and 1860s, in the perceptual theory of Hermann von Helmholtz, whom we have already mentioned. Helmholtz did not explicitly espouse the concept of either local signs or spatial feelings. From his writings, though, it is clear that he tacitly assumed something on the order of Lotze's local signs. Indeed, his interpretation of how spatial relationships get reconstructed was scarcely distinguishable from Lotze's, save that it was more thoroughgoing. Helmholtz agreed with Lotze that the process of reconstructing spatial relationships is surely an unconscious one. Where he differed was in pointing out that this unconscious process must be alike in nature to a process of *conscious inference.* Thus, Helmholtz argued, the process whereby punctiform sensations are transformed into structured, unified perceptions must be one of *unconscious inference.*

Helmholtz further argued that these "unconscious inferences" are strictly *inductive* in nature, being based upon "our usual experience, repeated a million times all through life."[10] And so it is, he suggested, that their inferential character is most clearly evident in the case of perceptual illusions. Here we have a case in which the "modes of stimulation of the organs of sense are *un*usual"; in consequence, "incorrect ideas of objects are apt to be formed."

> Obviously, in these cases there is nothing wrong with the activity of the organ of sense and its corresponding nervous mechanism which produces the illusion. Both of them have to act according to the laws that govern their activity once for all. It is rather simply an illusion in the judgment of the material presented to the senses, resulting in a false idea of it.[11]

The process, then, is distinctly one of inference. Still and all, Helmholtz was quick to point out, it differs from ordinary conscious inference in that its conscious product has about it the quality of perceptual immediacy. The process itself is "irresistible," grounded as it is in "the unconscious processes of association of ideas going on in the dark background of our memory." And it is for this reason that "its results are urged on our consciousness, so to speak, as if an external power had constrained us, over which our will has no control."[12] It perhaps goes without saying that Helmholtz had to see these results of unconscious inference as being perceptually immediate, for these "results" were precisely the immediate perceptions that he was trying to reconcile (by way of "unconscious inference") with the theory of punctiform sensations.

We shall see more of the theory of punctiform sensations in the next chapter. For the moment, we need only bear in mind that it was generated, quite directly, by the new, German physiological mechanism.

## NOTES

1.  I. Kant. *Critique of Pure Reason,* trans. N. K. Smith (London: Macmillan, 1953), pp. 41–42.
2.  J. F. Herbart, *A Text-Book in Psychology,* trans. M. K. Smith (New York: Appleton, 1891).
3.  J. F. Herbart. *Sämmtliche Werke,* ed. G. Hartenstein, vol. V (Hamburg and Leipzig: Voss, 1886), p. 20.
4.  M. W. Drobisch, *Empirische Psychologie nach naturwissenschaftlicher Methode* (Hamburg and Leipzig: Voss, 1898), p. 341.
5.  Ibid., pp. 348–349.
6.  S. Toulmin and J. Goodfield, *The Architecture of Matter* (New York: Harper & Row, 1962), p. 323.
7.  Ibid., p. 329.
8.  Ibid., p. 326.
9.  E. Du Bois-Reymond, *Zwei grosse Naturforscher des 19 Jahrhunderts: Ein Briefwechsel zwischen Emil Du Bois-Reymond und Karl Ludwig* (Liepzig: Barth, 1927), p. 19.
10. H. L. F. von Helmholtz, *Treatise on Physiological Optics,* trans. J. P. C. Southall, vol. III, sect. 26 (Rochester, N.Y.: Optical Society of America, 1925).
11. Ibid.
12. Ibid.

## FOR FURTHER READING

For an evaluation of Kant's influence upon nineteenth-century German psychological thought, see B. Wolman, "Immanuel Kant and His Impact on Psychology," in B. Wolman, ed., *Historical Roots of Contemporary Psychology* (New York: Harper & Row, 1968).

Excerpts from the more important psychological writings of Herbart and Drobisch will be found in G. Murphy and L. B. Murphy, eds., *Western Psychology: From the Greeks to William James* (New York: Basic Books: 1969); B. Rand, ed., *The Classical Psychologists* (Boston: Houghton Mifflin, 1912); W. S. Sahakian, *History of Psychology: A Source Book in Systematic Psychology* (Itasca, Ill.: Peacock, 1968). Herbart is one of those figures in the history of psychology who is often referred to but rarely studied in detail. An exception to this neglect is B. Wolman, "The Historical Role of Johann Friedrich Herbart," in B. Wolman, ed., *Historical Roots of Contemporary Psychology.*

A valuable background for our discussion of German physiological mechanism will be found in S. Toulmin and J. Goodfield, *The Architecture of Matter* (New York: Harper & Row, 1962). Some of the matters that we mentioned under the heading "physiological discovery" have been well chronicled in Chapter 2 of E. G. Boring, *A History of Experimental Psychology* (New York: Appleton-Century-Crofts, 1950).

The author knows of no complete English translation of Helmholtz' *"Erhaltung der Kraft."* Significant excerpts from it, however, will be found in L. Koenigsberger, *Hermann von Helmholtz,* trans. F. A. Welby (Oxford: Clarendon, 1906), which conveys something of the spirit of German physiological mechanism as well.

Well-chosen excerpts from the writings of Lotze, Hering, and Helmholtz on perception will be found in the Murphy, Rand, and Sahakian volumes mentioned above, as well as in the following: W. Dennis, ed., *Readings in the History of Psychology* (New York: Appleton-Century-Crofts, 1948), and R. J. Herrnstein and E. G. Boring, eds., *A Source Book in the History of Psychology* (Cambridge, Mass.: Harvard University Press, 1966).

# Chapter 6
## Psychophysics and the "New Psychology"

The whole of nature is a single continuous system of component parts acting on one another, within which various partial systems create, use, and transmit to each other kinetic energy of different forms, while obeying general laws through which the connections are ruled and conserved. Since in exact natural science all physical happenings, activities, and processes, whatever they may be called (not excluding the chemical, the imponderable, and the organic) may be reduced to movements, be they of large masses or of the smallest particles, we can also find for all of them a yardstick of their activity or strength in their kinetic energy, which can always be measured, if not always directly, then at least by its effects, and in any case in principle.

Gustav Fechner, *Elemente der Psychophysik* (1860)

Whenever we can show good reason for the belief that the peculiar form taken on by a stimulus-process in the sense-organs, the sensory nerves, and the sense-centers of the brain exercises a determining influence upon a particular sensation, we shall, of course, be constrained to take into consideration the character of the internal stimuli and the transformations which occur in the conversion of an external into an internal stimulus.

Wilhelm Wundt, *Vorlesungen über die Menschen- und Tierseele* (1863)

> All science begins with analysis. . . . Psychology is no
> exception to the rule. Our concrete mental experience, the
> experience of "real life," is always complex. However small
> a fragment we may seize upon—a single wish, a single idea,
> a single resolution—we find invariably that close inspection
> of it will reveal its complexity, will show that it is composed
> of a number of more rudimentary processes. The first object
> of the psychologist, therefore, is to ascertain the *nature and
> number of the mental elements*. He takes up mental experience,
> bit by bit, dividing and subdividing, until the division can
> go no further. When that point is reached, he has found a
> conscious element.
>
>                     E. B. Titchener, *An Outline of Psychology* (1897)

The more immediate psychological implications of the new German physiological mechanism may be summarized under two headings:

(1) *Conduction and conservation.* The nervous system is a conductor of electrical energy; its operations take place in accordance with the principle of the conservation of energy.

(2) *Stimulation and sensation.* Stimulation of a sense organ amounts to excitation of punctiform receptor units; these excitations are then conducted to their respective projection areas in the brain in a fairly direct and unilinear fashion. Accordingly, the resulting sensations must also be punctiform in character.

As we shall see presently, the first of these implications helped to spawn that often misunderstood psychological movement known as "psychophysics." The second, on the other hand, helped to promote a marriage between an old doctrine and a new one, whose issue was, up until a few decades ago, still reverently spoken of as the "New Psychology." We may consider each of these occurrences in turn.


### FECHNER AND PSYCHOPHYSICS

The story of the founding of psychophysics is a rather involved one, so we shall do well to go back and begin at the beginning.

Great men have great ambitions. And the great ambition of Gustav Theodor Fechner (1801–1887), the author of the psychophysical movement, was nothing less than to frame and promulgate a "grand unifying conception of the world." Of the general outlines of this scheme we need here say only that they involved a kind of refined hylozoism. As we have seen throughout the preceding pages of this volume, the trend of biological and psychological thought during the seventeenth, eighteenth, and early nineteenth centuries was to regard life and consciousness as *inherent functions of organized matter*. Fechner's "grand conception" simply carried this trend to one of its logical extremes. If life and consciousness are inherent correlates of organized matter, and if material systems differ from one another only in the *degree* of their organization, it then follows inescapably that *all* material systems are alive and conscious in varying degree! Thus, men are conscious, animals are conscious, plants are conscious, molecules are conscious, planets are conscious—indeed, the universe itself is conscious! Life and consciousness are invariably associated with matter; accordingly, we may say that "mind" and "matter" are simply two aspects of the same underlying reality.

This, then, is what Fechner spoke of as his *Tagesansicht*—his brighter, daylight view of the universe in which life and consciousness were seen to be coequal with matter. The alternative was a gloomy *Nachtansicht* which regarded life and consciousness as mere accidental by-products of matter. The *Nachtansicht* of the materialist considered the world only from one point of view; Fechner's *Tagesansicht* sought to take account of both. Thus:

> What will appear to you as your mind from the internal standpoint, where you yourself are this mind, will, on the other hand, appear from the outside point of view as the material basic of this mind. There is a difference whether one thinks with the brain or examines the brain of a thinking person. These activities appear to be quite different, but the standpoint is quite different too, for here one is an inner, the other an outer point of view. . . . The appearance of the mind to itself . . . is gained from the truly inner point of view of the underlying being regarding itself as in coincidence with itself, whereas the appearance of the material state belonging to it derives from a standpoint that is truly external, and not in coincidence.[1]

The general outlines of the *Tagesansicht* seemed to have dawned upon Fechner as early as 1820, when he was only nineteen. Shortly thereafter, curiously enough, his professional interests turned to that field of inquiry in which the opposing *Nachtansicht* was strongest. By 1824 he was lecturing in physics at the University of Leipzig; within a decade, he had been appointed to a full professorship in physics. He was forced by reason of health to resign this position in 1840, but by 1846 he was again lecturing at the University— ostensibly on physics, but in fact on a variety of matters, including matters psychological.

In 1847, Helmholtz published his paper "On the Conservation of Force." Three years later, presumably after having read this paper Fechner had a revelation. Lying in his bed on the morning of October 22, 1850, Fechner arrived at the idea that the way to vindicate his *Tagesansicht* of the world, both empirically and theoretically, was to make the "relative increase of bodily energy the measure of the increase of the corresponding mental intensity." The precise import of this revelation will become clear only as we go back to consider its origins and rationale.

### The Psychophysical Rationale

If the mental and the material are but two coequal aspects of the same underlying reality, then there is a certain inference that we may draw regarding the mutual relationships of the two. Consider, for example, the gravitational attraction of the earth upon the moon. According to Fechner's *Tagesansicht,* we may see the effect of this attraction from either or both of two points of view. From the "outside point of view," the effect will be that of one material system upon another. From the "internal standpoint," on the other hand, it will be more in the nature of a perception. In respect to their *quality,* then, the two views of the effect are radically distinct—so much so that we might almost imagine we are dealing with two different effects. In fact, it is just the same effect as seen from two different perspectives. Thus, even though the two views of the effect differ in quality, they must be *quantitatively* identical.

Here, then, was Fechner's grand strategy. His *Tagesansicht* demanded that mental and material effects be regarded as quantitatively identical; accordingly, a demonstration of this identity would serve (in part) as an empirical substantiation of his views. And thus were the seeds of psychophysics sown.

Fechner rightly recognized that the task involved two distinct problems: the first was a theoretical problem, the second, a practical one.

(1) The quantitative identity of the material and the mental cannot be demonstrated unless they can both be measured. Now, the measurement of material effects may at times present difficulties in practice, but only rarely does it present difficulties in principle. The measurement of the mental, on the other hand, was a problem in principle as well as in practice. Indeed, the task had traditionally been regarded as impossible—as well it might, for how can we begin to apply external standards of measurement to something which is evident only "from the truly inner point of view of the underlying being regarding itself, as in coincidence with itself"? We shall consider this matter at greater length in a later section; suffice it to say here that Fechner solved the problem, to his own satisfaction at least, through a variety of "internal" standards of measurement.

(2) In any case, our more immediate concern for the moment is with Fechner's second problem. In the human being, the material counterpart of the mental is to be found somewhere deep within the nervous system. In principle, the effects that take place deep within the nervous system could be measured; in practice, however, they could not. Thus, Fechner found himself in the curious position of being able to measure mental effects, but not their material counterparts! And, so long as this situation endured, the demonstration

of the quantitative identity between the mental and the material was as far away as ever.

It was in pondering this second problem that Fechner achieved his great insight of 1850. We may reconstruct his reasoning on the matter as follows: Although we cannot directly measure the material effects that take place deep within the nervous system, we know that their magnitudes must be "dependent functions" of the magnitudes of the external stimuli which bring them about. Thus, if we can show that their corresponding mental effects are also dependent functions of external stimuli, we shall then have established the quantitative identity between the mental and the material. Here, then, was Fechner's revelation—to make the "relative increase of bodily energy [i.e., stimulation] the measure of the increase of the corresponding mental intensity." Thus, as he wrote in the introductory section of his *Elements of Psychophysics* (1860):

> Even before the means are available to discover the nature of the processes of the body that stand in direct relation to our mental activities, we will nevertheless be able to determine to a certain degree the quantitative relationship between them. Sensation depends on stimulation; a stronger sensation depends on a stronger stimulus; the stimulus, however, causes sensation only via the intermediate action of some internal process of the body. To the extent that lawful relationships between sensation and stimulus can be found, they must include lawful relationships between the stimulus and this inner physical activity, which obey the same general laws of interaction of bodily processes and thereby give us a basis for drawing general conclusions about the nature of this inner activity.[2]

Accordingly, Fechner found it necessary to speak of both an "outer" and an "inner" psychophysics, depending upon "whether consideration is focused on the relationship of the psychical to the body's external aspects [i.e., to stimulation], or on those internal functions with which the psychic are closely related."[3] In practice, of course, Fechner could deal only with outer psychophysics. The processes of inner psychophysics were not open to inspection, and, for this reason, he repeatedly denied "making any assumptions about [their] nature." In fact, though, he made at least one quite considerable assumption.

Fechner's whole line of reasoning at this point was based upon the notion that effects within the nervous system are dependent functions of the magnitude of external stimulation. And we may now inquire into why he took this to be the case. Let us begin by recalling the more specific, neurological implication of the Helmholtzian constancy principle. (Remember also that Helmholtz' paper had been published only three years before and that Fechner, a physicist, must surely by that time have read it.) If the nervous system is purely a conductor, and if energy is neither gained nor lost in transformation, then we may expect the quantities of energy at the sensory end, at the center, and at the motor end of the neural circuit to be, if not identical, then at least proportional. Fechner took this new model of the nervous system entirely for granted; without it, indeed, he would never have seen the connection between his *Tagesansicht* and the measurement of "outer" psychophysical relationships. For, as he observed in the opening pages of his *Elemente:*

> Sensations are in a directly dependent relationship to certain processes in our brains . . . ; but sensations are merely in a mediated relationship to the external stimulus, which initiates these processes only via the intervention of a neural conductor. . . . The mediated functional relationships of body and mind fulfill completely the concept of a functional relationship only under the supposition that the mediation [i.e., the neural conductor] enters into the relationships.[4]

Fechner, in fact, was so taken with the Helmholtzian constancy principle that he devoted an entire chapter of his *Elemente* to its exposition. In one place, for example, he dilated:

> This is the great principle of the so-called conservation of energy, which while related to the law of the conservation of kinetic energy, is even more universal in its importance. This principle, while founded on long-known general principles of mechanics, was first clearly developed by Helmholtz, who pointed out its full meaning and explained its most important applications. Since then it has received the broadest consideration and use in the field of inorganic physics as well as biophysics. . . . Up to now no one has found reason to doubt its general applicability in the areas of the organic and the inorganic.[5]

Fechner conceded that "a general and exact proof of the extension of the validity of this law to cover psychophysical processes has not yet been demonstrated." But it can scarcely be doubted, he continued, "that all experiences . . . agree with this law and can be interpreted without trouble only by means of it. We will therefore have to take it into consideration," he concluded, "as long as there is no proof to the contrary."[6]

And well we might! For it was this principle of the conservation of energy, along with its attendant neurological implications, that constituted the rationale of Fechner's psychophysics:

> Kinetic energy employed to chop wood and kinetic energy used in thinking—that is, in the underlying psychophysical processes—are . . . not only quantitatively comparable, but each can be transformed into the other, and therefore both kinds of work are measurable on their physical side by a common yardstick. Just as it takes a certain quantity of kinetic energy to split a log or lift a given weight to a given height, so does it take a certain

quantity to think a thought of a given intensity; and the energy for one can be changed into energy for the other.[7]

### Psychophysical Measurement

Fechner's immediate concern was with outer psychophysics, the functional dependence of mental intensity upon stimulus intensity. And this relationship could not be established unless both intensities could be measured. The measurement of stimulus intensities, of course, presented no problems. The measurement of mental intensities was something else again. As Fechner saw the matter, there were only two ways in which mental intensities, in the form of sensations, could be "measured."

(1) First, we can state whether a given sensation is present or not present. Further, we can specify the average stimulus intensity at which the sensation first becomes present. Thus, we may speak of an *absolute threshold* of sensitivity to a stimulus (a *Reizlimen,* as Fechner called it).

The limitations of this first form of measurement are readily apparent. To establish a functional relationship between two variables, we must be able to specify, for any given value of one, the corresponding value of the other. But in the present case we are able to relate only one degree of sensation intensity (its minimal degree) to one value of stimulus intensity (its threshold value).

(2) A true functional relationship between stimulus and sensation requires that the respective values of each can be measured. On the stimulus side of things, this again presents no problems. Given any two intensities of a stimulus, we can readily determine whether, and in what degree, the one exceeds the other. On the side of sensation, however, the matter is a bit more involved. The legitimacy of Fechner's solution to the problem may be seriously questioned, but it was a brilliant stroke of genius nonetheless.

Granted, the measurement of sensation intensities is a difficult matter, but it is not (so Fechner argued) insurmountable. For there is a certain sense in which sensations can already be measured. Thus, given any two sensations, we can state whether the intensity of the first is greater than, less than, or the same as the intensity of the second. And on this same basis we can then determine the difference between stimulus intensities that gives rise to a just-noticeable difference between the intensities of the corresponding sensations. This we may speak of as a *differential threshold* of sensitivity (a *Differenzlimen*).

The limitation of this second form of measurement is again readily apparent. It is simply this: although we can readily specify whether two sensations differ from each other, we cannot directly measure the *degree* of their difference.

Fechner's strategy at this point was to argue that the measurement of degree could be made, if not directly, then indirectly, for:

The difference between one stimulus intensity and another can always be taken as a positive or negative increment to some stimulus magnitude. Therefore, the intensity of a single stimulus itself can be looked upon mathematically as the sum of positive increments starting with zero, with each increment imagined as added to previous sums until the total stimulus intensity is reached. Similarly, a sensation of difference can be looked upon mathematically as a positive or negative increment to one or the other sensation and . . . as such would be looked upon as the sum of positive increments starting with [a difference of] zero. Now if the functional relationship between the sum of stimulus increments starting from zero and the sum of the related sensation increments is known, the problem resolves itself for every degree of the stimulus and the resulting sensation.[8]

A close examination will reveal that this argument contains a very considerable assumption. It is brought into the argument right at the outset, where Fechner concludes: "[Therefore] the intensity of a single stimulus itself can be looked upon mathematically as the sum of positive increments starting with zero. . . ." The assumption, of course, was that there are such "increments" and, moreover, that they are equal. Thus, as he further elaborated:

In principle . . . our measure of sensation will consist of dividing every sensation into equal divisions (that is, equal increments), which serve to build it up from zero. The number of equal divisions we conceive as determined, like inches on a yardstick, by the number of corresponding variable stimulus increments that are capable of bringing about identical sensation increments. . . . In short, we determine the magnitude of a sensation, which we cannot do directly, by asking how many times it contains the same unit, an operation that we are able to perform directly, and we read off the result not as a number of sensations but as the stimuli that determines sensations.[9]

Now, even if we grant that the measurement of sensation intensities is solved in principle, there still remains the matter of solving it in practice. Or, to put the problem another way: If there *are* such equal increments of sensation intensity, where are they and what are they? Clearly, we cannot discover them by direct measurement, for we cannot measure them until we have a metric with which to do so. And we cannot construct such a metric until we have the equal increments themselves.

Fechner's answer was that we already have the equal increments of sensation at hand. Consider the case in which two different stimulus intensities, *a* and *b,* give rise to a just-noticeable difference between their corresponding sensations. Compare this, now, with the case in which two other different stimulus intensities, *c* and *d,* also give rise to a just-noticeable difference between corresponding sensations. In both cases, the differences between sensations are (a) *incremental,* in that they are the smallest possible of such differences; and

(b) *equal,* in the sense that they are both "just-noticeable." Here then, Fechner thought, were the equal increments that could be used to construct a metric for stimulus intensities. It now remained only to "derive the functional relationship of the sum of increments and, by relating it to the known stimulus, [to] determine the measure of sensation."[10]

### Psychophysical Laws

In the 1830s and 1840s, the Leipzig physiologist Ernst Heinrich Weber conducted a series of experiments involving the lifting of small weights. What he reported was that the just-noticeable difference between two weights depends not so much upon their absolute difference as upon their proportions. Thus, at the lower end of the scale, a relatively small absolute difference will be noticed, whereas, at the higher end of the scale, only a relatively large absolute difference will be noticed. Weber later found that the same was true for the just-noticeable differences between musical tones and the lengths of lines.

As Fechner recognized, Weber's observation was not a particularly new one, for "the law that stimulus increments for equal increases in sensation are larger at the upper end of a stimulus scale than at the lower, has been known for a long time, since it is a matter of everyday experience."[11] Weber's true contribution lay in his "exact formulation" of the law—in his statement "that the magnitude of the stimulus increment must increase in precise proportion to the stimulus already present, in order to bring about an equal increase in sensation."[12] In any case, Fechner considered Weber's law to be of fundamental importance to psychophysical theory. A moment's reflection will show us why this should be so.

If the nervous system were a *perfect* conductor, then the quantity of energy received at its sensory end would be *identical* with the amount conducted to its center. On the analogy of known electrical circuitry, however, it would have been wholly unreasonable to suppose that the nervous system was such a perfect conductor. For even the most efficient of known electrical conductors opposed a certain *resistance* to the passage of current, and there was at the time no reason to suspect that the nervous system might go about its business any differently. Thus, even before learning of Weber's law, Fechner would have had every reason to expect that the functional relationship between stimulus and sensation might not be one of direct covariation, but rather of proportional covariation. It is likely that Fechner looked upon Weber's formulation as a kind of Ohm's law of the nervous system. (Fechner imagined electrical phenomena to be of an essentially vibratory nature; this, however, did not materially alter the situation.)

In any case, Fechner took Weber's law to be the fundamental law of outer psychophysics. In mathematical notation, it may be written as

$$\frac{\delta R}{R} = \text{a constant for the just-noticeable difference}$$

where $R$ = the magnitude of a stimulus (*Reiz*) and $\delta R$ = the difference between $R$ and $R'$ ($R'$ being the magnitude of a comparison stimulus).

Now, as we noted earlier, Fechner assumed that these just-noticeable differences constituted the equal increments required for the measurement of sensation. On the basis of this assumption, he now went on to consider that Weber's law applies to stimulus intensities in general. The result was Fechner's *Fundamentalformel,* the basic functional relationship between stimulus and sensation:

$$\frac{\delta R}{R} c = \delta S$$

where $c$ = a constant of proportionality and $\delta S$ = an increment of stimulus intensity.

Integrating this equation (a process which Fechner regarded as legitimate on the assumption that just-noticeable differences are equal increments), he then arrived at the expression

$$S = c \, \log_e R + C$$

where $e$ = the base of natural logarithms and $C$ = the constant of integration. In principle, this equation would specify the magnitude of sensation $S$ for any given magnitude of stimulation $R$; in practice, however, it cannot, on account of the unknown constants $c$ and $C$. So, Fechner's next step was to substitute known values of $S$ and $R$ into the formula and solve for $c$ and $C$.

The crucial nature of this step can scarcely be overemphasized, for, as it happened, there was only one case in which the values of $S$ and $R$ were actually known. This was the case in which $R$ was at its absolute threshold value—a case in which $S = 0$, by definition. The result of the substitution was Fechner's *Massformel* (measurement formula):

$$S = k \, \log \frac{R}{r}$$

where $r$ = the threshold value of $R$.

As a final step, Fechner took $r$ as the unit of $R$, thus arriving at the well-known expression.

$$S = k \, \log R$$

Fechner spoke of this final expression as "Weber's law," though it is not certain that Weber would have immediately recognized it. In any event, it was precisely the sort of functional relationship between stimulus and sensation that Fechner set out to find. Whether or not it held true was, of course, quite another matter.

### Fechner's Contributions

As an empirical generalization, "Weber's law" has been found in the course of time to hold true only approximately, within a fairly narrow range of stimulus intensities. This, however, should not be allowed to obscure its significance. Fechner himself recognized that the law might have certain natural limits. But the important thing, he considered, was not whether "Weber's law" held true in every case, but rather that it was a first step in the right direction. And this direction was nothing less than to make of psychology an exact, experimental science, after the fashion of physics. Whether this direction was a feasible one in which to proceed is not here at issue; suffice it to say that Fechner's conviction took root, in a soil that was already well prepared for it, and that it has endured undiminished, even up to this day.

For the present, however, our principal concern must lie with Fechner's contributions to psychological theory. By way of conclusion, we may briefly touch upon three of these contributions.

(1) First and foremost, Fechner took the new German physiological mechanism and gave it psychological meaning. Thus, with Fechner, we find spread out before us in full-blown form the conception of organic functioning as a complex of energy exchanges and transformations. In one place, for example, he observed that "just as intensive thought necessarily interrupts all physical work, so a jump interrupts every train of thought." Nor is it merely accidental that this should be so, for the psychophysical processes within us conform to the same law of the conservation of energy that governs physical nature at large. Thus:

> The energy needed by the legs for their jump is taken from the flow of psychophysical processes needed for thinking. . . . [For] while we can divide disposable kinetic energy at will, we can reach a maximum for any one kind of activity only to the extent that we let other activities rest. Just as we must let one arm rest to gain maximum power for the other, so we must rest all the parts of the body in order to concentrate most energy in the head, and, vice versa, we must allow the activity in our heads to rest as much as possible in order to carry out the most energetic movements of our limbs. Thus also we see the deep thinker sit as much as possible and we never see someone who is running or lifting at the same time in deep thought. This is a contradiction; it cannot occur.[13]

All in all, Fechner concluded in good Helmholtzian fashion, the distribution of energy within the organism resembles that of a steam engine:

> Depending on how much steam the engine develops, its kinetic energy can rise high or fall low; but in normal operations neither the one nor the other will happen suddenly. One can, however, easily turn on one part of the machine and at the same time turn off another at will, by opening a valve here and shutting one there. The only difference is that in our organic machine the engineer does not sit on the outside but on the inside. . . .
> I do not mean by this to say that the kinetic energy of the body really distributes itself like steam in an engine, but only that the law of the conservation of energy leads to corresponding results.[14]

(2) Fechner's second contribution to psychological theory was his conception of sensory "thresholds." In all probability, no one ever really doubted that there are stimuli of too slight an intensity to give rise to sensations, or that there are some differences between stimuli too small to be noticed. Fechner, then, cannot be claimed to have originated the conceptions of absolute or differential sensory thresholds; what he did do was to make them explicit, thereby calling attention to them. In addition, he imposed upon the conception of sensory thresholds two significant elaborations: (a) As we have seen, he took the absolute threshold for a sensation as the mathematical zero-point for a scale of ascending sensory intensities; further, he regarded the values of the differential threshold as constituting the equal increments of this scale. As we shall see in a moment, these two assumptions, which were at the foundation of Fechner's psychophysical measurement theory, led to a most curious consequence. (b) The second elaboration was not so much an assumption as an observation. Fechner pointed out that sensory thresholds are not absolutely stable, but rather that they vary randomly around certain average values.

(3) Fechner's third contribution came as a result of his mathematical elaborations upon the concept of sensory thresholds. Recall for a moment the Fechnerian measurement formula:

$$S = k \ \log\frac{R}{r}$$

According to this formula, when $R$ is at its threshold value, the intensity of $S$ will be 0. This, of course, is simply an expression of the assumption that the threshold value of a sensation constitutes a mathematical zero-point of sensory intensity. But, from this expression, a certain curious conclusion follows. For it so happens that a stimulus can take on values which are below its sensory-threshold value; and, when these subthreshold values of $R$ are substituted into the formula, the resulting values of $S$ are necessarily *negative*.

For the interpretation of these "negative sensations," Fechner could have appealed to either of two different explanations. On the one hand, he could have argued that they were merely mathematical artifacts—that is, conclusions drawn from the mathematics of the case that have no correlate in reality. On the other hand, he could have argued that "negative sensations" are just what they claim to be—sensations of negative intensity. The interpretation to which he actually appealed was the latter: "As long as the stimulus . . . remains below threshold," he argued, "its perception is, as one says, unconscious." He was undoubtedly influenced in this matter by Herbart's "threshold of consciousness," but it would seem that he had other motives as well. In fact, he regarded these "negative sensations" as nothing less than the royal road to "inner psychophysics":

> Since other general higher phenomena of consciousness also have a point of expiration and a point of origination, we will be able to generalize the concept and expression of threshold to them. Examples of this type of phenomenon would be the level of awareness with respect to sleeping and waking, the way single thoughts become conscious, and the focusing of attention in a given direction. In these instances we cannot speak of a threshold value of an external stimulus responsible for lifting consciousness above threshold. But the question may be raised whether we would not have to assume a threshold value of the underlying psychophysical processes and whether stimulus thresholds, differential thresholds, and relative thresholds do not exist as far as sensations are concerned only to the extent that they can be translated into such processes.[15]

Fechner's notion, in a word, was that there are inner psychophysical processes that remain *unconscious*—not just physical processes, it must be emphasized, but *psycho*physical.

## WUNDT AND THE "NEW PSYCHOLOGY"

Fechner's hope was that his psychophysical inquiries would compel a sleeping world to wake up and embrace his "grand unifying conception." As it happened, his grand conception still went virtually unnoticed. His psychophysical inquiry itself, however, met with very great interest indeed, for here, it seemed to many, was a method by which psychology at long last could be made a *Naturwissenschaft*—an exact, experimental science after the fashion of physics.

And so, it was not long before laboratories were being established for the purpose of performing psychophysical experiments. Neither was it long before the workers in these laboratories began to consider whether other sorts of psychological questions might also yield to experimentation. The first, or at least one of the first, of these laboratories was founded in the late 1870s by Wilhelm Wundt (1832–1920) at Leipzig. During the next several decades, this same Wilhelm Wundt went on to become the most renowned psychologist in all Germany and the guiding light of the "New Psychology" both there and abroad.

Wundt's "New Psychology" was in fact *two* psychologies—one fairly new, the other really quite old. As was only natural for a *Gelehrter* of his day, Wundt considered that psychology is properly the study of sensations, that is, of their genesis in stimulation, of their vicissitudes, and of their interconnections in consciousness. Further, as he saw it, the task is a twofold one. "For in every sensation," he observed, "we distinguish two properties—one which we name its strength or intensity, and another which we call its quality." Neither of these, he added, can exist in the absence of the other, and yet the two *can be* independently varied. Thus:

> We can sound a musical note, e.g., at first quite softly, and then, by gradually increasing its strength, pass it through all possible degrees of intensity, while its quality remains unaltered. Or we can strike different notes one after the other, and so obtain different qualities, while we still keep, if we will, one and the same intensity of tone throughout.[16]

Fechner, of course, had already developed a method and rationale for investigating the *quantitative* aspect of sensation. Wundt took this method and rationale over virtually intact, making of it a principal component of his "New Psychology." There now remained only the task of developing an analogous method and rationale for studying the *qualitative* aspect of sensation. We have already examined Fechner's psychophysics at some length, and so, from this point on, we need consider only this second component of Wundt's "New Psychology." This component was later spoken of as "structural psychology" or "structuralism"; the name is not an entirely accurate one, but it will serve nonetheless to mark off the boundaries between it and psychophysics.

Wundt's structuralism was the result of a marriage between the new, German, physiological mechanism and the old, English, mental mechanism. This marriage, of course, was not a difficult one to bring about; indeed, we might almost say that the two "mechanisms" were made for each other. English mental mechanism was engendered, in part, by Newtonian physics; so also was German physiological mechanism. English mental mechanism spoke of simple, elementary sensations; German physiological mechanism spoke of punctiform sensations. Both doctrines, moreover, were faced with the task of explaining how simple, elementary, punctiform *sensations* get transformed into unified, structured *perceptions*. Surely, then, no troth was ever more inevitably plighted.

We should profit but little from a detailed consideration of the "New

Psychology" that issued from this marriage. There are, though, several general features of it which do require our attention.

### The Elements of Consciousness

Psychology is *Erfahrungswissenschaft*—the science of experience. And so, Wundt argued, since all science begins with analysis, the first task of psychology is to analyze the contents of experience into their elementary component parts. Now it is quite true, he conceded, "that these elements of mental life never occur separately, but always in connection with, always in dependence upon, one another."[17] Nonetheless, we know that they must exist, *as elements,* on account of "the peculiar form taken on by a stimulus-process in the sense-organs, the sensory nerves, and the sense-centres of the brain."[18]

Indeed, Wundt argued, there is a thoroughgoing correspondence, or *parallelism,* between the facts of consciousness and the processes of the nervous system. The nervous system is composed of many interconnected elements; so also are the various contents of consciousness. And thus, he observed, "the principle of the connection of elements may be understood in an anatomical, a physiological, and a psychological sense."

> Anatomically regarded, the nervous system is a unitary complex of numerous elements; and every one of these morphological elements stands in more or less close connection with others. . . . Physiologically, the principle of the connection of elements implies that every . . . [activity of the nervous system] is composed of a large number of elementary functions, the nature of which we may, under favorable circumstances, be able to infer, but which we can never completely isolate from the given complex activity. . . . Lastly, there is a psychological . . . formulation of the principle. It means, psychologically, that . . . the facts of consciousness always presuppose, as their physiological substrate, complex nerve processes, the result of the co-operation of many elementary parts. This complexity of the physical conditions of elementary psychical facts manifests itself in . . . [the observation that] the psychical elements, simple sensations or simple feelings, are always products of psychological abstraction, and never actually occur except in connections.[19]

For nearly two centuries, the tradition of mental mechanism has held that conscious contents could be meaningfully analyzed into "elements"; Wundt found confirmation of this view in what were now taken to be the "known facts of the nervous system."

### The Connection of Elements

The elements of consciousness never appear singly; they occur "always in connection with, always in dependence upon, one another." Accordingly, the task of psychology as *Erfahrungswissenschaft* is to study not just the elements themselves but also the modes and laws of their interconnection. On this point Wundt took over the doctrine of the association of ideas from the mental mechanists virtually intact. All forms of interconnection, he argued, may be listed under only two headings, these being the familiar association by *contiguity* and association by *similarity* ("assimilation"). And even these, he added, differ only as regards the results.

> In the matter of constituents there is, of course, no essential distinction to be drawn between the two forms. For it is obvious that just the same processes must be operative in successive association as in assimilation—the only difference between them being that the successively associated ideas are not combined into one simultaneous idea, but remain totally separate.[20]

By "constituents" Wundt of course had reference to the underlying "bodily substrate of the mental life." Indeed, how could anyone of Wundt's time have remained innocent of the compelling analog between the two—that is, between the interconnections of sensory elements and the interconnections of neural elements? Thus, he argued, the contents of consciousness

> may always be resolved into qualities of sensation and feeling that depend upon the functions of peripheral [neural] elements. In so far, therefore, as the central nervous system is concerned in the higher psychical processes, it must be occupied, not with the origination of new specific qualities, but solely with the indefinitely complex interrelation of these sensory elements of our mental life.[21]

Wundt's notion, then, was that association by contiguity and association by similarity were but different expressions of some single mode of connection between the underlying neural elements.

### Method, Discipline, and the "Stimulus Error"

At the time, a great part of the attraction of Wundt's "New Psychology" was that it was based upon the "experimental method." This held not just for its psychophysical aspect, but for its "structural" or qualitative side as well. Fechnerian psychophysics was experimental in that it varied stimulus conditions *quantitatively*. Wundt perceived that stimulus conditions could also be varied *qualitatively* and, thus, that here too the experimental method could be brought into the domain of psychology. On all counts, then, it seemed that psychology had at long last been transformed into a *Naturwissenschaft*—a science made in the image of physics.

And yet, Wundt noted, there is one respect in which the method of psychology must differ fundamentally from that of physics. Physics studies the objects of the external world, and though this study is necessarily mediated by experience, it is still not a study of experience itself. Psychology, on the other hand, is by definition *Erfahrungswissenschaft;* it is the science of experience *qua* experience. Physics, then, is based upon the method of external observation. Psychology, by contrast, must be based upon a method of *internal observation;* it must be based, in short, upon the method of *introspection (Selbstbeobachtung).* For while the physicist has only to observe *objects,* the psychologist must observe *experience.* Now it is true, of course, that two psychologists cannot observe the *same* experience in the same way that two physicists can observe the *same* object. But it is nonetheless possible for a psychologist to observe his own experience with as much objectivity and detachment as the physicist has for his objects. In addition, it is possible for two or more psychologists to compare notes about their observations.

As it happens, however, the sensory elements of which our complex perceptions and cognitions are composed do not immediately show themselves for what they are. Quite the contrary, their discovery requires a very special kind of training and discipline. First and foremost, then, the psychologist must acquire the capacity to attend strictly to sensations and never to confuse them with their meanings, or contexts. Otherwise said, he must discipline himself so as never to mistake the products of *Kundgabe,* or logical reflection for the sensory elements of which these products are composed. Edward Bradford Titchener (1867–1927), a student of Wundt's who did much to spread the "New Psychology" abroad in North America coined the phrase "stimulus error" to describe this "besetting sin of the descriptive psychologist." On account of logical reflection, he observed, "we are constantly confusing sensations with their stimuli, with their objects, with their meanings." And thus it is that "logical common-sense, *c'est l'ennemi.*" The purpose of the psychologist's training and discipline is to enable him to overcome this inveterate enemy, and so, to see experience as it *really is!*

We may close this chapter by remarking that, earlier in the century, James Mill had made similar observations on psychological method. All men are familiar with sensations, he wrote:

> but this very familiarity, as the mind runs easily from one well-known object to another, is a reason why the boundary between them . . . is not always observed. It is necessary, therefore, that the learner should by practice acquire the habit of reflecting upon his Sensations, as a distinct class of feelings; and should be hence prepared to mark well the distinction between them and other states of mind, when he advances to the analysis of the more mysterious phenomena.[22]

Mill's *Analysis* marked the culmination of "pure" mental mechanism; unlike Wundt, Titchener, and the other New Psychologists, he did not enjoy the advantage of German physiological mechanism and its attendant theory of punctiform sensation.

## NOTES

1.  G. T. Fechner, *Elements of Psychophysics: Volume I,* trans. H. E. Adler, eds. D. H. Howes and E. G. Boring (New York: Holt, Rinehart and Winston, 1966), p. 3.
2.  Ibid., p. 101.
3.  Ibid., p. 9.
4.  Ibid., pp. 8–9.
5.  Ibid., p. 29.
6.  Ibid., p. 31.
7.  Ibid., p. 36.
8.  Ibid., p. 49.
9.  Ibid., pp. 50–51.
10. Ibid., p. 50.
11. Ibid., p. 53.
12. Ibid., p. 54.
13. Ibid., p. 32.
14. Ibid., p. 35.
15. Ibid., pp. 199–200.
16. W. Wundt, *Lectures on Human and Animal Psychology,* trans. J. E. Creighton and E. B. Titchener (New York: Macmillan, 1894), p. 15.
17. Ibid., p. 13.
18. Ibid., p. 16.
19. W. Wundt, *Principles of Physiological Psychology: Volume I,* trans. E. B. Titchener (New York: Macmillan, 1904), pp. 320–321.
20. Wundt, *Lectures on Human and Animal Psychology,* p. 296.
21. Wundt, *Principles of Physiological Psychology,* p. 324.
22. J. Mill, *Analysis of the Phenomena of the Human Mind,* vol. I (London: Baldwin and Cradock, 1829), pp. 2–3.

## FOR FURTHER READING

For an alternative account of the origins of Fechner's psychophysics and Wundt's "New Psychology," see Chapters 14 and 16 of E. G. Boring, *A History of Experimental Psychology* (New York: Appleton-Century-Crofts, 1950). This book is the chief source of the tendency often found among psychologists to regard Fechner and Wundt as *the* pivotal figures in the history of psychology.

The first volume of Fechner's *Elemente der Psychophysik* has been translated into English as G. Fechner, *Elements of Psychophysics: Volume I,* trans. H. E. Adler, eds. D. H. Howes and E. G. Boring (New York: Holt, Rinehart, and Winston, 1966). It is an entirely readable translation, though the less eager student may still wish to confine himself to the excerpts that are to be found in W. Dennis, ed., *Readings in the History of Psychology* (New York: Appleton-Century-Crofts, 1948); R. J. Herrnstein and E. G.

Boring, eds., *A Source Book in the History of Psychology* (Cambridge, Mass.: Harvard University Press, 1966); B. Rand, ed., *The Classical Psychologist* (Boston: Houghton Mifflin, 1912); and W. S. Sahakian, ed., *History of Psychology: A Source Book in Systematic Psychology* (Itasca, Ill.: Peacock, 1968). In these same collections are to be found excerpts from the more important psychological writings of Wundt and his followers.

For an evaluation of psychophysics and the "New Psychology" by a not entirely sympathetic contemporary of Fechner and Wundt, see W. James, *The Principles of Psychology* (New York: Holt, 1890), especially Chapters 6, 9, 13, and 20. Some of James' views of these matters will be discussed in Chapter 8 of the present book.

# Chapter 7
# The Impact of Darwin

As many more individuals of each species are born than can possibly survive; and as, consequently, there is a frequently recurring struggle for existence, it follows that any being, if it vary however slightly in any manner profitable to itself, under the complex and sometimes varying conditions of life, will have a better chance of surviving and thus be *naturally selected*. From the strong principle of inheritance, any selected variety will [then] tend to propagate its new and modified form.

Charles Darwin, *Origin of Species* (1859)

These general considerations are here adverted to only to explain the general psychonomic law which assumes that we are influenced in our deeper, more tempermental dispositions by the life-habits and codes of conduct of we know not what unnumbered hosts of ancestors, which like a cloud of witnesses are present throughout our lives, that our souls are echo-chambers in which their whispers reverberate.

G. Stanley Hall, *Adolescence* (1904)

We come now to what was without question the most important intellectual event of the nineteenth century—the publication, in 1859, of Charles Darwins' (1809–1882) *Origin of Species*. Its significance can quite readily be compared with the publication, almost two centuries earlier, of Newton's *Principia*. In both cases, what we have is a theory which, though born within a specific realm of inquiry, was soon seen to have important implications for other realms

105

as well. Thus, Newton's theory was originally put forward to account for physical phenomena, but eventually it was expanded into a scheme of existence in general, applied alike to chemistry, biology, and even—as we have seen— psychology. Similarly, Darwin's theory was initially designed to account for biological phenomena, but soon it was taken to explain the evolution not only of organic species but also of the cosmos, of human social institutions, and even of individual human beings.

To appreciate the significance of Darwin's theory for psychology, we need only dwell for a moment upon what psychologists of an earlier generation reverently referred to as the "New Psychology" of the Germans. The endeavors of the new German psychology to become a *Naturwissenschaft* are all too apt to blind us to the fact that this psychology was in several respects still quite remote from present-day psychological thought and research. Even at its quantitative, experimental best, it was concerned solely, as E. G. Boring once put it, with the "generalized, human, normal, adult mind as revealed in the psychological laboratory." Nor was it merely accidental that this was so, for, however great its scientific enthusiasm, the "new" German psychology was guided throughout by two assumptions that were hoary with age and questionable at best: the first, that psychological processes find their clearest expression in the "human, normal, adult mind"; the second, that all such processes may be referred back to sensations and their vicissitudes in perception and thinking. Thus, there was nothing of "comparative" psychology, nothing of "developmental" or "abnormal" psychology, and precious little of motivation, learning, and emotion. These are distinctly modern emphases in psychological thought and research. They were rarely to be found in the "New Psychology" of the Germans, for they came mainly through the mediation of Darwin's theory of organic evolution. Chronologically, the new German psychology belonged to the latter half of the nineteenth century; in effect, though, it was an essentially *pre*-Darwinian enterprise.

## ORGANIC EVOLUTION

In the realm of living creatures, there is nothing so obvious as the stability of species. Any individual member of a species tends to resemble its parents; its parents, in turn, resemble their parents; and so on, back as far as one might care to trace it. The relation of resemblance is a transitive one; and for this reason, it is not at all irrational to assume that organic species have existed in their present form since the very beginning—in a word, since Creation. This, indeed, is precisely the assumption that held sway in the Western world up to, and including, the time of Darwin. Organic species were considered to be both *specially created* and *immutable*. The authority for this view, if any in addition to that of common sense were needed, was readily to be found in the first chapter of the Biblical account of Genesis:

> And God said: "Let the earth bring forth the living creature after its kind, cattle and creeping thing, and beast of the earth after its kind." And it was so. And God made the beast of the earth after its kind, and the cattle after their kind, and everything that creepeth upon the earth after its kind; and God saw that it was good. . . . And God saw everything that He had made, and, behold, it was very good. And there was evening and there was morning, the sixth day.

Prior to the eighteenth and nineteenth centuries, the idea of organic evolution—that species might have evolved into their present forms from earlier and perceptibly different forms—is scarcely to be found. Even the ancient Greeks, to whose speculative genius so very much of the furniture of the modern intellect may be traced, conceived of it only dimly, if at all. The source of this omission was probably the same as we have mentioned above: there was no reason to believe that species evolve, and every reason to believe that they do not. At any rate, the idea was not explicitly entertained or systematically pursued until the late eighteenth and early nineteenth centuries. And then, as so often happens in the history of thought, it was arrived at by several different persons independently. This, of course, is readily understandable when we consider the mood and temper, the ideas and enthusiasms, of the age. The eighteenth century had been an age in which deism and mechanism prevailed among the intellectual elite, and in which it was openly considered that all things might have their proper place in some vast, continuous *scala naturae.* From here, it was a relatively short step to the further thought that this Great Chain of Beings might have a genetic dimension to it. Thus, the Englishman Erasmus Darwin (the grandfather of Charles) and the Germans Immanuel Kant and J. W. von Goethe are often spoken of as pre-Darwinian evolutionists.

The first full-blown theory of organic evolution was put forward in 1809 by a Frenchman, Jean Baptiste de Lamarck. As we have seen, the eighteenth century's Great Chain of Beings was drawn out along a line characterized by varying degrees of complexity. Thus, to repeat the words of Denis Diderot, it extended "from the inert molecule, . . . to the living molecule, to the miscroscopic animal, to the plant-animal, to the animal, to man"—the latter being the most complexly organized of all. Lamarck's evolutionary addition to this conception was contained in the idea that all beings strive to increase their degree of complexity and thus to ascend further up along the chain. If this were not so, Lamarck reasoned, then why should the Great Chain of Beings exist at all? It can only be that all beings endeavor to increase their complexity, and that different beings (actually, different bloodlines) have been successful in varying degrees. Thus, in Lamarck's view, the stability of species is a mere appearance concealing a deeper, underlying reality.

Lamarck properly recognized that organic species differ from one another in respects other than that of complexity. This led him to distinguish between essential organs, which are directly involved in the striving toward greater complexity, and inessential organs, which develop chiefly in response to environmental exigencies. It is quite clear, Lamarck argued, that the continued use of an organ (in response to environmental demands) tends to strengthen that organ, while disuse tends to weaken it. And, so far as he could see, there was no reason to believe that these acquired modifications might not be passed on to succeeding generations. This, then, was what Lamarck took to be the secondary factor in the process of organic evolution—the inheritance of acquired characteristics. (Lamarck, of course, did not invent the idea that acquired modifications might be inheritable; it was an accepted, common-sense belief that can be traced as far back into history as we might wish to pursue it.)

Though Lamarck's theory excited much interest at the time, it nonetheless soon withered on the vine. Naturally, it was not acceptable to the special creationists on the grounds that it contradicted the Biblical account of Creation. Oddly enough, it was not acceptable to the mechanists either, for the upward striving toward complexity that it implied was seen to be a distinctly teleological notion. Further, both camps could reject it out of hand, and with a clear conscience, on the grounds that it was unsupported by any evidence, save that of rather fanciful anecdote.

Darwin's theory, published just fifty years later, suffered only from the first of these disadvantages. It was unacceptable to the special creationists, of course. To the mechanists, on the other hand, it was not only acceptable but welcome, for it provided an explanation of organic evolution in terms of blind, unthinking, "mechanical" principles. (In his younger years, Darwin was much awed by the "mechanical view of nature.") In both camps, moreover, it was a theory to be reckoned with and hardly to be dismissed out of hand, for Darwin shrewdly interwove it with a vast array of data to demonstrate that organic species do, in fact, evolve. Thus, as Julian Huxley has observed: "He was concerned both to establish the fact of evolution and to discover the mechanism by which it operated; and it was precisely because he established both aspects of the problem simultaneously that he was so successful."[1] For our purposes, we need be concerned only with the latter of these, the *mechanism*.

In 1798, the *laissez-faire* economist Thomas Malthus published his famous volume *Essay on the Principles of Population*. His argument ran roughly as follows: Population increases geometrically whereas available food supply can increase only arithmetically; in consequence, there will eventually develop a scarcity of food and an ensuing struggle for existence. Malthus drew all manner of debatable economic implications from this argument, but with these we need not now be concerned. What is important is how Malthus' "struggle for existence" suggested to Darwin what might be the mechanism of organic evolution. "In October, 1838," Darwin later recounted in his autobiographical *Life and Letters,*

> that is fifteen months after I had begun my systematic enquiry [into the possibility of organic evolution], I happened to read for amusement *Malthus on Population,* and being well prepared to appreciate the struggle for existence which everywhere goes on from long-continued observations of the habits of animals and plants, it at once struck me that under these circumstances favorable variations would tend to be preserved and unfavorable ones to be destroyed.[2]

Thus, in his *Origin of Species* of 1859, Darwin based his theory of the mechanism of evolution upon four points, of which the first two were distinctly Malthusian:

(1) *Overproduction.* Most species reproduce in numbers far exceeding what can be supported by the environment.

(2) From this, conjoined with the observation that the populations of species remain relatively constant, we must infer that there is a *struggle for existence* raging throughout nature. Darwin was very careful to point out that he used the phrase "struggle for existence" "in a large and metaphorical sense, including dependence of one being on another, and including (which is more important) not only the life of the individual, but success in leaving progeny."[3]

(3) *Survival of the fittest.* Those individuals which are best fitted to meet the exigencies of life are the ones most likely to survive.

(4) *Natural selection of adaptive variations.* This was the heart of the theory. It is an indisputable fact of nature, Darwin observed, that the members of a given species differ from one another in certain—presumably inheritable—respects. Given a certain environment, some of these variations will prove "favorable," or adaptive, while others will not. Moreover, those individuals possessed of such adaptive variations will tend to survive longer, and so will have a greater chance of propagating "after their kind." In effect, then, adaptive variations within a species will be "selected," and the proportion of their distribution within the species will steadily increase. This was Darwin's great principle of natural selection, which he took to be the fundamental mechanism underlying the process of organic evolution.

Curiously enough, the idea that organic evolution takes place by means of "natural selection" occurred almost simultaneously to a countryman of Darwin's, Alfred Russell Wallace (1823–1913). For twenty years prior to 1858, Darwin had been working on the theory that was soon to be presented in his *Origin of Species.* Then, unexpectedly, he received a memoir from Wallace in which the theory of natural selection had been anticipated in every detail. (It was Wallace, in fact, who seems to have coined the phrase "natural selection.") The result of this coincidence was that the theory of organic evolution by means of natural selection was first announced to the scientific world in 1858, in joint papers by Darwin and Wallace read before the Linnean Society of London.

Wallace, too, had arrived at his ideas as a result of reading Malthus' *Essay on the Principles of Population.* In his autobiography of 1905, he recorded that the issues raised by Malthus had led him to consider:

> Why do some die and some live? And the answer was clearly that on the whole the best fitted live. From the effects of disease the most healthy escape; from the enemies the strongest, the swiftest, or the most cunning; from famine the best hunters or those with the best digestion; and so on. Then it suddenly flashed upon me that this self-acting process would necessarily *improve the race,* because in every generation the inferior would inevitably be killed off, and the superior would remain—that is, *the fittest* would survive."[4]

This influence of Malthus' work upon both Darwin and Wallace has prompted a number of writers to suggest that their theories were in large measure a reflection *laissez-faire* economic theory. There is no doubt a certain truth in this, although it could equally be argued that *laissez-faire* economic theory was but an anticipation of what Darwin and Wallace later discovered to be the contingencies of organic development in general. In any case, a detailed consideration of the question lies outside our present purposes.

The reception of "Darwinism" following 1859 is a fairly well-known story. The first printing of *The Origin of Species by Means of Natural Selection: or, the Preservation of Favoured Races in the Struggle for Life* was sold out on the very first day it appeared. The implications of the theory clearly touched upon tender nerves in all quarters, and all educated persons soon found themselves becoming *either* Darwinians *or* anti-Darwinians almost *in toto.* Of course, there were many axes to be ground on both sides. Thus, the well-known dictum of the English statesman Disraeli:

> What is the question now placed before society with a glib assurance the most astounding? The question is this: Is man an ape or an angel? My Lord, I am on the side of the angels.[5]

Scarcely to be outdone, the Darwinians often responded with equal spite and irrationality. Thus, the German biologist Weismann dilated:

> We accept natural selection not because we are able to demonstrate the process in detail, not even because we can with more or less ease imagine

it, but simply because we must—because it is the only possible explanation that we can conceive. We must assume natural selection . . . because all other apparent principles of explanation fail us, and it is inconceivable that there could be yet another capable of explaining the adaptation of organisms without assuming the help of a principle of design.[6]

All in all, then, the French biologist Mivat was quite correct when he observed in 1871: "If the *odium theologicum* has inspired some of [Darwinism's] opponents, it is undeniable that the *odium antitheologicum* has possessed not a few of its supporters."[7]

## THE BROADER IMPLICATIONS

Let us now inquire into the broader implications of evolutionary theory, particularly insofar as these bore upon the enterprise of psychology. The implications fell under three general headings: continuity, instinct, and adaptation.

### Natura Non Facit Saltum

Darwinian theory held, first, that existing organic species have *evolved* from earlier forms of life and, second, that the *direction* of this process has been, in the main, from simplicity to complexity. Thus, any given species may be supposed to have passed through a number of earlier and simpler stages in the course of evolving up to its present position along the great *scala naturae*. This, of course, was considered to hold as true for the human species as for any other. Man did not come full-formed from the womb of nature. Rather he has evolved, and in the process he has accumulated a great host of earlier, simpler ancestors. From this fact, too, derives his kinship with other existing organic species. Man and the anthropoid apes, for example, were both regarded by Darwin as having evolved from a common ancestral stock (though not from one another, as so many of Darwin's opponents imagined); and it was on this basis that the manifest affinities between them were to be readily understood.

Now, if this had been all there was to it, the theory of evolution—specifically, of phylogenesis—could have had no very profound implications for psychology, for in the absence of a certain mediating assumption, it is of no psychological consequence whatever whether one has ancestors in common with apes, elephants, snails, or turnips. As it happened, though, this assumption was supplied straightaway by the Darwinian doctrine of phylogenetic *continuity*. In causing organic species to evolve from simpler into ever more complex forms, Darwin had written, *"natura non facit saltum"*—nature does not move by leaps, but through continuous gradations. The alterations within a species from one generation to the next are minute at most, and in all cases they amount to nothing more than modifications of already existing characteristics. Thus, the evolution of a species into higher forms is to be seen as a continuous progression of variations, of ever-increasing complexity, upon the simpler themes provided by that species' earlier, lower ancestors. These earlier themes remain within the species throughout its existence; it is only that, in the course of evolution, they become more complex.

With this, of course, the relevance of evolutionary theory to the psychological enterprise could scarcely be escaped, for it could now be imagined that an individual's ancestry, his heredity, his entire phylogenetic past are *immanent* within him. Thus, man and the anthropoid apes have a common ancestor, but now, more importantly, it could be imagined that they both have this same ancestor thumping, as it were, within their breasts. This particular message of evolutionary doctrine was received by a great many psychologists of the period, but none received it more grandiloquently than G. Stanley Hall (1844–1924). "The general psychonomic law," he observed in one characteristic passage,

> assumes that we are influenced in our deeper, more temperamental dispositions by the life-habits and codes of conduct of we know not what unnumbered hosts of ancestors, which like a cloud of witnesses are present throughout our lives, that our souls are echo-chambers in which their whispers reverberate.[8]

It should go without saying that this line of thought naturally gave rise to a great many excesses, of which more than a few were committed or encouraged by Darwin himself. In the long run, though, it was an unquestionably healthy influence if for no other reason than that it served somewhat to deintellectualize psychology. Up to this point, psychology had been a study almost exclusively of the "mind." Now, however, it could not help but become a study of the "passions" as well, for what, indeed, is more characteristic of the animal stock from which man derives than the passions by which the beasts are moved to feed, fight, and mate? Toward the end of this chapter, and in later ones as well, we shall see how this process of deintellectualization within psychology took place.

### Comparative Psychology

All of this, however, is not intended to suggest that psychology became deintellectualized entirely. On the contrary, one of the most vigorous of post-Darwinian psychological movements came into being largely as an attempt to understand, to explain, and in some cases to explain *away* human "intellectual functions." This was the movement known, then as now, as *comparative* psychology.

The explication of comparative psychology's Darwinian rationale was first provided by George John Romanes (1848–1894) in his volume of 1882, *Animal Intelligence*. If organic species evolve, he argued, then it may also be said that *aspects* of organic species evolve. Thus, we may speak of the evolution of an organ, such as the stomach, or of the evolution of a physiological process, such as digestion. And if we may speak of the evolution of physiological processes, then surely we may speak of the evolution of mental processes as well. For is it not a certainty that the process of thinking, for example, evolved in the human species just as surely as did the processes of digestion and elimination? Thus, Romanes observed, if we take the theory of evolution seriously, we must then conclude that there is a "psychological, no less than physiological, continuity extending throughout the length and breadth of the animal kingdom."[9] We find mentality in man; we must therefore expect to find it spread out in continuous gradations throughout his phylogenetic lineage. Here, then, is the ultimate task of an evolutionary psychology: to trace psychological processes back to their hintermost origins or, in Romanes' own words, to trace the "probable genesis of mind from non-mental antecedents."[10]

Now, if mentality *is* continuously spread out along the phylogenetic scale, then one can undertake to study it comparatively either from the bottom to the top or from the top to the bottom. That is, he can view higher mental processes in the light of lower ones, or lower ones in the light of higher. Neither of these procedures would be unacceptable, of course, unless they were allowed to run to excess. As it happened, though, this came to pass in fairly short order.

The extreme of viewing higher mental processes in the light of lower ones was the more common because it was more strictly in keeping with the mood of Darwinian theory. The reasoning ran as follows: If the direction of evolution is from simple to complex, and if the higher mental processes have thus continuously evolved from lower ones, then it must be that these higher processes are even now but complex forms of some utterly simple basal process. This seemingly incontestable conclusion naturally sent many able investigators in search of such a basal process. Naturally, too, it was not long before they found it, or at least imagined that they did, and then set about to explain all the higher mental processes in its terms.

One of the best illustrations of this tendency is to be found in the writings of Romanes' younger contemporary Jacques Loeb (1859–1924). After making a thorough study of "comparative brain physiology and comparative psychology," Loeb concluded that all of the higher mental processes are but complex variations upon the simple theme of "associative memory." And this, he further contended, is in turn nothing more than a variation upon an even simpler process which may be found to underlie the automatic reflexes of animals and even the tropisms of plants. Indeed, he seems to have concluded, this latter process is so simple and fundamental, so easily to be understood as a mere physical-chemical process, that it must surely have been present even in that abiotic, primordial *Urschleim* from which we may suppose all life to have evolved.

The second extreme is best illustrated by Romanes himself. Of course, Romanes shared with Loeb the desire to trace the higher mental processes *back* to their primordial "non-mental antecedents." This, however, did not prevent him from seeing that the supposed continuity of the phylogenetic scale extends in both directions, that is, from the top to the bottom as well as from the bottom to the top. Thus, he reasoned, if mentality is spread continuously throughout the phylogenetic scale, then it must be that the psychological processes of the lower animal species differ from those of man only in degree. And from this it follows that the "mental states" of the lower species can be understood, at least to a degree, on the analogy provided by their human counterparts!

> Therefore, having full regard to the progressive weakening of the analogy from human to brute psychology as we recede through the animal kingdom downwards from man, still, as it is the only analogy available, I shall follow it throughout the animal series.[11]

And follow it he did—a practice from which he has since been often criticized and seldom praised.

Loeb and Romanes both followed the Darwinian assumption of phylogenetic continuity to an extreme; the only difference was that they followed it in different directions. The extreme reached by Loeb was the more strictly in keeping with the mood of Darwinian theory and, for this reason, the more common. For this reason, too, it was the less recognizable as an extreme and thus, attracted less criticism from within the scientific community. The extreme of Romanes, on the other hand, was very visible indeed, leading as it did to statements such as the following:

> If we observe an ant or a bee apparently exhibiting sympathy or rage, we must either conclude that some psychological state resembling sympathy or rage is present, or else refuse to think about the subject at all.[12]

It is scarcely surprising, then, that Romanes' approach to comparative psychology became the target of criticism almost immediately.

The most effective and perhaps also the most misunderstood of such criticism was put forward by Romanes' countryman, C. Lloyd Morgan (1852–1936). Now, Morgan did not doubt for a moment that "subjective induction" was an entirely valid procedure in the study of comparative psychology. What he did doubt was that it could be followed, uninterruptedly, "throughout the animal series." And so it was, in the face of this doubt, that he proposed what he thought should be taken as the "basal principle" of inquiry in comparative psychology:

> In no case may we interpret an [animal] action as the outcome of the exercise of a higher psychical faculty, if it can be interpreted as the outcome of the exercise of one which stands lower in the psychological scale.[13]

This was Morgan's initial statement of his famous "canon" of 1894.

Morgan's canon has often been portrayed as simply a restatement of Occam's Razor—the principle of parsimonious explanation—*vis-à-vis* comparative psychology. Morgan himself, however, went well out of his way to deny this interpretation, for, as he observed, "surely the simplicity of an explanation is no necessary criterion of its truth."[14] This latter observation of Morgan's may or may not be accurate. But it is clear in either case that his canon was based upon an idea of an entirely different sort.

Consider for a moment the assertion that a certain "psychical faculty" is not to be found—even in simple, rudimentary form—in any species lower than man. As Morgan rightly recognized, this assertion would not be warmly received by the orthodox Darwinians, such as Loeb and Romanes, on the grounds that *natura non facit saltum.* Thus:

> It may, however, be objected that this [canon] is contrary to the principles of evolution, since the presence of any faculty in higher types involves the germ of this faculty in lower types. This criticism only holds good, however, on the assumption that the [discontinuous] evolution of higher faculties out of lower faculties is impossible. Those evolutionists who accept this assumption as valid are logically bound to believe either (1) that all forms of animal life from the amoeba upwards have all the faculties of man, only reduced in degree and range . . . . or (2) that in the higher forms of life the introduction of the higher faculties has been effected by some means other than that of natural evolution.[15]

As may be readily surmised, then, Morgan was not prepared to accept this assumption of the orthodox Darwinians without qualification. Comparative psychology had been brought into being by the doctrine of phylogenetic continuity; what Morgan's canon held was that the discipline should also be prepared to recognize phylogenetic *dis*continuity, if ever it should be found. For it is clear, he argued,

> that any animal may be at a state where certain higher faculties have not yet evolved from their lower precursors; and hence we are logically bound not to assume the existence of these higher faculties until good reasons shall have been shown for such existence.[16]

Morgan did not make use of the terms "emerge" or "emergent" until later, but it is plain even here that his sympathies lay on the side of an evolutionary subdoctrine—emergentism—which was at that time just beginning to take shape in the minds of a number of diverse thinkers.[17] Briefly stated, the doctrine of emergentism accepted organic evolution, but rejected all notions of a strict, thoroughgoing phylogenetic continuity.

We noted earlier that Morgan's canon was directed principally against the anthropomorphic excesses of Romanes. It should be clear as well, though, that its emergentist implications would have applied equally against the "method of reduction" of such a person as Loeb. For once the possibility of phylogenetic *dis*continuity is accepted, then any attempt to explain higher processes in terms of lower ones must bear the full burden of proof. As it happened, this particular effect of the canon was not very clearly seen at the time. Indeed, even today the principle which it espouses is to be counted among those venerated institutions which are often cited, rarely understood, and almost never studied.

### The Psychological Study of Children

One can, of course, study the psychology of lower animals for its own sake, in and of itself, simply because it is interesting. Human concerns being what they are, though, it is more likely that the study will be pursued because of the light that it might cast upon human psychology. This observation goes far to explain the fact that, prior to Darwin, the psychological study of lower animals was virtually nonexistent, for until the theory of evolution came upon the scene, there was no very compelling reason to suppose that animal psychology might have any light to cast upon anything at all. Darwin's theory provided this reason through its doctrine that higher, more complex forms evolve continuously from lower, simpler forms. As we have seen, the pursuit of comparative psychology did not require that the continuity of this evolution be absolute and unqualified, but it did require at least a partial or piecemeal continuity.

Much the same may be said about the psychological study of children. Before the coming of evolutionary theory, there was really no reason to suppose that the psychology of the child might have any light to cast upon human psychology in general. Afterwards, on the other hand, there was reason to suspect that it might cast a very great deal of light indeed.

It is true that evolutionary theory, as such, was not primarily concerned with ontogenesis—the development, or "evolution," of the individual member of a species. Even when it did speak of ontogenesis, as with the formula "ontogeny recapitulates phylogeny," it did so mainly as a means to the end of studying phylogenesis. Still and all, a theory so vast and promising as that of organic evolution cannot help but spill over, now and again, into other pots. And so, the underlying evolutioary rationale of developmental psychology was not long in coming: if human psychology might be illuminated by a study of its phylogenesis, as was the hope of comparative psychology, then might it not also be illuminated by a study of its ontogenesis?

To anyone caught up in the evolutionary enthusiasm of the day, the answer could only be in the affirmative. For to all those who had ears to hear it, the larger message of evolutionary theory was just this: all things—from the cosmos-at-large to the individual human being—evolve continuously from earlier to later stages and from simpler to more complex forms. Clearly, then, all things can be seen in their fullness only when shown in an evolutionary, or developmental, light. G. Stanley Hall, one of the principal figures in post-Darwinian developmental psychology, put the matter quite succinctly as follows:

> Our ideals of what the most perfect knowledge of any fact or object really is, are coming to be more and more genetic. We really know things only when we trace their development from the farthest beginning through all their stages to maximal maturity and decay.[18]

Here, then, was a large part of the rationale for the greatly increased interest in the psychology of the child that followed upon the appearance of evolutionary theory. To be sure, no one had ever really doubted that adults "evolve" from children and that they do so through fairly continuous gradations. But never, before Darwin, had the message been so forcefully driven home: "We really know things only when we trace their development."

There was another feature of evolutionary theory that was also conducive to an increased interest in the psychological study of children. In the 1870s, Darwinian theory had appended to it the so-called "Fundamental Biogenetic Law" of Ernst Haeckel. The immediate origins of this "law" lay in some rather specific embryological observations; its significance, however, was imagined to extend into far more general realms. The embryological developmental of a living organism may be observed to pass through a succession of fairly distinct stages. Further, if one is not too pedantic with regard to details, these stages somewhat resemble the phylogenetic stages through which the organism's species may be supposed to have passed in evolving into its present form. Thus, the "fundamental biogenetic law": ontogenesis, the development of the individual, *recapitulates* phylogenesis, the development of the species.

Now it is true that this doctrine was originally intended to apply to ontogenesis only in its bare anatomical and physiological aspects. But it requires little imagination to see how it might readily have been extended to apply to ontogenesis in its *psychological* aspect as well. If the anatomical and physiological development of the individual in its early stages recapitulates the phylogenesis of the species, then might not the same be true of early psychological development? To the extent that psychological processes are based upon physiological processes, the answer must surely be yes. From this, of course, it was but a short step to the conclusion that the psychological development of the child stands as the "great revealer of the [psychological] past of the race."

The words that we have just quoted were those, again, of G. Stanley Hall, who was without question the foremost proponent of the doctrine of psychological recapitulation. In brief, Hall's notion was that "original [psychological] tendencies" appear in the development of the individual in approximately the same sequence and proportions as they appeared initially in the evolution of the species. Thus, in its evolution, the human species may be supposed to have passed at one time through a fish-like stage. Anatomically, this ancestry is recapitulated by the gill-like formations which appear at one point in the development of the human embryo. Psychologically, it is recapitulated by such instances as the following:

> A babe a few days old . . . made peculiar paddling or swimming movements. . . . In children and adults . . . we find swaying from side to side or forward or backward, not infrequent. This suggests the slow oscillatory movements used by fish. . . . Children . . . after the first shock and fright take the greatest delight in water. . . . Others older or less active can sit by the hour seeing and hearing the movements of water in sea or stream.[19]

Hall found many additional instances of recapitulation in other spheres. He perceived, for example, that man's primate ancestry is recapitulated by such things as the prehensile reflexes of the newborn, the infant's tendency to fall asleep when rocked, the child's fear of thunder, lightening, snakes, high winds, and open spaces, his "untaught horror of water[!]," and the like. Indeed, there were few things about the child that Hall did *not* see as instances of recapitulation.

It goes without saying that the doctrine of psychological recapitulation could survive only so long as the biological doctrine, on which it rested, remained in good repute. Both doctrines fell, at length, from their original favor—and this is perhaps just as well.


### Nature, Nurture, and Instinct

We saw in the earlier chapters of this book how the psychological thought of the seventeenth and eighteenth centuries culminated in a kind of wholesale environmentalism. Human nature and the human mind, it was held, are largely—indeed, exclusively—the products of immediate environmental circumstances. True, this tendency abated somewhat in the post-Kantian psychology of the Germans, but it was still, all the same, a force to be reckoned with.

(Helmholtz, for example, took pride in the fact that his perceptual theory was an "empiristic" one.)

The effect of evolutionary theory was, of course, to send the pendulum of opinion swinging back again toward the "nature" end of the nature-nurture controversy. As we have noted, the mechanism of evolution was taken to be "natural selection"; its medium, on the other hand, was none other than "heredity." Thus, to the degree that psychological inquiry was guided by evolutionary considerations, it could not help but incline toward nativism.

One of the best indications of this swing back toward nativism is to be found in the prominence accorded by biological and psychological writers of the late nineteenth century to a thing called "instinct." In his famous and widely read *Principles of Psychology* of 1890, for example, William James (1842–1910) included an entire chapter on instinct—and well he might, for in his post-Darwinian view there was simply no doubting either the existence of instinct or its biological and psychological importance. "Instinct," he wrote,

> is usually defined as the faculty of acting in such a way as to produce certain ends, without foresight of the ends, and without previous education in the performance. That instincts, as thus defined, exist on an enormous scale in the animal kingdom needs no proof. They are the functional correlatives of structure. With the presence of a certain [structure] goes, one may say, almost always a native aptitude for its use.[20]

It is fairly well known that James and his like-minded contemporaries were rather liberal in their estimation of the extent of such "native aptitudes." Thus, James hesitated not a bit to list under the heading of "special human instincts" such things as "vocalization," "emulation or rivalry," "pugnacity," "sympathy," "the hunting instinct," "fear of high places," and even "cleanliness." This, though, is simply one more illustration of the rule that, given sufficient enthusiasm, things are apt to be carried to extremes. The point is that evolutionary theory served to bring the notions of "native aptitude," "innate disposition," and the like, within the pale of legitimate psychological inquiry.

James' *Principles* appeared about thirty years after the publication of Darwin's *Origin of Species*. And, by this time, the notion of "instinct" had already been crystallized into two fairly distinct forms. In the first of these, which was the one more in keeping with the definition given above, an instinct was taken to be a more or less complex concatenation of specific reflexive reactions. Thus, James wrote by way of illustration, when a cat engages in the complex and seemingly purposeful act of chasing a mouse,

> He acts in each case separately, and simply because he cannot help it; being so framed that when that particular running thing called a mouse appears in

his field of vision he *must* pursue . . . His nervous system is to a large
extent a preorganized bundle of such reactions—they are as [predetermined]
as sneezing, and as exactly correlated to their special excitants.[21]

This was "instinct" in the stronger sense of the term.

The second sense of "instinct," which seems to have been elaborated upon
mainly by German writers, was a rather weaker one, for it held an instinct
to consist not so much in specific reflexive reactions as in a kind of generalized,
goal-directed impulsion (*Trieb*). Most of the things that James listed as special
human instincts were of precisely this sort. When he asserted, for example,
that there is a human instinct for cleanliness, he was suggesting only that
there is an innate *impulse* to avoid substances which are "natively repugnant."
Instinct in a case of this sort is nothing more than an impulsion to achieve a
certain goal (viz., the avoidance of repugnant substances). The impulsion and
its goal are innately determined; the means of achieving the goal, however,
are not. It is to be noted, then, that "instinct" in this second and weaker
sense is not so inflexible a thing as in the first. As James observed with
respect to the cleanliness instinct:

> It is true that the shrinking from contact with these things may be inhibited
> very easily, as by a medical education; and it is equally true that the impulse
> to clean them away may be inhibited by so slight an obstacle as the thought
> of the coldness of the ablution, or the necessity of getting up to perform it.
> It is also true that an impulse to cleanliness, habitually checked, will become
> obsolete fast enough.[22]

We have said that the notion of "instinct" had already been crystallized,
by the time James published his *Principles,* into these two distinct forms. This
is true, but it must be added that James and his contemporaries were not
entirely cognizant of the distinction. James, for example, wrote at great length
about instincts of the impulsion type, which could scarcely be seen as
concatenations of specific reflexive reactions, and yet he hesitated not at all in
asserting that "the actions we call instinctive all conform to the general reflex
type." This confusion, however, was only a matter of time. In later chapters,
we shall see how both of these senses .of "instinct" entered quite fully and
distinctly into the mainstream of psychological thought.

### The Idea of Adaptation

Darwin had argued that variations within a species tend to be preserved,
or "selected," only insofar as they are adaptive—that is to say, only insofar as
they conduce to the survival of the individual or the propagation of the species.
From this, the converse inference was readily drawn: namely, that each and

every aspect of an extant species' native endowment must have some *adaptive function*. Exceptions, such as the vermiform appendix, were of course recognized, but these, in the main, were taken to be merely exceptions that proved the rule. And that rule, presumably, held as true for a species' psychological endowment as for its anatomy and physiology. This was the evolutionary rationale for that late nineteenth-century movement within psychology known as "functionalism."

The functionalist approach to psychology was well summarized by James Rowland Angell (1869–1949) in a paper of 1907. "The psychologist of this stripe," he wrote,

> is wont to take his cue from the basal conception of the evolutionary movement, i.e., that for the most part organic structures and functions possess their present characteristics by virtue of the efficiency with which they fit into the extant conditions of life broadly designated the environment. With this conception in mind he proceeds to attempt some understanding of the manner in which the psychical contributes to the furtherance of the sum total of organic activities.[23]

This functionalist approach to psychology was just that—an *approach*. It never developed into a full-blown theoretical movement, and so we need not pause here to examine it in detail. Suffice it to say that its emphasis upon the "function," or adaptive significance, of psychological processes quickly became one of the main currents of post-Darwinian psychological thought. The conviction upon which the emphasis was based was simply this: that psychological processes have come into existence through evolution, and that they have done so by virtue of their *usefulness* in preserving the life and propagating the species of their possessor.

In the present chapter, we have touched only upon those psychological consequences of evolutionary theory that were fairly conspicuous and immediate. There were others, of course; but consideration of these is best put off until later.

### NOTES

1. J. Huxley, *Evolution: The Modern Synthesis* (New York: Harper, 1942), p. 13.
2. P. G. Fothergill, *Historical Aspects of Organic Evolution* (London: Hollis and Carter, 1952), p. 108.
3. C. Darwin, *The Origin of Species by Means of Natural Selection* (New York: Bert, 1898), p. 59.
4. Fothergill, *Organic Evolution,* p. 118.
5. In a speech delivered at Oxford University, 1864.
6. Fothergill, *Organic Evolution,* p. 118.

7. Ibid., p. 121.

8. R. E. Grinder, ed., *A History of Genetic Psychology: The First Science of Human Development* (New York: Wiley, 1967), p. 214.

9. R. J. Herrnstein and E. G. Boring, eds., *A Source Book in the History of Psychology* (Cambridge, Mass.: Harvard University Press, 1966), p. 461.

10. Ibid., p. 457.

11. Ibid., p. 461.

12. Ibid.

13. Ibid., p. 468.

14. Ibid., p. 465.

15. Ibid., p. 468.

16. Ibid.

17. See, for example, Morgan's 1922 Gifford Lectures, *Emergent Evolution* (London: Williams and Norgate), 1923.

18. Grinder, *Genetic Psychology,* p. 215.

19. G. S. Hall, *Adolescence,* vol. II (New York: Appleton, 1904), pp. 192–195.

20. W. James, *The Principles of Psychology,* vol. II (New York: Henry Holt, 1890), p. 383.

21. Ibid., p. 384.

22. Ibid., p. 434.

23. J. R. Angell, "The Province of Functional Psychology," *Psychological Review,* 14 (1907).

## FOR FURTHER READING

A number of good histories of evolutionary theory exist. The most readable of these happens also to be the one best suited to our purposes: P. G. Fothergill, *Historical Aspects of Organic Evolution* (London: Hollis and Carter, 1952). Good background accounts of the matters that we have discussed are also contained in J. C. Green, *The Death of Adam: Evolution and Its Impact on Western Thought* (Ames: Iowa State University Press, 1959); J. Huxley, *Evolution: The Modern Synthesis* (New York: Harper, 1942); and W. Irvine, *Apes, Angels, and Victorians: The Story of Darwin, Huxley, and Evolution* (New York: McGraw-Hill, 1955).

For an alternative account of the influence of evolutionary theory upon psychological thought and research, see Chapter 8 et passim of G. Murphy, *Historical Introduction to Modern Psychology* (New York: Harcourt, Brace, and World, 1949).

Well-chosen excerpts from the writings of Romanes, Morgan, and other comparative psychologists of the early post-Darwinian period will be found in R. J. Herrnstein and E. G. Boring, eds., *A Source Book in the History of Psychology* (Cambridge, Mass.: Harvard University Press, 1966), and W. S. Sahakian, ed., *History of Psychology: A Source Book in Systematic Psychology* (Itasca, Ill.: Peacock, 1968).

A number of lengthy excerpts from the writings of authors who fall within or alongside the tradition of genetic psychology are to be found in R. E. Grinder, *A History of Genetic Psychology: The First Science of Human Development* (New York: Wiley, 1967).

# Chapter 8
# William James

It is an argument from analogy, drawn from rivers, reflex actions and other material phenomena where no consciousness *appears* to exist at all, and extended to cases where consciousness seems the phenomenon's essential feature. The consciousness doesn't count, these reasoners say; it doesn't exist for science, it is nil; you mustn't think about it at all. The intensely reckless character of all this needs no comment. It is making the mechanical theory true *per fas aut nefas*. For the sake of that theory we make inductions from phenomena to others that are startlingly *un*like them; and we assume that a complication which Nature has introduced (the presence of feeling and of effort, namely) is not worthy of scientific recognition at all. Such conduct may conceivably be *wise*, though I doubt it; but scientific, as contrasted with metaphysical, it cannot seriously be called.

William James, *Principles of Psychology* (1890)

In 1878 William James (1842–1910), then an assistant professor of physiology at Harvard, contracted with the New York publisher Henry Holt to write a textbook in psychology. Holt wanted the manuscript delivered within a year; James thought he might be able to have it ready in two. As it turned out, the book was not finished for twelve years. The delay was occasioned by a number of things: the duties of teaching, the exigencies of an academic career (during the twelve years James went from assistant professor of physiology to professor of philosophy), troublesome eyesight, and just plain procrastination of the sort that every author knows only too well. But most of all it was occasioned by the difficulty of the work itself. Once into it, James found that every problem "bristles with obstructions," that every paragraph presented "some unforeseen snag," that every sentence had to be forged "in the teeth of irreducible and stubborn facts."[1]

Of course, this was partly because the science of psychology was "in such a confused and imperfect state." But in large measure it was also because James felt very keenly some of the problems—existential problems, let us call them—that this new science engendered. Beginning in the seventeenth century, the whole drift of psychological thought had been in the direction of mechanism. By James' time the mechanistic view was stronger than ever, for it could now refer to a large body of detailed physiological information that seemed to support it. Then, too, there was the strengthening provided by the post-Darwinian preeminence of "instinct" and "reflex." At any rate, although there were differences in detail among the various psychological "isms" that abounded in James' day, the predominating vision was plain enough: the human animal is an automaton, a biological machine, whose every thought and act is determined by inexorable mechanical laws of cause and effect. What then of "will" and "freedom"? Mere illusions! Of consciousness? An irrelevancy! Human "dignity"? A mere conceit of animal automata grown too big for their biological breeches! And what of love, enthusiasm, aspiration, suffering, illumination, devotion, and all the other things that mankind has so long regarded as constituting the most substantial and important part of itself? They are all mere shadows of the automatisms of the body, in particular the nervous system, in its interactions with that larger mechanism known as external reality.

And here, in brief, was James' situation. On the one hand he found the physiological and evolutionary arguments in favor of psychological mechanism to be quite compelling; but on the other hand he was not at all comfortable with their existential (he called them "ethical") implications. The result was that a large part of his two-volume *Principles of Psychology,* twelve years in the making, can be seen as an effort to defend psychological mechanism with the one hand while combating it with the other—or to take from it what he could not in good conscience refuse, yet insisting that there might still be "something more."

This aspect of James' *Principles* is not always clearly visible at first reading, for the text of the work runs to 1,377 pages, and the organization of its many parts is far from systematic. (James himself, in a moment of postpartum despondency, described it as a "loathsome, distended, tumefied, bloated, dropsical mass."[2]) A careful reading of the book, however, will show clearly enough that this is the theme that runs throughout—giving mechanism what seemed to be its due, while yet insisting that "your delights and sorrows, your loves and hates, your aspirations and efforts are real combatants in life's arena, and not impotent, paralytic spectators of the game."[3] James clearly recognized a truth that the rest of us ignore only at our peril: that the theories we spin, "besides offering us objects able to account satisfactorily for our sensible experience," are also likely to bear on our "aesthetic, emotional, and active needs."[4] In examining how this worked itself out in James' own case, we will not only gain a sense of what the predominating psychological vision of human nature was toward the end of the nineteenth century; we will also have a glimpse of the existential tension engendered by this vision in those who, like James, saw clearly how it tended to belittle and vitiate "all that makes life worth living."

## HABIT AND THE MECHANICS OF THE NERVOUS SYSTEM

One of the things that compelled James to give mechanism its due was a certain irreducible and stubborn fact that impressed him very deeply. It was the observation that a great many human and animal actions, even many that appear purposeful, seem to be performed more or less automatically, with little or nothing in the way of conscious direction. Take, for example, the act of walking down a flight of stairs. Although quite commonplace, it is an act of exceeding complexity. At every moment, and from one moment to the next, the composite movements of the body must be coordinated with one another, with the terrain of the stairs, and perhaps also with the movements of other persons. And yet the task is performed with a minimum of conscious direction. Perhaps there is the general decision to go from up here to down there, but beyond that it is almost all automatic. There are no conscious directions to the effect of "left leg bend at the knee," "fall forward," "check fall," "right leg down," and so on. The same is true of many other acts as well: "standing, walking, buttoning and unbuttoning, piano-playing, talking, even saying one's prayers"—these and many others can all be done more or less automatically. "The performances of animal instinct [also] seem semiautomatic, and the reflex acts of self-preservation certainly are so."[5]

And this, of course, is what mechanism had been claiming all along—that humans and animals are basically automata. James was reluctant to make the transition from "automatic" to "automata," but he did concede that one of the most obvious and important characteristics of living creatures is that they are "bundles of habits." Indeed, he found this conception of "habit" so compelling that he made it one of the central points of his psychology. One of the chief reasons it was so compelling was that it seemed to fit in quite neatly with what was then known—or thought to be known—about the basic processes of the nervous system. James is often quoted as defining psychology as "the science of Mental Life, both of its phenomena and their conditions."[6]

But of course it was not just in "mental life" that he was interested; he was also keenly interested in what we would nowadays call "behavior," that is, acting and doing. At any rate, be sure to note that his interest was not just in the bare phenomena of mental life and behavior, but also in their *conditions*— the laws and processes by which they are governed. And first and foremost among these conditions, in James' view, were the workings of the nervous system. The importance of the nervous system was simply not to be denied, especially not by someone who, like James, had been trained as a physiologist (actually, as a physician, although he never practiced medicine). His psychology, therefore, was in the first instance a psycho*physiology*. Indeed, in the very first chapter he warned the reader that "the whole remainder of the book will be more or less of a proof" of the postulate that psychological phenomena "are explicable only by the fact that the brain laws are a codeterminant of the result."[7]

There is a certain irony in this, though it is visible only from the perspective of the present. In most areas James was not a man to accept without question the conventioanl wisdom on a subject; we will see several examples of this before the present chapter is finished. When it came to the nervous system, however, he accepted part and parcel, with hardly any questioning at all, the then conventional mechanistic view of things. This did not mean that his confrontation with psychological mechanism was lost before it began, but it did mean that he had a steeper hill to climb than would have been the case had he been in a position to question the basic assumptions of the mechanistic view of the nervous system. It also meant that his possibilities for admitting a nonmechanistic "something more" into life's arena were fairly limited.

The basic assumptions of the mechanistic view of the nervous system were the following:

(1) First was the assumption that the nervous system is fundamentally a reflex apparatus—that everything it does is but a variation, simple or complex, on the basic theme of reflexive "discharge." This notion of a reflexive nervous system had been growing ever since Descartes, who imagined the reflexive operations to be accomplished by the interplay of hydraulic pressures within the tube-like structures of the system. By James' day they were presumed to be accomplished by "currents," electrical or electrochemical, running along nervous "pathways" and eventually "discharging" into glands or muscles or, alternatively, into the lower or higher centers of the brain. The nerve currents are occasioned in the first place by stimulation of the sensory organs, and when they are discharged immediately into the motor organs, without involving the higher centers of the brain, the result is a reflexive action pure and simple. When they run first to the higher brain centers, and only then out to the motor organs, the result might be more complex and variable, perhaps even displaying purpose and intelligence; but it is a reflex action all the same. It

is "only a difference of degree and not of kind, and does not change the reflex type. The conception of *all* action as conforming to this type is the fundamental conception of modern nerve-physiology."[8]

(2) The second assumption concerned the role of the higher brain centers, in particular the cerebral hemispheres. The mechanistic neurophysiology of the late nineteenth century made one fatal assumption about these higher centers, namely, that they are fundamentally *passive*—that they do nothing but *receive* impressions from the sensory organs and *reflect* them back to motor organs. The only complication is that the higher centers contain a great variety of interconnections that are to some extent modifiable by experience. But here again it is "only a difference of degree and not of kind." For the interconnections, however complex or modified by experience they might be, contribute nothing active to the process. They do not *act;* they merely *reflect*. It is, James wrote, "like the great commutating switchboard at a central telephone station. No new elementary process is involved; no [new] impression nor any [activity] peculiar to the hemispheres."[9] It is just a switching operation, performed not by "operators," but automatically in accordance with the mechanics of the nervous system and the modifications wrought upon it by experience.

(3) Finally there were several assumptions that were not just physiological but *psycho*physiological, as they concerned the supposed relationships between the mechanics of the nervous system and the phenomena of mental life. The nature of these supposed relationships will offer no surprise. Take the assumptions concerning the mechanics of the nervous system that we have just examined, add to them the main features of the traditions of mental mechanism and associationism, and you will have it in fairly complete detail. The phenomena of mental life are the results that occur in consciousness when currents within the nervous system are discharged into various specific locations in the higher brain centers. And since these currents can only be initiated by stimulation of the sensory organs, it follows that *all* of the phenomena of mental life must ultimately derive from sensory experience. In short, they are all *sensations*. The only question is whether they are immediate sensations of objects now present to the senses, or "remote sensations" (memories, ideas, etc.) of objects that were present to the senses at some time in the past. In the latter case what we have is an instance of what had traditionally been called "association of ideas." James preferred the phrase "association of objects," because in his view the phenomena of mental life—sensations, ideas, and all the rest—are not really "associated" at all, except indirectly. The only substantial associations that exist are the associations of temporal contiguity between the objects of sensory experience. If object A and object B impress themselves upon the senses at approximately the same time, the nerve currents that they initiate will discharge themselves into the higher brain centers also at approximately the same time. This of course entails that the mental impressions

of the two objects will be "associated" in conscious experience. But more importantly it means that the two discharges, occurring more or less simultaneously, will tend to reinforce each other as they spread outward, thus increasing the "permeability" of the neural connections between their two locations. Thus it will happen that on some future occasion the sensory impression of one of the objects might arouse in consciousness the "remote sensation" of the other, even though the latter is not present. The "association" occurs because a portion of the sensory discharge into the first brain location will be propagated along the now permeable connective pathway to the second location. This was James' paradigm for all mental phenomena that were not just the immediate sensory impressions of present objects, including such complex things "as we call feelings, desires, cognitions, reasonings, decisions, and the like." However varied and complex they might be, however remote from particular sensory experience they might seem, they are all the result of "the laws of habit in the nervous system."[10]

This is a good place to point out that James used the term "habit" in two senses. In the one sense the term referred only to sequences of behavior that are more or less automatic, that is, unaccompanied by conscious direction. In the other it referred to "the laws of habit of the nervous system" and accordingly, much more broadly, to everything that falls under the governance of these laws. This of course includes all instances of behavior that are "habit" in the first sense of the term. But it also includes even those behaviors that *are* accompanied by conscious direction. For as we have just seen, the events of consciousness are themselves governed by these laws. In this sense *all* complex behavior is habit, and *everything* psychological is automatic!

James saw habit, in both the broad and narrow senses of the term, to be of considerable advantage. For the broad sense, the laws of habit of the nervous system are what allow the organism to adjust its actions to the exigencies of its particular environment. Without them (as in the case of a decerebrate animal) the "lower machinery" of the nervous system shows only a limited range of fairly stereotyped actions. But let the great commutative switchboard be added, let the permeability of its connections be modifiable by experience, and you have the makings of "an endless consequent increase in the possibilities of behavior on the creature's part."[11] It will still be true that "the entire nervous system is nothing but a system of paths between a sensory *terminus a quo* and a muscular, glandular, or other *terminus ad quem*."[12] But the possible permutations are now vastly increased, all to the adaptive advantage of the organism.

For the narrow sense of habit, the advantages come from the sharpening, focusing, and consequent increased efficiency of behavior. Consider again the act of walking down a flight of stairs. No one is born with the ability to perform this complex act. All of the specific movements and coordinations involved in it must be practiced again and again, bit by bit, with much effort and many errors. Those parts of the act most essential to it will be the ones most often repeated and most often associated with one another either simultaneously or in sequence. Their corresponding neural connections will accordingly be the ones most often traversed by current, and thus they will become the ones that are most permeable to the passage of current on future occasions. In a word, practice makes perfect; the essential components are retained, sharpened, and focused, while the irrelevant components drop away. Thus the first advantage of habit in the narrow sense: it "simplifies the movements required to achieve a given result, makes them more accurate, and diminishes fatigue."[13] The second advantage is that the more habitual the act becomes, the less it need be accompanied by conscious attention. Here again there is a neurological underpinning. Although the neural events corresponding to conscious attention might be necessary in the initial practice stages of the act, they are eventually superseded by a more streamlined network of connections in which "what instigates each new muscular contraction in its appointed order is not a thought or a perception, but [merely] the sensation occasioned by the muscular contraction just finished."[14] James saw the great majority of human actions as being of this habitual type, and he was not dismayed by so great an incursion of mindless automatism into life's arena. On the contrary, he saw it as one of the greatest benefits of the laws of the nervous system; for "the more of the details of our daily life we can hand over to the effortless custody of automatism, the more our higher powers of mind will be set free for their own proper work."[15] In view of the thoroughgoing automatism that James embraces up to this point, we might wonder just where he is going to find room—or need—for the operation of such "higher powers of mind." We must lay a bit more mechanistic groundwork before answering that question.

### REFLEXIVE EMOTIONS AND IDEO-MOTOR ACTIONS

James' espousal of mechanistic psychophysiology reached its highest point in his theories of emotion and action. First, his theory of emotion. Common sense says that first we feel grief and then cry, or fear and then run, and so on—in short, that the emotion precedes and causes the emotional behavior. James' theory was the exact opposite; in fact it could not have been otherwise in view of his psychophysiological first principles. An emotion is a state of mind. And since every state of mind is a sensory experience, either immediate or "remote," it must be that an emotion is also a sensory experience. But a sensory experience *of what?* If a person meets a bear in the woods, that individual's fear of the bear is clearly not the same as the mere perception of the bear. For by itself the perception is "purely cognitive in form, pale, colorless, destitute of emotional warmth." The emotion comes in only after the perception has evoked reflexive bodily changes such as turning, running, trembling, and various modes of visceral arousal. These bodily changes produce sensations, and they in turn are what constitute the felt emotion. Thus "the more rational statement is that we feel sorry because we cry, angry because we strike, afraid because we tremble, and not that we cry, strike, or tremble because we are sorry, angry, or fearful."[16]

James of course recognized that this was a crude way of putting it, for he did not suppose that some isolated bit of behavior, such as crying, striking, or trembling, was by itself sufficient to produce the full emotional color of grief, anger, or fear. Rather he saw the entire body as an emotional "sounding board," consisting of changes "so indefinitely numerous and subtle," so rich in "permutations and combinations," that "no shade of emotion, however slight, should be without a bodily reverberation as unique, when taken in its totality, as is the mental mood itself." Each emotion involves an immense number of subtle as well as gross bodily modifications, and that is why it is

> so difficult for us to produce in cold blood the total and integral expression
> of any one of them. We may catch the trick with the voluntary muscles,
> but fail with the skin, glands, heart, and other viscera. Just as an artificially
> imitated sneeze lacks something of the reality, so the attempt to imitate an
> emotion in the absence of its normal instigating cause is apt to be rather
> "hollow."[17]

And from the lowest and coarsest emotion to the highest and finest, each tells the same story. The fear of a bear and the love of justice, if it is truly a love and not just a cold, bloodless, "intellectual perception"—both are tunes played on the keyboard of the body, differing only in key and melody and, of course, in the objects that excite them. Each emotion is but the "resultant of a sum of . . . organic changes," and each of these changes is but the "reflex effect of the exciting object."[18]

The existential implication of this view of emotion was exactly what James had set out to avoid; for it suggested that "your delights and sorrows, your loves and hates," really are only "impotent, paralytic spectators of the game." But he embraced the theory enthusiastically all the same, clearly recognizing that there was only one alternative. That would be to "deny the view [of the nervous system] that is current, and hold the cortex to be something more than" a merely passive organ of projection and connection. He was not prepared to do this, but chose rather to abide by the conventional and at that time authoritative view that there is nothing involved "beyond the ordinary reflex circuits, and the local centres admitted in one shape or another by all to exist."[19] On that view, emotion *must* be a sensation, and there is nothing for it to be a sensation *of,* except the bodily changes.

The same can be said of James' ideo-motor theory of action: in view of his psychophysiological first principles, there was really no alternative. All actions originally occur as the reflexive results of external stimulation. The ideo-motor theory explains how these actions can also come to be instigated by ideas—actually, by the neural "discharges" of which ideas are the mental reflection. Here is how it happens. The performance of the act produces sensations; so too do any consequences to which the act might recurrently lead. These various sensations occur at approximately the same time as the act itself; the connective pathways between the locations of their respective neural discharges become more permeable; and so, eventually, all that is needed to produce the act will be the "idea" of the act and its consequences. Here again it is a matter of habit and automatism. Once the new connections have been formed, the action follows the idea just as reflexively as it once followed the external stimulus. This is true even when the act is delayed, or fails to come at all, as a result of what appears to be deliberation or irresolution. All that is involved in such cases is the simultaneous presence of a second idea whose reflexive action would be incompatible with the reflexive action of the first. It is all just the mechanical working-out of the laws of the nervous system: "The inhibition of a movement no more involves an express effort or command than its execution does; . . . just as the bare presence of one idea prompts a movement, so the bare presence of another idea will prevent its taking place."[20]

This is the place where James came closest to a view of what we would nowadays call "psychodynamics." Only a few years later another psychologist trained as a physiologist-physician, Sigmund Freud, was to promulgate a similar view, although in much greater detail and with some assumptions regarding the conscious and unconscious status of "ideas" that James was not prepared to accept. We will see later that the following, though written by James, could easily have been written by Freud:

A waking man's behavior is thus at all times the resultant of two opposing neural forces. With unimaginable fineness some currents among the cells and fibres of his brain are playing on his motor nerves, whilst other currents, as unimaginably fine, are playing on the first currents, damming or helping them, altering their direction or their speed. The upshot of it all is that whilst the currents must always end by being drained off through *some* motor nerves, they are drained off sometimes through one set and sometimes through another; and sometimes they keep each other in equilibrium so long that a superficial observer may think they are not drained off at all. Such an observer must remember, however, that from the physiological point of view a gesture, an expression of the brow, or an expulsion of the breath are movements as much as an act of locomotion is. A king's breath slays as well as an assassin's blow; and the outpouring of those currents which the . . . streaming of our ideas accompanies need not always be of an explosive or physically conspicuous kind.[21]

Or consider this passage, also by James, which could almost serve as a summary of Freud's views of inhibition, displacement, and neurotic symptom formation:

> [The behavioral expression of emotion], being the natural channel of discharge, exhausts the nerve-centres, and emotional calm ensues. But if fears or anger are simply suppressed, whilst the object of grief or rage remains unchanged . . . , the current which would have invaded the normal channels turns into others, for it must find some outlet of escape. It may then work different and worse effects later on. Thus vengeful brooding may replace a burst of indignation; a dry heat may consume the frame of one who fain would weep, or he may, as Dante says, turn to stone within; and then tears or a storming fit may bring a grateful relief. This is when the current is strong enough to strike into a pathological path when the normal one is dammed.[22]

We will see later that the similarity is perfectly understandable and, in fact, only to be expected. For James and Freud began with almost identical sets of assumptions concerning the basic nature of the nervous system. So, for that matter, did almost every other psychologist and physiologist of the time.

But for all its psychodynamics and its appreciation of complexity and "unimaginable fineness," James' psychology up to this point is still a thorough-going, unmitigated mechanism. Even his writing of it he saw as the work of an automaton. I am writing, he wrote, "simply because I have once begun, and being in a state of intellectual excitement which keeps venting itself in that way, find that I *am* writing still." He went on to mention some other human activities, and then concluded: "We do all these things because at the moment we cannot help it; our nervous systems are so shaped that they overflow in just that way."[23] What an awkward position to be in for a man who set out to write a nonmechanistic—indeed, an antimechanistic—psychology! We now turn to see how James tried to get himself off the mechanistic hook.


## CONSCIOUSNESS, ATTENTION, AND WILL

We must begin by saying that, although the foregoing account of James' psychology is accurate so far as it goes, it is a bit lopsided. For the fact is that James began qualifying his acceptance of mechanism at the very start. The distinction here is between a piecemeal mechanism and a thoroughgoing mechanism. James could readily accept that *some* of the facts were capable of being subsumed under the categories of what he called "the automaton theory." What he could not accept—not without question, anyway—was the wholesale assertion that *all* of the facts could be fit into these categories. It all came down to the question of *consciousness*. Does it do anything, or does it not? Does it have a worthwhile role to play in the life of the individual, or is it merely an irrelevant epiphenomenon of neural activity? The answer of automaton theory was unequivocal: "Consciousness doesn't count . . . ; it doesn't exist for science; it is nil; you mustn't think about it at all." It held well enough when the only facts at issue were "reflex actions and other material phenomena where no consciousness appears to exist at all." Let it try to cast its net more widely, however, and it becomes a mere dogma, "a sort of philosophic faith, bred like most faiths from an esthetic demand." This is especially apparent when the theory is extended "to cases where consciousness seems the phenomenon's essential feature."[24] Are we really to believe, for example, that "if we knew thoroughly the nervous system of Shakespeare, and as thoroughly his environing conditions, . . . we should understand the rationale of every erasure and alteration [in his manuscripts] . . . without in the slightest degree acknowledging the existence of thoughts in Shakespeare's mind"? Is it really possible that "we might exhaustively write the biography of those two hundred pounds, more or less, of warmish albuminoid matter called Martin Luther, without ever implying that it felt"?[25]

The questions are of course purely hypothetical. The neuroscience of James' day—ours too, for that matter—could not know thoroughly the nervous system of Shakespeare or anyone else. And even if the nervous system were thoroughly known, its innermost workings might turn out to be something quite different from what anyone ever suspected. At any rate, James' answer was also unequivocal: "It is to my mind quite inconceivable that consciousness should have *nothing to do* with a business which it so faithfully attends."[26] He would not have denied that this too was a philosophic faith bred from an esthetic demand; but that is not to say that it had no rational basis. The chief argument was along the lines of what we described in the preceding chapter as functionalism. In its barest form, it was simply this: If consciousness did not *do* something—something that could not be done by the nervous system alone—then why should it exist at all! The question is, what does it do?

Not surprisingly, James found the answer among the properties of the nervous system. We have already seen him speak of the "unimaginable fineness" with which currents among the cells and fibres of the higher brain centers interact with one another, "damming or helping them, altering their direction or speed." The machinery is extremely delicate and, for that reason, highly unstable. Now in general, the more delicate and unstable something is, the more its performances are likely to approach randomness. And so it is with the "hair-trigger organization" of the complex nervous system:

A low brain does few things, and in doing them perfectly forfeits all other uses. The performances of a high brain are like dice thrown forever on a table. Unless they be loaded, what chance is there that the highest number will turn up oftener than the lowest?[27]

But of course the highest number *does* turn up more often than the lowest, and the useful act *is* the one most likely to be performed. Might this not be because consciousness increases the efficiency of the machine and the reliability of its performances by "loading the dice" in favor of useful outcomes? James' answer was yes. At any given moment, the balance of processes within the higher brain centers can be tipped "at a very slight hint" in any one of several possible directions. It is the role of consciousness to provide this hint by selecting from all the possibilities the one most closely connected with its interests, and then "emphasizing and accentuating [it] and suppressing as far as possible all the rest"?[28]

The next question is, how might this be done? This is not the large question of how is it possible for consciousness to produce effects upon the body at all. James acknowledged that to be an utter mystery, and he was not perturbed by the objection that "we can form no positive image of the *modus operandi* of a volition or other thought affecting the cerebral molecules."[29] One could equally ask how it is possible for the nervous system to produce effects in consciousness. We haven't the slightest idea of how it is possible; but obviously it is possible, because it happens. No, the question is the smaller one of how the supposed dice-loading efficacy of consciousness fits in with what we already know about psychophysiology.

In earlier sections of this chapter we represented James as believing that consciousness is the merely passive reflection of underlying neural "discharges." And in fact he did believe this, but only up to a point. There was one place in particular, a small but extremely important place, where consciousness seemed to him to be something more than a mere passive reflection. This was the process of attention. Now certainly there are many instances in which attention is merely passive: we attend quite automatically, for example, to a loud, abrupt noise. But there are also many instances in which it presents itself as voluntary and active, "taking possession . . . , in clear and vivid form, of one out of what seem several simultaneously possible objects or trains of thought." And here is the place where "an antimechanical psychology must, if anywhere, make its stand." Everything else, James conceded, "is pretty certainly due to cerebral laws," for consciousness "can certainly not create ideas or summon them *ex abrupto.*"[30] It can, however, selectively attend to what is already there, focusing on some ideas while neglecting others; and thus, by way of ideo-motor connections, it can tip the scale in favor of some particular behavioral outcome.

This is what is chiefly involved in the process that we call Will. It is nothing more than active, selective attention.[31] Nothing more, but also nothing less; and that is quite a lot! For there was nothing in the mechanics of the nervous system, nor in their offspring automaton theory, that could possibly account for such an active, selective process. This was James' "something more" that seemed to offer at least the possibility that consciousness is not, after all, only an impotent, paralytic spectator of the game, but an active participant.

The remaining question is whether selective attention is "free" and "spontaneous," in the traditional sense of free will, or only another automatism of a different order. The only compelling answer here is that there is no answer; for the question is "insoluble on strictly psychologic grounds" and probably on any other grounds as well. The most that a believer in determinism can do is to show that his views are plausible. The most that a proponent of free will can do is to show that the deterministic arguments are not compelling. Although James admitted that he sometimes found these deterministic arguments "seductive," he nonetheless cast his lot on the side of free will. Indeed, the lot had been cast a number of years earlier. During his middle and late twenties, James had gone through a personal crisis that was intimately bound up with the existential implications of the free-will versus determinism issue. Its resolution came in 1870 when he found in the writings of the French philosopher Charles Renouvier a conception of free will that succeeded in allaying the doubts with which he had been struggling. Renouvier's argument was no more logically compelling than those of the determinists, but it did at least convince James that free will was *possible,* even within the context of a mechanistic material universe and a mechanistic nervous system. We need not go into the details of Renouvier's conception, except to say that it was much the same as James espoused in his *Principles* when he wrote: "The essential achievement of the will, . . . when it is most "voluntary,' is to *attend* to a difficult object and hold it fast before the mind." [32]

James' reasoning beyond this point was a kind of Pascal's wager. Free will is possible; but so too, of course, is determinism. All one can do is cast his lot and take his chances. The question is, what are the best chances to take? The thoroughgoing determinist, if he is true to his belief, is obliged to see himself as a helpless pawn and his every action as determined by inexorable material causation. Perhaps he will admit that in the day-to-day living of life it sometimes *feels* as though one's choices are free; but as he believes this to be an illusion, he will not be likely to make much of it. Now what does he gain and what does he lose, according to whether his belief is right or wrong? If he is right he gains nothing, at least, nothing worth gaining; while if he is wrong he loses everything! The free-willist, on the other hand, will see himself as an active participant in life, capable of making free choices, and he will act accordingly. If he is wrong he loses nothing, and if he is right he gains everything! Granted that this reasoning is not logically compelling, nor did James claim it to be so. He did, however, find it existentially compelling. "My first act of free will," he had written in his diary after reading Renouvier, "shall be to believe in free will." [33] In the *Principles* he was understandably more restrained; he put himself on record "for the alternative of freedom," but declined to go into his reasons on the grounds that they were "ethical rather than psychological." He did, however, go so far as to say that if free will *were* true, then "freedom's first act should be to affirm itself."[34]

## OUR ACCOUNTS WITH REALITY

In considering James' encounter with mechanism, we must be careful not to dwell so closely on details as to lose sight of the larger issue. On the one hand there were the claims of science—or at least of what called itself "science"—that we are automata. On the other hand were the claims of consciousness that we are more than that; for consciousness does *feel* as though it is doing something; and voluntary effort does *feel* as though it is no illusion. James of course knew perfectly well that feelings of this sort do not prove anything; but they are facts nonetheless, and on that account they must be taken very seriously. Here indeed was a guiding principle of almost everything James ever wrote. By all means let us spin our grand, all-encompassing theories-of-everything; but as we do it, let us remember that our first allegiance should not go to theories or interpretations, but to the raw facts of immediate experience. And of all such facts, the rawest and most immediate are the facts of consciousness. It simply will not do to assume at the outset that these facts are of no account; that is just begging the question. Nor should we be impressed if this assumption is claimed to be required in order for psychology to be properly "scientific"; for humbug in the name of science is humbug all the same. The facts of consciousness are just as real and worthy of scientific consideration as the "twitching of frog's legs." And if these facts seem to conflict with some grand theory-of-everything, the proper course is not to bend them until they fit, or alternatively just to ignore them, but to question the theory.

Here is where James was at his best—as a questioner of theories, doctrines, and dogmas, and as a gadfly insisting that we must keep our accounts with reality open until every last fact has had its say. "It is astonishing," he wrote, "what havoc is wrought in psychology by admitting at the outset apparently innocent suppositions that nevertheless contain a flaw. The bad consequences develop themselves later on, and we are irremediable, being woven through the whole texture of the work."[35] The chief part of the havoc is that once the assumptions become established, "as they have a way of doing in our very descriptions of the phenomenal facts," [36] the facts themselves are then systematically cut and shaped to fit them; and the contrived fit is then taken as verification.

James saw clearly that this is exactly what had happened in the "New Psychology" of Wundt and the Wundtians, the chief psychological orthodoxy of the late nineteenth century. It had accepted at the outset, without question, the assumption of the tradition of mental mechanisms that conscious experience is composed of simple elements. And then, determined to find these elements and disentangle them from one another, it developed an elaborate "experimental" methodology through which the trained observer could take the raw, jumbled, fused diversity of experience and break it down into its pristine atomic constituents. "This method taxes patience to the utmost," James wrote, "and could hardly have arisen in a country whose natives could be *bored*."[37] Worse still, it bends its facts to suit its theories, and so ends up with nothing but contrivance and artificiality. For the only empirical reality of experience is precisely the raw, jumbled, fused diversity that the Wundtian method tries to disregard. Consciousness is a "teeming multiplicity," fluid and ever-changing like the waters of a stream; and nowhere within it do we find even the hint of some simple "element" that might be dissected out from the rest of the flow. We might just as well pull buckets of water from a river and say "here are its elements." The divisions are purely arbitrary, and they are no longer part of the river in any case. This was James' great compelling image of the "stream of consciousness," the most often quoted of his many quotable phrases. Consciousness does not come to us "chopped up in bits." It is not a "chain" or a "train." "It is nothing jointed; it flows. A 'river' or a 'stream' are the metaphors by which it is most naturally described."[38]

The two volumes and 1,377 pages of James' *Principles of Psychology* were published in 1890—and they are still in print! His other major psychological work, *The Varieties of Religious Experience* (1902), is also still in print. Both works deal at length with aspects of the stream of consciousness, and certainly one of the main parts of their continued appeal is that James was such an extraordinarily keen (and artful) observer of the stream's flow, in both himself and others. This is especially true of his *Varieties,* which is as sensitive and perceptive a treatment of first-person experience as one is ever likely to find. It is also in the *Varieties* that we find indications of an exceedingly important change in James' basic understanding of the stream of consciousness. When James spoke about the stream of consciousness in the *Principles,* it was a stream of very little depth. And here was one respect in which he himself, at least for a while, had not left his own accounts with reality open. As with all fine ideals, it is one thing to urge it upon others, and quite another to perform it oneself. Early in the *Principles* he had taken up the question: Can states of mind be unconsciousness? His answer there was an unequivocal and rather contemptuous "No!" The idea has no merit whatever; it is mere humbug, "the sovereign means for believing what one likes in psychology, and of turning what might become a science into a tumbling ground for whimsies."[39]

One reason for this adamant rejection was that the idea of unconscious mental states, in particular the Helmholtzian notion of "unconscious inference," had been recruited to the service of the mental elements theory. How can discrete, punctiform sensory elements become organized into structured, unified perceptions? Obviously it must be through a nonperceptual process of inference; and the fact that we are not conscious of such a process does not mean that it does not exist, but only that it is *un*conscious. We may recall that the notion of unconscious mental states had also been invoked by Fechner, whose "patient whimsies" included the suggestion that subthreshold stimuli must produce subthreshold (i.e., unconscious) sensations. Then, too, there were the seeming extravagances of certain philosophers, such as Leibniz, Schopenhauer, and especially Eduard von Hartmann, author of a widely read book of the day, *The Philosophy of the Unconscious* (1869). James wrote of the latter that he "fairly boxes in the compass of the universe with the principle of unconscious thought. For him there is no namable thing that does not exemplify it." These associations with the notion of unconscious mental states apparently inspired in James an attitude something like that of the man whose horse got its foot caught in the stirrups: "If you are getting on, then I am staying off."[40]

But there was another reason, too, and it was an outright intellectual prejudice. The whole notion of unconscious mental states is "simply unintelligible and fantastical." For there is only one condition in which a mental state can be, "and that is a fully conscious condition. If it is not in that condition, then it is not at all." In brief, James had accepted without question the ancient assumption that "mind" and "consciousness" are coextensive; and so he took it for granted that a mental state, being "mental," simply *could not* be unconscious. He did allow that some mental states might give the appearance of being unconscious because they are conscious only momentarily, then quickly forgotten. But it is only an appearance: for so long as these actually exist as mental states they are conscious; and as soon as they cease being conscious, they also cease to exist as mental states. A similar point can be made for those cases where "ideas in an unconscious state" seem to be "exerting a steady pressure and influence" upon the ongoing processes of consciousness and behavior. What is involved here is not really an unconscious mental state at all. It is only a brain process that has been strongly enough aroused to exert its pressure on consciousness and behavior, but not so strongly as to produce its own characteristic conscious idea. In both of these cases it is possible to speak of unconscious mental states only if we "throw away the logical principle of identity in psychology, and say that . . . the mind is a place in which a thing can be all kinds of other things without ceasing to be itself as well." The same point applies to the allegation that our motivations can exist as unconscious mental states. Certainly it is true that we sometimes find among our motives "jealousies and cupidities which we little suspected to be there." But when we find them they are conscious, and when we do not find them they are not mental states.[41]

And yet, throughout it all, there were certain irreducible and stubborn facts that simply would not fit. Some of them were perfectly ordinary, such as the observation that

> Every hour we make theoretic judgements and emotional reactions, and exhibit practical tendencies, for which we can give no explicit logical justification. . . . We know more than we can say. Our conclusions run ahead of our power to analyze their grounds. . . . Most of our knowledge is at all times potential. We act in accordance with the whole drift of what we have learned, but few items rise into consciousness at the time.[42]

Others were less ordinary, but irreducible and stubborn all the same. There were two kinds of facts in particular that especially impressed James in this regard. One included the remarkable alterations of consciousness found among the phenomena of hypnosis (especially posthypnotic suggestion), psychopathology (especially hysteria), trance (especially mediumistic trance), mystical and religious ecstasy, as well as altered states of consciousness induced by chemical and other means. The second included the phenomena of fairly radical personality transformations, such as are reported in cases of both religious and nonreligious "conversion" experiences. There were many other such facts as well, both common and extraordinary, all seeming to point in the same direction: that there is more to "the mind" than is ever evident on the surface and in the clearly defined center of conscious at any given moment.

Although we do not have an exact record of how the transformation occurred, it is clear that by the time James wrote his *Varieties of Religious Experience,* only twelve years after the publication of the *Principles,* his views on the subject of unconscious mental states had changed entirely. Consider the contrast between the following passage from the *Varieties* and his earlier statements in the *Principles:*

> As our mental fields succeed one another, each has its centre of interest, around which the objects of which we are less and less attentively conscious fade to a margin so faint that its limits are unassignable. . . . The important fact which this "field" formula commemorates is the indetermination of the margin. Inattentively realized as is the matter which the margin contains, it is nevertheless there, and helps both to guide our behavior and to determine the next movement of our attention. It lies around us like a "magnetic field," inside of which our centre of energy turns like a compass-needle, as the present phase of consciousness alters into its successor. Our whole past store of memories floats beyond this margin, ready at a touch to come in; and the

entire mass of residual powers, impulses, and knowledges that constitute our empirical self stretches continuously beyond it. So vaguely drawn are the outlines between what is actual and what is only potential at any moment of our conscious life, that it is always hard to say of certain mental elements whether we are conscious of them or not.[43]

James continued to dislike the term "unconscious," perhaps because of the objectionable associations mentioned earlier. In its place he used such terms as "subconscious," "subliminal," and "extra-marginal." Whatever the terms, the meaning was quite the same: "there is not only the consciousness of the ordinary field, with its usual centre and margin; but an addition thereto in the shape of a set of memories, thoughts, and feelings which are extra-marginal and outside of the primary consciousness altogether, but yet must be classed as conscious [mental?] facts of some sort, able to reveal their presence by unmistakable signs."

We saw earlier a certain parallel between James and Freud; and here, of course, is another. The differences, however, were far greater than the similarities. As we will see in more detail later on, Freud saw both conscious and unconscious as the products of a reflexive, automatistic "psychical apparatus" of precisely the sort that James rejected in the *Principles*. Moreover, the mind and personality that they constituted had definite limits, already fairly well known (Freud supposed), beyond which there was simply nothing. For James, on the other hand, the boundaries were not yet in sight, and our accounts, accordingly, could not yet be closed. Of course James had his own suspicions of what the remoter regions of psychological reality might turn out to be; but that is not the point. What matters is his insistence, for himself as well as others, that the accounts be kept open. In this respect he is not just an interesting though "dated" figure in the *history* of psychology, but a man for all seasons.

### THE REMOTER SCHEMES AND HOPES

Let us linger for just a few final words on James' existential encounter. Although the details of the matter have changed considerably since his day, the general issue is the same now as then. Psychological theories have implications for how we shall understand *ourselves;* they make claims about what we basically are, and about what is possible and what is not. In that degree they set the context for what we shall understand to be the significance of our own lives and of human life in general. In the practical life of the individual, James observed in the *Varieties,*

we know how his whole gloom and glee about any present fact depends on
the remoter schemes and hopes with which it stands related. Let it be known
to lead nowhere, and however agreeable it may be in its immediacy, its glow
and gilding vanish. . . . Place round [our experiences] the curdling cold and
gloom and absence of all permanent meaning . . . , and the thrill [of life]
stops short or turns rather to an anxious trembling.[44]

There are some, of course, in every generation who appear to be not much
concerned with such remoter schemes and hopes. James, for better or worse,
was not one of them.

## NOTES

1.  R. B. Perry, *The Thought and Character of William James*, 2 vol. (Boston: Little, Brown, and
    Co., 1936), vol. II, p. 40.
2.  Ibid., vol. I, p. 48.
3.  Ibid., vol. II, p. 31.
4.  W. James, *Principles of Psychology*, 2 vol. (New York: Henry Holt and Co., 1890), vol. II,
    p. 312.
5.  Ibid., vol. I, p. 5.
6.  Ibid., vol. I, p. 1.
7.  Ibid., vol. I, p. 4.
8.  Ibid., vol. I, p. 23.
9.  Ibid., vol. I, p. 26.
10. Ibid., vol. I, p. 562.
11. Ibid., vol. I, p. 26.
12. Ibid., vol. I, p. 108.
13. Ibid., vol. I, p. 112.
14. Ibid., vol. I, p. 115.
15. Ibid., vol. I, p. 122.
16. Ibid., vol. II, p. 450.
17. Ibid., vol. II, p. 450.
18. Ibid., vol. II, p. 453.
19. Ibid., vol. II, pp. 473–474.
20. Ibid., vol. II, p. 527.
21. Ibid., vol. II, p. 527–528.
22. Ibid., vol. II, p. 466.
23. Ibid., vol. II, p. 553.
24. Ibid., vol. I, pp. 134, 454.
25. Ibid., vol. I, pp. 132–133.
26. Ibid., vol. I, p. 136.
27. Ibid., vol. I, p. 140.
28. Ibid., vol. I, pp. 139–140.
29. Ibid., vol. I, p. 135.
30. Ibid., vol. I, pp. 403–404.

31.  Ibid., vol. II, pp. 559–569.
32.  Ibid., vol. II, p. 561.
33.  Perry, *Thought and Character*, vol. I, p. 323.
34.  James, *Principles*, vol. II, p. 573.
35.  Ibid., vol. I, p. 224.
36.  Ibid., vol. I, p. 145.
37.  Ibid., vol. I, p. 192.
38.  Ibid., vol. I, p. 239.
39.  Ibid., vol. I, p. 163.
40   Ibid., vol. I, pp. 168–170.
41.  Ibid., vol. I, pp. 170–176.
42.  Ibid., vol. I, p. 167.
43.  W. James, *The Varieties of Religious Experience* (New York: Longmans, Green, and Co., 1902), pp. 231–232.
44.  Ibid., p. 141.

## FOR FURTHER READING

The most richly detailed published source of biographical information about James was compiled by his student, friend, and colleague, Ralph Barton Perry: *The Thought and Character of William James*, 2 vols. (Boston: Little, Brown, and Co., 1936). Less detailed, but more probing and integrative, is the very fine biography by Gay Wilson Allen, *William James* (New York: Viking Press, 1967).

Of course, James was well known not only as a psychologist but also a philosopher. And just as his psychological writings were often infused with philosophizings, so too were his philosophical writings often psychological. Some of the more psychologically interesting of these are the following: *Essays in Radical Empiricism* (New York: Longmans, Green, and Co., 1912); *A Pluralistic Universe* (New York: Longmans, Green, and Co., 1909); *Pragmatism* (New York: Longmans, Green, and Co., 1907); and *The Will to Believe, and Other Essays in Popular Philosophy* (New York: Longmans, Green, and Co., 1931).

Another aspect of James' interests that must be mentioned is his long-standing preoccupation with psychical research, which he pursued much to the ridicule of some of his contemporaries. Here, incidentally, is yet another indication of his tendency to leave his accounts with reality open until every last fact—even the most despised or bizarre—has been considered. Although he saw clearly enough that this field of investigation was open to the encroachment of humbug, he could not close the door on the possibility that there might still be something there worth examining. A good sourcebook for studying this side of James is the volume compiled and edited by Gardner Murphy and Robert Ballou *William James on Psychical Research* (New York: Viking Press, 1960).

# Part III

# The Threshold of the Present

The chapters of Part III attempt to bring our account of psychological theory as far up to date as space and historical distance will allow. Their focus is on the twentieth century; and since the influence of this more recent past upon the present is far more immediate and pervasive, we will naturally be entering into it in greater depth and detail. Indeed, the "past" with which we are now dealing often shades so imperceptibly into the present that it is impossible to tell where the one ends and the other begins.

The first two chapters of Part III focus on Freud's development of the psychoanalytic theory: Chapter 9 points out some often unrecognized roots of the theory, and Chapter 10 then goes on to examine its more familiar trunk and branches. Chapter 11 describes the origins and development of Gestalt theory, both as a specific theory of perception and as a framework for a theory of psychological functioning in general. Then come two chapters on the behavioristic movement. The first of these, Chapter 12, reviews some of the pre-twentieth-century parentage of behavioristic theory, describes the early development of the movement at the hands of John B. Watson, and overall sets the stage for the more recent development of behaviorism as delineated in Chapter 13. Most of Chapter 13 is devoted to the elaborate and quite sophisticated behavioristic theorizings of Clark Hull, though at the end it will also offer a few observations on the purportedly "nontheoretical" behaviorism of the movement's current luminary, B. F. Skinner.

The book concludes with Chapter 14, in which we will raise some questions that apply not just to this or that particular theory, but to psychological theorizing in general.

# Chapter 9
# Psychoanalysis I: Sources

A man like me cannot live without a hobby-horse, a consuming passion—in Schiller's words a tyrant. I have found my tyrant, and in his service I know no limits. My tyrant is psychology; it has always been my distant, beckoning goal and now, since I have hit on the neuroses, it has come so much the nearer.

Sigmund Freud, letter to Wilhelm Fliess (1895)

I hope that Freud and his pupils will push their ideas to their utmost limits, so that we may learn what they are. They can't fail to throw light on human nature, but I confess that he made on me personally the impression of a man obsessed by fixed ideas. I can make nothing in my own case with his dream theories, and obviously "symbolism" is a most dangerous method.

William James, letter to Théodore Flournoy (1909)

When Sigmund Freud was born in 1856, John Stuart Mill was still very much alive, as were Helmholtz, Fechner, and any number of others whom we have mentioned in earlier sections of this book. Darwin's *Origin of Species,* Fechner's *Elemente der Psychophysik,* and the American Civil War were all still several years in the future. When Freud's *Interpretation of Dreams* was published in 1900, John B. Watson, the "father of behaviorism," was not yet out of graduate school. In Germany, Max Wertheimer was just beginning his studies in law at the age of twenty, while his later associates, Köhler and Koffka, were still in their early teens. Freud was forty-four at the time, his youth and formal education far behind him. If we seek a transition, then, between the remoter past and the present, it is with psychoanalysis that we shall do well to begin.


## FREUD'S "TYRANT"

In 1873 Freud entered the University of Vienna as a medical student; yet, he recorded some fifty years later, "neither at that time, nor indeed in my later life, did I feel any particular predilection for the career of a [physician]." [1] Elsewhere he observed:

> After forty-one years of medical activity, my self-knowledge tells me that I have never really been a [physician] in the proper sense. I became a [physician] through being compelled to deviate from my original purpose; and the triumph of my life lies in my having, after a long and roundabout journey, found my way back to my earliest path. [2]

We may begin our consideration of the psychoanalytic theory by asking just what *was* Freud's "original purpose" and "earliest path"?

Freud entered the University of Vienna, as we have said, in 1873, at the age of seventeen. During his first three years there, he was driven, he later recorded, by a restless "youthful eagerness" to master all subjects at once. In the autumn of 1876, however, this restlessness came to an end, for he had been accepted by the University's famed and somewhat glamorous Physiological Institute in the post of *Famulus,* a sort of junior research assistant. There he remained until 1882, spending what he later described (in the ripeness of age) as "the happiest years of my youth."

The importance of these years in Freud's life may be seen under several aspects. First is the fact that, during his earlier years at the University, his interests and enthusiasms had been far-reaching but diffuse. In the Physiological Institute he found a focus for these interests and enthusiasms. Under this same heading, we might also mention the fact that when Freud first entered the University he "experienced some appreciable disappointments. Above all, I found that I was expected to feel myself inferior and an alien because I was a Jew." [3] In the Physiological Institute, on the other hand, overt anti-Semitism of this sort seems to have been at a minimum. All in all, then, Freud's years at the Physiological Institute appear to have provided him not only with a focus for his interests but also with "a nook and cranny in the framework of humanity" as well.

It was here also that Freud had his most sustained and impressive encounter with "hard" laboratory science. The Physiological Institute was presided over by "the great [Ernst] Brücke himself"—a man of imposing scientific competence and reputation. The great Brücke was apparently a man of imposing personal stature as well, for Freud, even in later life, declared him to be "the greatest authority I ever met." It may even be suggested that Brücke served as Freud's scientific "father image" (he was indeed about the same age as Freud's father), and thus as the author of his scientific "superego." Be this as it may, it is quite clear that Freud imbibed deeply of the scientific *esprit* of the Physiological Institute.

Up to this point we have done nothing more than elaborate upon Freud's statement in his *Autobiographical Study* of 1925: "At length, in Ernst Brücke's physiological laboratory, I found rest and full satisfaction—and men, too, whom I could respect and take as my models."[4] We may now go beyond this statement and point out that the activities of the Physiological Institute were decked from top to bottom with theoretical, even ideological, trappings. As we have seen in earlier chapters, there had been in progress since the seventeenth century a movement within physiology toward what we may describe as "physicalism"—that is, the conviction that the phenomena of life could be subsumed under the then recognized principles of physics. These principles were none other than those contained in Newton's *Principia*—mass, motion, attraction and repulsion, and the like—along with such later elaborations as Helmholtz' "conservation of energy." In the nineteenth century, this movement reached its crest with what we have spoken of as German physiological mechanism.

At this point, the name of Ernst Brücke will perhaps strike a familiar chord, for it was he who in 1842 pledged with Emil Du Bois-Reymond "a solemn oath to put into effect this truth. . . ." In view of the importance of physicalism in Freud's later activities, the substance of "this truth" may be profitably repeated:

> No other forces than the common physical-chemical ones are active within the organism. In those cases which cannot at the time be explained by these forces one has either to find the specific way or form of their action by means of the physical-mathematical method or to assume new forces equal in dignity to the chemical-physical forces inherent in matter, reducible to the force of attraction and repulsion.[5]

As we shall see later, a good deal of light is thrown upon Freud's later development of psychoanalysis by the last part of this oath: ". . . or to assume new forces equal in dignity to the chemical-physical forces inherent in matter, reducible to the force of attraction and repulsion."

By way of summary, then, let us say that what Freud found in Brücke's Physiological Institute was not just "rest and full satisfaction," but a whole new way of looking at things—a way, moreover, which promised to bring biological phenomena at long last into the purview of genuine natural science. As Bernfeld has observed, in the 1870s "that part of German university teaching which was held to be the most interesting, the most far-reaching, and the most modern, was the physiology of the Helmholtz school. It fascinated the student of that time in somewhat the same way as atom smashing appeals to the students of today [1944]."[6] This way of looking at things, though dressed in the garb of physiology, was nothing more nor less than the philosophy of physicalism.

Freud's association with the Physiological Institute was reluctantly terminated in 1882. As there was no salary attached to the post of *Famulus,* he had been dependent upon his father's "generous improvidence" throughout. And his father's resources had begun to run dry. Mopreover, he was now contemplating marriage, and it seemed unlikely that any salaried position to which he might in the foreseeable future attain with the Physiological Institute would be sufficient to support a family. Thus, with his heart in the Institute and no particular taste for the practice of medicine, Freud embarked upon a medical career, for which he had belatedly qualified in 1881. The story of Freud's life from this point on is fairly widely known, at least in broad outline. After trying his hand in several clinical departments of medicine, he soon found his way back into the laboratory by way of cerebral anatomy. He found this work highly satisfying, but to his regret it did not go very far in solving the financial problem. And so, Freud recounted, "with an eye to pecuniary considerations, I began to study nervous diseases."[7] From "nervous diseases," he proceeded to a study of the neuroses; and from these, ostensibly, he launched his psychoanalytic theory around 1900.

Freud's own account of these intervening years gave rather short shrift to the possible influence of the Physiological Institute upon the psychoanalytic theory. It is only within relatively recent years, through the discovery and publication of Freud's letters to Wilhelm Fliess,[8] that materials have come to light from which we might gain a truer impression of this influence. Occupying the years between 1887 and 1902, from his thirty-first to his forty-sixth year, Freud's correspondence with Fliess affords, as Ernst Kris has remarked, an intimate personal glimpse of him "during the years in which he applied himself—tentatively at first—to a new field of study, psychopathology, and acquired the insight on which psychoanalysis, both as a theory and a therapy, is based."[9] Far more important than this personal glimpse, however, is the fact that Freud's letters to Fliess present a detailed chronology of his *transition* from physiologist to psychologist.

Wilhelm Fliess (1858–1928), the recipient of these letters, was a Berlin physician who was widely admired for "his wealth of biological knowledge, his imaginative grasp of medicine, his fondness for far-reaching speculation and his impressive personal appearance."[10] From the very beginning, the intellectual bond which held Freud and Fliess together was their common espousal of the physicalistic principles of the "Helmholtz school" and their common interest in seeing psychological phenomena—specifically, psychopathological phenomena—brought under the scope of these principles. In a letter cited at the beginning of this chapter, Freud characterized this common interest in the bluntest way possible. "I am plagued," he wrote (May 25, 1895), "with two ambitions: to see how the theory of mental functioning takes shape if quantitative considerations, a sort of economics of nerve-force, are introduced into it; and secondly, to extract from psychopathology what may be of benefit to normal psychology."[11]

## "PROJECT FOR A SCIENTIFIC PSYCHOLOGY"

The ostensible culmination of these ambitions came with Freud's drafting of what has since come to be known as the "Project for a Scientific Psychology."[12] Although the final form of the "Project" dates from September of 1895, it is clear that the essential structure of this work had been arranging itself in Freud's thoughts for some time prior to that date. In a letter to Fliess dated April 27, 1895, for example, he wrote of his being "so deep into the 'Psychology for Neurologists' that it quite consumes me, until I have to break off out of sheer exhaustion." It is also clear that this work was not for Freud a mere exercise, for he continued: "I have never been so intensely preoccupied by anything."[13]

The "Psychology" continued at its own pace until the occasion of Freud's visit with Fliess in September of 1895. Freud apparently found this visit so stimulating that he immediately set about the writing of the "Project," the first part of which he composed on the train in return from Berlin to Vienna. Shortly after his return, he informed Fliess that he had thus begun the "Project" and that he was counting upon the latter for "criticism" and for "adapting the theory to the general laws of motion."[14] This appeal to "the general laws of motion" served well to set the mood for what was to follow. For, whatever else the "Project" might have been, it impresses one immediately as being sharply out of keeping with the temper of Freud's more familiar writings. The difference, however, is one of mood and temper only, for it was in the "Project" as nowhere else that Freud gave rather explicit expression to those physicalistic conceptions which were to serve him largely unchanged throughout the remainder of his theoretical career.

Freud's expressed intention in writing the "Project" was to "furnish us with a psychology which shall be a natural science: its aim, that is, is to represent psychical processes as quantitatively determined states of specifiable material particles and so to make them plain and void of contradiction."

Toward this end, he began with three assumptions: (1) that what is basically involved in psychological processes is a "quantity [of energy] subject to the general laws of motion"; (2) that "the material particles in question are the neurons"[15]; and (3) that "each single neuron is . . . a model of the neuronic system as a whole."[16] The third assumption will readily be seen as an instance of what we described in Chapter 5 as the neurological fallacy of composition, that is, the fallacy of attributing to the nervous system as a whole the properties of its individual parts. At any rate, the chief implication that Freud drew from these assumptions was what he spoke of as the "principle of neuronic inertia." It held that the neuronic system as a whole, like each of its individual parts, is an essentially *reflexive* apparatus: that its basic principle of operation is to *receive* energy at one end, to *conduct* it to the other end, and there to *discharge* it. Freud claimed that this reflexive principle of neuronic inertia was suggested to him by "pathological clinical observations,"[17] and perhaps it was; but quite obviously its main source was the tradition of German physiological mechanism. We shall see in the next chapter that Freud made the same claim for his psychoanalytic theory, which also began with a reflexive principle, though shorn of this earlier neurological fleece.

Freud's reasoning on this point was based upon the notion that, "as the internal complexity of the organism increases, the neuronic system receives stimuli from the somatic element itself—endogenous stimuli, which call equally for discharge." He had in mind, here as later, internal needs, such as hunger, which give rise to internal stimulation ("tension") that can be relieved only through the realization of certain rather definite conditions in the external world. To allow its vessel, the organism, to survive under these conditions, "the neuronic system is consequently obliged to abandon its initial trend toward inertia. . . . It must learn to tolerate a store of [energy] sufficient to meet the demands for specific action." Thus, "all the performances of the neuronic system are to be comprised under the heading either of the primary function [of discharging energy] or of the secondary function [of storing energy] imposed by the exigencies of life."[18]

The supposed neurophysiological basis of this secondary process of storing energy was the relatively recent recognition that the functional units of the nervous system, the neurons, do not have direct anatomical connections with one another, but are rather separated by microscopic "contact barriers." Some of these might be "permeable" and thus readily permit the discharge of energy from one neuron to another; while others might be relatively impermeable and therefore *resist* the transmission. Freud supposed the "contact barriers" of the second class to be responsible for opposing the tendency toward immediate reflexive discharge and thus for storing up the quantities of energy needed for producing effective reality-oriented action.[19]

Only two further developments need concern us here. As in his later, psychoanalytic theory, Freud's "project" made much ado about the respective functions of pain and pleasure. Considering what we have already seen of his principle of neuronic inertia, it will come as no surprise that he regarded pain as the "irruption of large quantities [of excitation] . . . into [the system of relatively impermeable neurons]. . . ."[20] Conversely, he regarded pleasure as the relatively rapid diminution, or discharge, of such quantities. The significance of these two kinds of experiences is that they leave behind them *residues*: "A wishful state [i.e., the residue of the experience of pleasure] produces what amounts to a positive *attraction* to the object of the wish, or rather to its memory-image; an experience of pain results in a *repulsion*, a disinclination to keep the hostile memory-image cathected [i.e., invested with energy]. Here we have primary wishful attraction and primary defense."[21] Although Freud's theory of pleasure (as the absence of stimulation) and pain (as an excess of stimulation) might appear implausible from the perspective of the present, in the late nineteenth century it seemed to make perfectly good sense. Indeed, if the nervous system is purely and simply a receiver, conductor, and discharger of energy, there is really nothing else that pleasure and pain *can* be. We may also take note here of this first appearance in the "Project" of Freud's abiding preoccupation with the imagery of attraction and repulsion.

In the final development which we shall consider, the relevance of Freud's "Project" to his later, psychological writings becomes particularly evident. This had to do with his introduction of the term "ego." "Both of these processes [wishful attraction and defense]," Freud argued, "indicate that an organization has been formed in [the system of relatively impermeable neurons] . . . whose presence interferes with the passage [of energy]." This organization is called the "ego." The manner in which the ego achieves this interference is as follows:

> The [energy] which enters a neuron from anywhere will pursue its path through the contact-barrier which shows the greatest facilitation [i.e., the least resistance], and will give rise to a current flowing in that direction. . . . Thus the course taken depends on the [magnitude of the energies] and on the relative strength of the facilitations. . . . If [however] an adjoining neuron is simultaneously cathected [and assuming "that a quantity [of energy] . . . passes more easily . . . to a cathected neuron than to an uncathected one"], this acts like a temporary facilitation of the contact-barriers between the two neurons, and modifies the course of the current, which would otherwise have followed the direction of the only facilitated contact-barrier. A "lateral" cathexis thus acts as an *inhibition* of the passage of quantity.[22]

More precisely, Freud's "lateral cathexis" amounted to a *diversion* of the passage of quantity. It was the task of the ego to effect this diversion.

In any case, what Freud meant to suggest by all this was that the "ego"— a system of "relatively impermeable neurons"—could selectively divert and thus *direct* the course of conduction within the nervous system. And so it was that he developed in the "Project" the dynamics of what came later to be known as "repression." As he further noted,

> Inhibition of this kind is decidedly to [the psychical system's] . . . advantage. [For] we can now easily see how, with the help of a mechanism which draws the ego's attention to an imminent fresh cathexis of the hostile memory-image, the ego can succeed in inhibiting the passage of quantity from the memory-image to the release of unpleasure, by a copious lateral cathexis which can be increased as circumstances dictate.[23]

The ego's task, in short, is to forefend the "release of unpleasure" by diverting excitation away from the "hostile memory-image"; the hostile image is thereby, in effect, "repressed."

While these observations have not covered Freud's "Project" in every detail, there nonetheless emerges from them a fairly clear picture of the essay's essential structure. Its chief pillar was the "principle of neuronic inertia"—a borrowing from German physiological mechanism which held that individual neurons (and thus "the neuronic system as a whole") tend to divest themselves of quantity. This, Freud asserted, is the primary function, or process, of the nervous system. In the face of life's exigencies, however, this primary function comes to be supplemented by a secondary one, whose aim is to store up quantity toward the realization of rather definite conditions in the external world Otherwise stated, this secondary function arises in the service of reality, or self-preservation. That organization of relatively impermeable neurons which accomplishes this secondary, inhibitory function is known as the "ego." It is the task of the ego not only to preserve the organism by coping realistically with life's exigencies, but also to provide strategies for avoiding unpleasure in general. This it does by closing off the gates of action to hostile memory-images, that is, by inhibiting the passage of the memory-image into consciousness. This inhibition, in turn, is accomplished through a more or less complex system of "lateral cathexes," through which the hostile memory-image is "displaced" onto less threatening pathways and thus, in effect, "repressed."

On the face of things, then, it would seem that the "Project" came as close as one might wish to fulfilling the pledge made by Brücke, Freud's earlier mentor, and Du Bois-Reymond: ". . . reducible to the force of attraction and repulsion." This reduction was accomplished by the hypothesis of contact-barriers. If there existed at the contact-barrier between two neurons a state of facilitation, then energy was in effect attracted from one to the other; if, on the other hand, there existed a state of resistance, then energy from one was in effect repulsed by the other. The "repression" through "displacement" achieved by Freud's contact-barriers and lateral cathexes affords an exceptionally clear instance of the interaction of repulsion and attraction.

But however close the "Project" might have come to fulfilling Freud's physicalistic ambitions, it did not come close enough, for he soon abandoned its neurophysiological designs in favor of purely psychological explanation. Apparently, the major difficulty lay in his attempt to account neurophysiologically for the "mechanism which draws the ego's attention to an imminent fresh cathexis of the hostile memory-image." When, in the final extant part of the "Project," Freud attempted to give an accounting of this "mechanism of psychical attention," he wrote:

> I find it hard to give any mechanical (automatic) explanation of its origin. I believe, therefore, that it is biologically determined: that is, that it has been left over in the course of psychical evolution because any other behavior on the part of [the nervous system] has been excluded owing to its generating unpleasure.[24]

Inasmuch as this "mechanism" was nothing less than the crux of repression, or "the inhibition of the passage of quantity," it may readily be appreciated how Freud's inability to explain it neurophysiologically might have opened the doors to abandoning neurophysiological explanation altogether. In this connection, we may note that the "Project" consisted of three extant parts and a fourth part, on repression, which was evidently never completed. As Freud wrote to Fliess in a letter of October 8, 1895:

> I am not ready to send [it to] you yet, because it only takes the subject to a certain point. From that point I had to start from scratch again, and I have been alternately proud and happy and abashed and miserable, until now, after an excess of mental torment, I just apathetically tell myself that it does not hang together and perhaps never will.[25]

In any case, following his submission of it to Fliess in September of 1895, Freud's attitude toward the "Project" went from confidence to doubt to utter rejection. The high-water mark of his enthusiasm seems to have been reached about the middle of the following month when he wrote to Fliess:

> One strenuous night last week, when I was in that stage of painful discomfort in which my brain works best, the barriers suddenly lifted, the veils dropped, and it was possible to see from the details of neurosis all the way to the very conditions of consciousness. Everything fell into place, the cogs meshed, the thing really seemed to be a machine which in a moment would run of itself. . . . I can hardly contain myself with delight.[26]

This mood of elation over the ideas put forward in the "Project" did not last long, however, for at the end of October he wrote to Fliess:

> I cannot borrow yet on my own million. I think it hangs together as a whole, but I do not really trust the individual parts. I keep changing them,

and do not dare submit the whole structure to a wise man. What you have is also partially discredited—it was intended more as a trial run than anything else—but I hope something will come of it.[27]

Finally, at the end of November, Freud wrote to Fliess his last appraisal of the value of the "Project": "I no longer understand the state of mind in which I concocted the psychology; I cannot conceive how I came to inflict it on you. I think you are too polite; it seems to me to have been a kind of aberration."[28]

### THE PHYSICALISTIC BASES OF PSYCHOANALYTIC THEORY

In his first letter of the year 1896, Freud made one last, rather half-hearted attempt to revise the "Project." Following this, he spoke in detail of the "psychical apparatus" only in psychological terms. The "Project," and the attempt at neurophysiological explanation which it embodied, was something which Freud had, as it were, to get out of his system. Due in large measure, no doubt, to the results of his own abortive struggle, Freud's later view of such attempts was a dim one. In his later paper on "The Unconscious" (1915), for example, he wrote:

> Research has given irrefutable proof that mental activity is bound up with the function of the brain as it is with no other organ. . . . But every attempt to go on from there to discover a localization of mental processes, every endeavor to think of ideas as stored up in nerve-cells and of excitations as traveling along nerve-fibers, has miscarried completely. . . . Our psychical topography has for the present nothing to do with anatomy; it has reference not to anatomical localities, but to regions in the mental apparatus, wherever they may be situated in the body.[29]

Thus, after abandoning the "Project," Freud never again attempted such a synthesis between neurophysiology and psychology. We need not look far, though, to find that those physicalistic principles to which Freud gave expression in the "Project" were to recur time and again in his later, psychological writings. It is true that he abandoned speaking of neuronic systems in favor of psychical systems, but there remained throughout the dynamics of facilitation and resistance, displacement and repression, attraction and repulsion. We shall take this matter up again in this next chapter.

### THE NEUROSES

We may recall at this point that Freud's "tyrant" had two faces. The first, which we have just considered, was "to see how the theory of mental functioning takes shape if quantitative considerations, a sort of economics of nerve-force, are introduced into it." The second, which we must look into now, was "to extract from psychopathology what may be of benefit to normal psychology." As it turned out, these two faces of the tyrant were—in Freud's eyes, at least—entirely suited to each other.

Freud began his study of "nervous diseases" in the early 1880s, at a time when there was still an almost utter ignorance of this strange rag-bag of disorders. Indeed, "nervous diseases" were generally held to be just what their name declared them to be—diseases of the nervous system. (There were exceptions to this, of course, but they were few and far between.) To medical specialists of the time, one of the more common of these "diseases" was the disorder known as *hysteria,* a condition whose principal clinical symptoms were localized paralyses or anesthesias. The word "hysteria" derives from the Greek word meaning "womb." Certain physicians of classical antiquity were of the considered medical opinion that some women's wombs are capable of coming loose from their proper moorings and wandering freely about within the body, thus causing malfunctions at whatever points they might happen to lodge. The more enlightened physicians of the nineteenth century no longer subscribed to the wandering-womb theory, but it was still widely believed that hysteria was the result of organic pathology and that it was a disorder peculiar to females.

Through this dense fog of ignorance and misconception, Freud wrote in his *Autobiographical Study,* there glimmered in the distance "the great name of Charcot."[30] Jean-Martin Charcot was at that time professor of neuropathology at the University of Paris and director of the famed Salpêtrière clinic for chronic "nervous diseases." In 1885, Freud received a traveling fellowship which enabled him to go to Paris and study under Charcot for the period of a year. Later he wrote of this period:

> What impressed me most of all while I was with Charcot were his latest investigations upon hysteria, some of which were carried out under my own eyes. He had proved, for instance, the genuineness of hysterical phenomena [i.e., that they were not deliberate deceptions on the part of the patient] and their conformity to laws, the frequent occurrence of hysteria in men, [and] the production of hysterical paralyses and contractures by hypnotic suggestion.[31]

From the genuineness of the phenomena, Freud was led to suspect (though not yet very explicitly) that hysterical disorders were *not* deliberate, conscious productions. From the fact that men, too, were subject to the disorders, he was led to suspect that they were not due to some peculiarity of the female nervous system. And finally, from the fact that hysterical symptoms could be induced hypnotically, he was led to suspect that they might be the result of something other than organic pathology—specifically, that they might be psychological in origin. One of these suspicions was dramatically reinforced in 1889 when Freud, with the idea of perfecting his hypnotic technique, spent several weeks at the clinic of Liébeault and Bernheim at Nancy. For it was here, he later worte, that "I received the profoundest impression of the possibility that there could be powerful mental processes which nevertheless remained hidden from the consciousness of men."[32]

In 1895, the same year in which he drafted the "Project for a Scientific Psychology," Freud joined with Joseph Breuer (1842–1925) in the publication of *Studies on Hysteria*. Breuer, like Freud, was a Viennese physician who took an interest in "nervous diseases." Like Freud also, he held the view that hysterical disorders could be traced to psychological sources. The *Studies on Hysteria* was an attempt to portray several hysterical cases in just this light. The book is of interest to us at this point for two reasons: first, because it was physicalistic to the core, a kind of psychological companion piece to the "Project"; second, because it casts an interesting light upon Freud's views, published only later, of the importance of sexuality.

As with Freud, Breuer's theoretical sympathies lay squarely within the tradition of physicalism—specifically, of German physiological mechanism. Indeed, it was at Brücke's Physiological Institute that Breuer and Freud had first met. The physicalistic leanings of the two men were clearly visible in the conceptions which made their appearance in the *Studies*. In the course of working with hysterical patients, for example, both had observed that the disorder could usually be traced to some "traumatic," emotion-laden experience. The memory of this experience, they noted, was usually not consciously available to the patient. Under hypnosis, however, it *could* be recovered to consciousness, whereupon the patient, as it were, relived the initial, traumatic experience. After this reliving of the experience, the patient's hysterical symptoms tended to remit.

Now, of course, what was physicalistic about the *Studies* was not these observations themselves, but rather the interpretation that was put upon them. Any experience, Breuer and Freud agreed, corresponds to some sort of excitation within the nervous system; and the first task of the nervous system is to "discharge" any and all such excitation by way of an "energic reaction"—that is, through "voluntary or involuntary reflexes." If this reaction takes place in a sufficient amount, they continued, then "the affects [quantities of excitation] are discharged." If the reaction is "suppressed," however, "the affect remains attached to the memory."[33] And it is precisely this retained affect, this undischarged excitation, which gets "converted" into hysterical symptoms. In view of these considerations, they concluded, "it will now be understood how it is that the psychotherapeutic procedure which we have described . . . has a curative effect. It brings to an end the operative force of the idea [i.e., the excitation] which was not abreacted [i.e., discharged] in the first instance, by allowing its strangulated affect to find a way out through speech."[34]

This plainly physicalistic idea that symptom formation comes about through the "conversion of affect" was thoroughly worked over by Breuer in his lengthy theoretical chapter of the *Studies*. In his initial presentation of the idea, Breuer attributed its origins to Freud. Freud later averred, however, that "the conception came to us simultaneously and together." In any case, the "conversion of affect" was clearly based upon some "principle of neuronic inertia," whatever might have been its empirical moorings.

And now to the matter of sexuality. In his later *Autobiographical Study*, Freud observed that

> In the case histories which I contributed to the *Studies* sexual factors played a certain part, but scarcely more attention was paid to them than to other emotional excitations. Breuer wrote of the girl, who has since become famous as his first patient, that her sexual side was extraordinarily undeveloped. [But] it would have been difficult to guess from the *Studies on Hysteria* what an importance sexuality has in the etiology of the neuroses.[35]

This must seem a rather curious remark when we consider that Freud, by 1895, was already quite convinced that the etiology of the anxiety neuroses and neurasthenia, at least, was of an exclusively sexual nature. The earlier Fliess correspondence reveals this quite clearly. In February of 1893, for example, he drafted an argument to the effect that "neurasthenia is always only a sexual neurosis."[36] (He prefaced the argument by advising Fliess, "You will of course keep the draft away from your young wife.") In November of the same year, he was again able to write to Fliess: "The sexual business is becoming more and more firmly consolidated, and the contradictions are fading away."[37]

Now, the interesting point to be made here is this: the Fliess correspondence shows fairly clearly that Freud's initial suspicions regarding the sexual etiology of the neuroses were based largely on theoretical grounds. And these grounds were none other than the familiar philosophy of physicalism—though in the guise, of course, of German physiological mechanism. In an argument drafted for Fliess around June of 1894, he spelled it all out quite plainly. In sexual abstinence, he wrote,

> we may lay it down that we are dealing with a physical accumulation of excitation—an accumulation of physical sexual tension. The accumulation is due to discharge. . . . Anxiety neurosis is thus, like hysteria, a neurosis due to dammed-up excitation.[38]

Freud's notion here was that "physical sexual tension" is continuously released into the nervous system, where it remains and accumulates until such time as it is "discharged." The psychopathological difficulty arises from the fact that sexual tension, unlike most other forms of excitation, often encounters factors which militate against its discharge.

Like any other form of excitation, then, this accumulated "physical sexual tension" *tends* to be discharged through direct reflex action; this, however, is not always entirely possible. As Freud put it:

> Physical sexual tension, when it rises above a certain degree, arouses physical libido which then leads to copulation, etc. If the specific reaction [copulation] does not follow, the psychophysical tension (the sexual affect) increases to an immeasurable extent.[39]

And it is here, he concluded, that the accumulated tension may be "converted" into anxiety. Freud at this point was not yet convinced that hysteria was of an exclusively sexual origin. He did, however, see an important similarity between the two. Thus:

> There is a kind of "conversion" at work in anxiety neurosis just as there is in hysteria . . .; only in hysteria it is a *psychical* excitation [the initial traumatic experience] which takes a wrong path in an exclusively somatic direction, whereas in anxiety neurosis it is a *physical* tension [sexual], which is unable to find a psychical outlet and consequently continues along a physical path [anxiety].[40]

If, now, it were found that the traumatic experience giving rise to hysteria is always of sexual significance, anxiety neurosis and hysteria could then be portrayed as but two different forms of the *same* underlying process of "conversion."

Here, then, was Freud's theory circa 1894 of the sexual etiology of the neuroses. He admitted to Fliess that it was incomplete and that "the gaps sorely need filling in." Still, he was confident that "the foundation is right. It is still completely unsuitable for publication, of course. Suggestions, amplifications, indeed refutations and explanations, will be received with extreme gratitude."[41]

## NOTES

1.  S. Freud, *An Autobiographical Study,* in *The Standard Edition of the Complete Psychological Works of Sigmund Freud* (ed. and trans. J. Strachey), vol. XX (London: Hogarth, 1959), p. 8.
2.  S. Freud, *The Question of Lay Analysis,* in *Standard Edition,* vol. XX, p. 253.
3.  S. Freud, *Autobiographical Study,* p. 9.
4.  E. Du Bois-Reymond, *Zwei grosse Naturforscher des 19. Jahrhunderts: Ein Briefwechsel zwischen Emil Du Bois-Reymond und Karl Ludwig (Two Great Natural Scientists of the Nineteenth Century: The Correspondence of Emil Du Bois-Reymond and Karl Ludwig)* (Leipzig: Barth, 1927), p. 19.
5.  S. Bernfeld, "Freud's Earliest Theories and the School of Helmholtz," *Psychoanalytic Quarterly,* 13 (1944).
6.  S. Freud, *Autobiographical Study,* p. 11.

7. S. Freud, *The Origins of Psychoanalysis: Letters to Wilhelm Fliess, Drafts and Notes: 1887–1902,* eds. M. Bonaparte, A. Freud, and E. Kris, trans. E. Mosbacher and J. Strachey (London: Imago, 1954). First published as *Aus den Anfängen der Psychoanalyse* (London: Imago, 1905).

8. Ibid., p. 3.

9. Ibid., p. 4.

10. Ibid., pp. 119–120.

11. Ibid., pp. 355–445. "Entwurf einer Psychologie" was the German title accorded by the editors of the Fliess correspondence to this originally untitled draft.

12. Ibid., p. 118.

13. Ibid., pp. 123–124.

14. Ibid., p. 355.

15. Ibid., p. 359.

16. Ibid., p. 356.

17. Ibid., p. 358.

18. Ibid., pp. 359–360.

19. Ibid., p. 368.

20. Ibid., p. 383.

21. Ibid., pp. 384–385.

22. Ibid., p. 385.

23. Ibid., p. 417.

24. Ibid., pp. 125–126.

25. Ibid., p. 129.

26. Ibid., p. 131.

27. Ibid., p. 134.

28. S. Freud, "The Unconscious," in *Standard Edition,* vol. XIV (1957), pp. 174–175.

29. Freud, *Autobiographical Study,* p. 11.

30. Ibid., p. 13

31. Ibid., p. 17.

32. J. Breuer and S. Freud, *Studies on Hysteria,* in *Standard Edition,* vol. II (1955), p. 8.

33. Ibid., p. 17.

34. Freud, *Autobiographical Study,* p. 22.

35. Freud, *Origins of Psychoanalysis,* p. 66.

36. Ibid., p. 79.

37. Ibid., p. 90.

38. Ibid., p. 91.

39. Ibid., p. 94.

40. Ibid.

41. Ibid.

## FOR FURTHER READING

The account that this chapter has presented of the origins and early development of psychoanalytic theory is of course only one of many. Some of the first were offered by Freud himself: *On the History of the Psycho-Analytic Movement,* in *Standard Edition,* vol. XIV (1957); and *An Autobiographical Study,* in *Standard Edition,* vol. XX (1959). These and other Freudian pronouncements set the stage for most of the interpretations that have since been offered by Freud's pupils and followers. Two good sources for becoming acquainted with the pro-psychoanalytic understanding of origins and early development are: E. Jones, *The Life and Work of Sigmund Freud*, vol. I (New York: Basic Books, 1953); and J. E. Gedo and G. H. Pollock, eds., *Freud, the Fusion of Science and Humanism: The Intellectual History of Psychoanalysis* (New York: International University Press, 1976). The latter contains a number of articles by different authors, who approach the subject from a variety of directions. Two other treatments of the subject that might be consultd as counterpoise to the account of the present chapter are: Kenneth Levin, *Freud's Early Psychology of the Neuroses* (Pittsburgh: University of Pittsburgh Press, 1978); and F. J. Sulloway, *Freud, Biologist of the Mind: Beyond the Psychoanalytic Legend* (New York: Basic Books, 1979). And then, for sheer charm and imagination, one might wish to read D. Bakan, *Sigmund Freud and the Jewish Mystical Tradition* (Princeton, N.J.: Van Nostrand, 1958).

Other recommendations for further study on Freud and psychoanalysis will be given at the end of Chapter 10.

The English version of Freud's Fliess correspondence, which well repays all study invested in it, is S. Freud, *The Origins of Psychoanalysis: Letters to Wilhelm Fliess, Drafts and Notes: 1887–1902*, trans. E. Mosbacher and J. Strachey, eds. M. Bonaparte, A. Freud, and E. Kris (London: Imago, 1954). A slightly variant translation is to be found in volume I of J. Strachey, ed. and trans., *The Standard Edition of the Complete Psychological Works of Sigmund Freud* (London: Hogarth, 1966). The same volume contains a number of Freud's other early psychological writings as well. The interested student would also do well to look into the *Studies in Hysteria* (*Standard Edition*, vol. II, 1955).

Other recommendations for further study on Freud and psychoanalysis will be found at the end of Chapter 10.

# Chapter 10
## Psychoanalysis II: The General Theory

> Yet Brücke would have been astonished, to put it mildly, had he known that one of his favorite pupils, one apparently a convert to the strict faith, was later, in his famous wish theory of the mind, to bring back into science the ideas of "purpose," "intention," and "aim" which had just been abolished from the universe. We know, however, that when Freud did bring them back he was able to reconcile them with the principles in which he had been brought up; he never abandoned determinism for teleology.
>
> Ernest Jones, *The Life and Work of Sigmund Freud* (1953)

Freud's vision of the "psychical apparatus" made its first public appearance in *The Interpretation of Dreams* of 1900. The book itself was an attempt to frame a psychological explanation of the process of dreaming, and it was in the course of this attempt that Freud found himself "obliged to set up a number of fresh hypotheses which touch tentatively upon the structure of the apparatus of the mind and upon the play of forces operating in it."[1] As we shall see directly, these hypotheses were not nearly so "fresh" as Freud seems to have imagined. From the fact that he held to them, virtually unchanged, throughout the remainder of his theoretical career, we may judge that they were not particularly "tentative" either.

## THE PSYCHICAL APPARATUS

In introducing his theory of the psychical apparatus, Freud declared that he would "remain upon psychological ground" and "entirely disregard the fact that the mental apparatus with which we are here concerned is also known to us in the form" of a nervous system.[2] How well he succeeded in this resolve may be judged from what he put forward as the primary characteristic of the psychical apparatus. "The first thing that strikes us" about this apparatus, he wrote, is that it

> has a . . . direction. All our psychical activity starts from stimuli (whether internal or external) and ends in innervations. Accordingly, we shall ascribe a sensory and a motor end to the apparatus. At the sensory end there lies a system which receives perceptions; at the motor end there lies another, which opens the gateway to motor activity. Psychical processes advance in general from the perceptual end to the motor end.[3]

The reader will surely see in this characteristic a reflection of Freud's earlier "principle of neuronic inertia." Freud perhaps did, too, for he went on to observe that

> This, however, does no more than fulfill a requirement with which we have long been familiar, namely that the psychical apparatus must be constructed like a reflex apparatus. Reflex processes remain the model of every psychical function.[4]

It was in *The Interpretation of Dreams* that Freud drew the valuable distinction between the *manifest content* of a dream and its *latent content.* By way of analogy, we may here draw a like distinction between the manifest content of a *theory* and its latent content. In the present case, the manifest content is the "primary process" of the psychical apparatus—namely, to receive stimulation at one end and to discharge it, reflexively, at the other. The latent content, on the other hand, is the earlier "principle of neuronic inertia," which we may safely assume lay at the heart of Freud's "requirement with which we have long been familiar."

In any case, it is fair to say that Freud's "psychical apparatus" of 1900 and thereafter was structurally similar to his earlier "neuronic system" in almost every respect. In the "Project," for example, he had argued that "the exigencies of life" oblige "the neuronic system . . . to abandon its initial trend toward inertia. . . . It must learn to tolerate a store of quantity . . . sufficient to meet the demands for specific action." In *The Interpretation of Dreams* he put forward the same argument in almost the same words:

> Hypotheses, whose justification must be looked for in other directions[!], tell us that at first the apparatus's efforts [are] directed toward keeping itself so

far as possible free from stimuli; consequently its first structure [follows] the plan of a reflex apparatus, so that any sensory excitation impinging upon it [can] be promptly discharged along a motor path. But the exigencies of life interfere with this simple function, and it is to them, too, that the apparatus owes the impetus to further development. The exigencies of life confront it first in the form of the major somatic needs. The excitations produced by internal needs seek discharge in movement. . . . [Thus] a hungry baby screams or kicks helplessly. But the situation remains unaltered, for the excitation arising from an internal need is not due to a force producing a momentary impact but to one which is in continuous operation.[5]

In short, somatic needs—the "exigencies of life"—require *specific* action, and from this Freud went on once again to argue that the apparatus must learn to avoid an "unnecessary expenditure of energy . . . [which would] drain away to no useful purpose and diminish the quantity available for altering the external world."[6] Thus, "psychical energy" exists within the apparatus in two forms: "free" or "mobile" and "bound" or "quiescent."

In the "Project," this secondary function of storing energy required the formation of a system of impermeable neurons "whose presence interferes with the passage [of energies]." Similarly, in the psychical apparatus of 1900 and thereafter, it required a "second system [which] succeeds in retaining the major part of its cathexes of energy in a state of quiescence." Concerning the underlying "mechanics of these processes," Freud averred that they

are quite unknown to me; anyone who wished to take these ideas seriously would have to look for physical analogies to them and find a means of picturing the movements that accompany excitation of neurons. All I insist upon is the idea that the activity of the first $\psi$-system is directed toward securing the free discharge of the quantities of excitation, while the second system, by means of the cathexes emanating from it, succeeds in inhibiting this discharge and in transforming the cathexis into a quiescent one.[7]

Freud spoke of the functions of the first system as "primary processes," those of the second system as "secondary processes." Under the former were to be included all activities of the apparatus that amount to direct, reflexive discharges of "psychical energy." Secondary processes, on the other hand, were to include all activities, such as planning, reasoning, and the like, that are involved in coping with life's exigencies. Taken together, Freud argued, these two processes exhaust all psychological functioning.

## CONSTANCY AND THE PLEASURE PRINCIPLE

As we have just seen, the first and foremost tendency of the psychical apparatus—its "primary process"—is to discharge as promptly as possible any excitation that it might receive. In time, of course, this tendency becomes overlaid with a "secondary process," but still the overall aim of the apparatus is to keep the excitation within it at a minimum. Some twenty years after the publication of *The Interpretation of Dreams,* Freud spoke of this superordinate tendency as "the principle of constancy." Its importance lay in the fact that it led straightaway to the formulation of his well-known "pleasure principle."

In the "Project" of 1895, Freud held that pain consists in an excess of excitation, pleasure in an absence of excitation. This idea, of course, had been a fairly common one since the days of thoroughgoing environmentalism in the eighteenth century. In any case, the same notion appeared in the psychical apparatus of 1900 and thereafter, and it can readily be seen how, in conjunction with the "constancy principle," it leads directly to yet another version of psychological hedonism. If pain is simply excitation, and pleasure its absence, and if, further, the primary tendency of the psychical apparatus is to keep excitation at a minimum, it then inescapably follows that the chief "aim" of the apparatus will be to achieve pleasure and avoid pain. This, in the proverbial nutshell, is Freud's "pleasure principle."

In and of itself, the "pleasure principle" is a notion of almost pristine simplicity. Placed within its broader theoretical context, however, it quickly gives way to complication, of which there are two major varieties:

(1) *The requirements of specific action.* When confronted with the stimulation of an organic need. Freud held, the first tendency of the psychical apparatus is

> to recathect the mnemic image of the perception [of a previous satisfaction of that need] and to re-evoke the perception itself [as a hallucination]. . . .
> An impulse of this kind is what we call a wish; the reappearance of the perception is the fulfillment of the wish; and the shortest path to the fulfillment of the wish is a path leading direct from the excitation produced by the need to a complete cathexis of the perception.[8]

Freud took this "recathexis" of the memory image (of previous satisfactions) to be a primitive, reflexive activity of the psychical apparatus—an activity by which at least some of the excitation produced by the need is discharged. As he was quick to point out, however, the hallucination of a previous satisfying experience does not go far toward starving off starvation, slaking thirst, or finding a suitable sexual object. And so it is that the "bitter experience of life must have changed this primitive thought-activity into a more expedient secondary one."[9]

Now the key word in the above sentence is "expedient." For, as it happens, the excitation ("unpleasure") of an organic need can be terminated only through specific action. And this requires that excitation be bound, or retained, rather than immediately discharged. Thus, the initial simplicity of the pleasure principle is complicated in the first instance by the necessity of storing up excitation-unpleasure. In effect, the apparatus sacrifices a smaller pleasure for the achievement of a greater one; otherwise said, it tolerates a smaller pain in order to avoid a greater one.

(2) *Defense, repression, diversion.* Another complication of the pleasure principle is occasioned by the remarkable ability of the psychical apparatus to be placed in dilemmas. Imagine, for example, the case of an organic need whose satisfaction would result in punishment. If the need is *not* satisfied, then the excitation-unpleasure deriving from it will increase. And yet, if it *is* satisfied, there will also be an increase of excitation-unpleasure. It is at this point that the apparatus must take two kinds of defensive measures:

(a) The first thing it must do is to prevent the "hostile wish" from finding expression in action. This, however, can be accomplished only if the hostile wish is kept out of consciousness, for it is consciousness that stands at "the gateway to motor activity." Accordingly, the hostile wish must be *repressed.*

(b) Through repression, then, the hostile wish is denied access to consciousness, and thus its expression is action is prevented. This serves to avoid whatever punishment might follow in consequence of action, but at the same time, alas, it leaves the original organic need unsatisfied. And so long as this need remains, the excitation-unpleasure resulting from it will persist and even increase. Accordingly, if an intolerable increase of tension is to be prevented, some *indirect* outlet for the accumulating excitation must be found. This, of course, will not satisfy the need as such, but it will provide a kind of escape valve through which the excitation might, as it were, seep out. Freud spoke of this process under a variety of labels, the most often used being "displacement" and "substitution." For our own purposes, we may call it simply "diversion." In any event, it is the more general case of what we spoke of earlier as "conversion."

We have spoken of repression and diversion as though they were two independent processes. In fact, Freud argued, they are not; they are rather like the two sides of the same coin. In the earlier "neuronic system," the matter of repression was handled by the twin hypotheses of "contact-barriers" and "lateral cathexis." If there existed at the contact-barrier between two neurons a state of "facilitation," then excitation was in effect attracted from one to the other; if, on the other hand, there existed a state of "resistance," then the energy from one was in effect repulsed by the other. Thus, through an appropriate lateral cathexis, a "hostile memory-image" could be diverted onto less threatening neural pathways and, thereby, denied access to consciousness and action. The process, in any case, was a twofold one, requiring the simultaneous operation of facilitation and resistance, attraction and repulsion, diversion and repression.

Here again, now, we have a latent theoretical content which became manifest in Freud's later vision of the psychical apparatus. In his "metapsy-chological" paper "On Repression" (1915), for example, he observed that

> It is a mistake to emphasize only the repulsion which operates from the direction of the conscious upon what is to be repressed; quite as important is the attraction exercised by what was primally repressed upon everything with which it can establish a connection. Probably the trend toward repression would fail in its purpose if these two forces did not cooperate, if there were not something . . . ready to receive what is repelled by the conscious.[10]

Repression and diversion, repulsion and attraction, are accordingly but two different views of the same underlying "mechanism of defense." And thus, as Freud was able to conclude in the same paper, "the essence of repression lies simply in turning something away, and keeping it at a distance, from the conscious."[11]

## THE DREAM-WORK

We may at this point summarize the major activities of the psychical apparatus by reviewing Freud's theory of the psychology of dreaming.

When sleep comes, motor activity stops; stimulation, however, does not. It is true, of course, that *external* stimulation is sharply diminished in sleep. But what of *internal* stimulation? The man may sleep, but his organic needs never do; they are there all the while, ever increasing until such time as they are satisfied. Clearly, they cannot be satisfied in the absence of motor activity, and yet, if the tension which they produce continues to accumulate, it will soon become so great as to threaten sleep. This, of course, would be unacceptable, since sleep is itself an organic need. Obviously, then, if organic needs cannot be satisfied during sleep, and if sleep must nonetheless be preserved, it follows that the excitation produced by these needs must be, somehow, drained off. Dreaming, in Freud's view, constitutes the "somehow" by which the accumulating excitation is allowed to seep out of the apparatus. As we noted earlier, the first tendency of the psychical apparatus (when confronted with endogenous stimulation) is to "recathect" the memory-image of a previous satisfaction. It is to this primitive process that the psychical apparatus reverts in sleep. It has no means of achieving a *present* satisfaction of the need, and so, it revives the memory of a *previous* satisfaction. A dream, then, is but the hallucinatory fulfillment of a *wish*.

The description of the dream process given above applies to wishes in general. What, now, may be said about wishes that are ordinarily repressed? We may recall that a hostile wish is repressed from consciousness because it is consciousness that stands at the "gateway to motor activity." In sleep, however, this gateway to action is already fairly tightly shut. Even the most hostile wish could not lead to action, and so, its complete exclusion from consciousness is no longer necessary. The result is that even the normally repressed wish is allowed entry into dream consciousness—the only restriction being that it must come in disguise, so that its true identity will not be revealed. Freud's aim in *The Interpretation of Dreams* was to break the code of this process of disguise, to reveal the true identity, and so to embark upon what he saw as the "royal road to a knowledge of the unconscious activities of the mind."[12]

Of course, the dream process was not the only road to knowledge of the unconscious. Another was the process of neurotic symptom formation, and still others included those aspects of thought and action that Freud somewhat later described as the "psychopathology of everyday life." Here, too, it is possible to speak of a disguised "manifest content," which is the symptom, thought, or action itself, and a hidden "latent content," which is the underlying constellation of impulses and inhibitions.

## ID, EGO, AND SUPEREGO

Up until the publication of *The Ego and the Id* in 1923, Freud had spoken of three psychical systems: the conscious, the preconscious, and the unconscious. The last two of these, the preconscious and the unconscious, he had treated in a fairly unequivocal manner. Thus, he had consistently portrayed the unconscious as the system that contains repressed psychical contents; similarly, he had described the preconscious as containing materials which, though temporarily unconscious, are nonetheless capable of becoming conscious. Freud's treatment of the conscious system, on the other hand, had been in many ways confused and ambiguous. By way of example, let us take again his portrait of the psychical apparatus in *The Interpretation of Dreams*. In one place he rhetorically asked, "But what place is there left to be played in our scheme by consciousness, which was once so omnipotent and hid all else from view?" His answer, italicized for emphasis, was: *"Only that of a sense-organ for the perception of psychical qualities."*[13] The assertion was clearly intended to suggest that the conscious system plays a purely passive role. And yet, as we have seen, Freud argued in almost the same breath that the system of consciousness must have some sort of censoring function attached to it—a rather active function, to say the least. We may recall, too, his notion of the "secondary process"—a process charged with the rather complex and demanding task of coping with life's exigencies. Here as well was a function that could scarcely be handled by a mere "sense-organ for the perception of psychical qualities."

It was in *The Ego and the Id,* his last major theoretical work, that Freud made his most elaborate and sustained attempt to dispel this ambiguity. What he did was to posit three additional psychical systems: the id, the ego, and the superego. We may consider each of these new systems in turn:

(1) The word "id" is the Latin counterpart of the English and German neuter pronouns "it" and *"Es."* The phrase that Freud used, of which "the id" is the familiar translation, is *das Es.* Its literal translation into English would be "the It." Freud got the phrase *das Es* from a certain Georg Groddeck, "who is never tired of insisting that what we call our ego behaves essentially passively in life, and that, as he expresses it, we are 'lived' by unknown and uncontrollable forces." [14] Groddeck, in turn, probably got the phrase, if not the idea, from Nietzsche. Freud conceived of the id as lying within, and being contained by, what he had formerly spoken of as "system *Ucs*"—the unconscious. As we shall see in a moment, however, he did not take the id to be coextensive with system *Ucs.* Briefly, we may characterize the id as the repository of instinctual urges—more precisely, of instinct-derived wishes.

(2) In the "Project" of 1895, Freud spoke of "the ego" as an organized system (of neurons) "whose presence interferes with the passage" of excitation. Its task was a threefold one: (a) to store energy for the purpose of coping realistically with life's exigencies; (b) to evolve strategies for so coping; and (c) by means of "lateral cathexes," to repress hostile psychical contents. Thus, the "ego" of the "Project" was both active and partially unconscious. For reasons known only to himself, however, Freud made no use of this conception for nearly three decades following the "Project"; instead, he used the term "ego" mainly in the rather bland sense of "self" or "self-image." It was not until *The Ego and the Id* of 1923 that he returned to this vision of the "ego" as a subsystem of the (psychical) apparatus, partially unconscious and distinctly active.

The task of Freud's earlier "ego" (ca. 1895) had been to interfere with, and thus to guide and direct, the course of excitation within the neuronic apparatus. His later "ego"—the one of 1923 and thereafter—had quite the same task to perform within the *psychical* apparatus. In both cases, the function of the ego was to exercise control over the "gateway to motor activity." Thus, he observed in *The Ego and the Id,* "the functional importance of the ego is manifested in the fact that normally control over the approaches to motility devolves upon it. Thus in its relation to the id it is like a man on horseback who has to hold in check the superior strength of the horse." [15] The difference between the two relationships is this: the horse exists for the sake of the rider, whereas the ego exists for the sake of the id. Specifically, the ego comes into being in order to bring the demands of the id into line with the contingencies of the external world. Indeed, the ego is but a part of the id which becomes differentiated for this purpose.

[It] is that part of the id which has been modified by the direct influence of the external world through the medium of the [perceptual-conscious system]. . . . It seeks to bring the influence of the external world to bear upon the id and its tendencies, and endeavors to substitute the reality principle for the pleasure principle which reigns unrestrictedly in the id. . . . The ego represents what may be called reason and common sense, in contrast to the id, which contains the passions.[16]

(3) In any case, it should be clear that Freud's newer "ego" had at least the first two functions of the older one: (a) to "bind" energy for the purpose of coping realistically with life's exigencies and (b) to evolve strategies for so coping. What, now, may be said of the third function—the repressive function? That Freud also attributed this third function to his newer "ego" will probably come as no surprise; it may prove of interest, though, to see just how he went about doing it. It was as a result of long psychoanalytic experience, he stated, that "we find ourselves in an unforeseen situation." For in the course of psychoanalytic therapy, it is commonly found that, "when we put certain tasks before the patient, he gets into difficulties; his associations fail when they should be coming near the repressed [materials]." Freud had long recognized this "resistance" of the patient during the "analytic" process. It was only now, though, that he took theoretical advantage of the "unforeseen situation" to which it led. "There can be no question," he wrote,

but that this resistance emanates from his ego and belongs to it. . . . We have [thus] come upon something in the ego itself which is also unconscious, which behaves exactly like the repressed—that is, which produces powerful effects without itself being conscious and which requires special work before it can be made conscious.[17]

And so it was that "from this ego proceed the repressions, too." We may see, of course, that Freud's "situation" in this respect was not so "unforeseen" as he portrayed it.

Freud spoke of this repressing portion of the ego as the "superego." Its origins he attributed to the "mother-identification" and "father-identification" consequent upon the child's resolution of the celebrated "Oedipus complex." Owing to the child's "bisexual" nature, Freud argued, he cannot help but develop "object-relations" (erotic attraction) toward both parents. For this reason, it is inevitable that he will come to see each parent as a hostile rival for the erotic love of the other. Thus, the child will be both attracted and repelled, so to speak, by each parent. All this, of course, takes place in varying degrees, depending upon the "relative strength of the [initial] masculine and feminine sexual dispositions" of the child. But, in any case, it is from this situation that the Oedipus complex evolves, and it is toward a resolution of this complex that the superego comes into being. Thus, the male child identifies himself with the father and thereby enjoys, vicariously but with impunity, the erotic love of the mother. (In lesser degree, he identifies also with the mother, thereby satisfying the feminine side of his "bisexual" nature). At the same time, though, he must pay a certain price for this vicarious erotic satisfaction, for to identify with a parent requires that the child incorporate into himself the ostensible moral standards of that parent. These standards form a kind of "precipitate" in the ego, and so it is that the superego comes into being as the internal representative of external, parental authority. This superego remains largely unconscious because its origin is "intimately connected with the Oedipus complex, which belongs to the unconscious."

## INSTINCT THEORY AND ITS VICISSITUDES

In English editions of Freud's writings, the German word *Trieb* is usually given as "instinct." This translation is not entirely off the mark, but it is not entirely felicitous either, for the English word "instinct," though derived from a Latin word (*instinctus*) whose meaning is fairly close to that of *Trieb,* holds several meanings which Freud did not intend to convey. In the sense in which Freud used it, *Trieb* would be best translated by such phrases as "driving force," "motive power," "drive," "urge," "impetus," and the like. Its sole claim to being translated as "instinct" is that Freud applied it only to such "urges" as derive from *innate* somatic needs. We may in the present account continue to speak of "instincts" and "instinct theory," provided we bear in mind precisely what is intended by these terms.[18]

It should be clear from the above that an "instinct," *vis-à-vis* the psychical apparatus, is simply the "endogenous stimulation" with which we are already familiar. We are familiar, too, with the means by which the psychical apparatus strives to ease itself of the "pressure" (*Drang*) produced by such an instinct. It now remains to consider Freud's reflections upon the varieties of instincts and the relationships between them. His theorizing on these matters passed through three fairly distinct stages.

(1) The notion of "instinct"—more generally, of "innate inclination"—had been ushered into prominence by the Darwinian theory of evolution. Following Darwin, biological and psychological writings upon the subject were generally agreed that all such instincts in man (and the other higher animals) could be listed fairly neatly under two headings: (a) those which helped to ensure the survival of the individual and (b) those which tended toward the propagation of the species. It was to this rather fashionable Darwinian classification of human instincts that Freud first turned. Thus, initially, he portrayed psychological functioning as the product of a struggle between the instincts of self-

preservation on the one hand and the erotic instincts on the other. As we have seen already, and as we shall see again later, Freud was much given to seeing "struggles" between opposed forces—be they attraction and repulsion, primary process and secondary processes, self-preservation and erotic instincts, or what have you. In the present case (Freud argued), the struggle derives from the fact that, in human society, the demands of self-preservation often require that the erotic instincts be compromised. In any event, Freud coined the word "libido" to denote the "psychical energy" which pertains to the erotic instincts.

(2) By 1914, Freud had come to have second thoughts on the matter. For reasons that we need not enter into just now, it was at this point that he introduced the concept of "narcissism." He had, in fact, used the term "narcissism" before. But in his metapsychological paper "On Narcissism" (1914), it came to denote not just a "perversion, but the libidinal complement to the egoism of the instinct of self-preservation."[19] To put the matter very briefly, what Freud argued here was that the self-preservative instincts, the "ego-instincts," are themselves but differing expressions of the erotic instincts. Thus, when libido is invested in the external world, it may be spoken of as "object-libido"; when it is directed back toward the self, it is "ego-libido." In either case, the *Trieb,* the urge, the driving force, is libido—the "pressure" of the erotic instincts.

This conception of "primary narcissism" helped Freud to find his way clear of some mild theoretical difficulties that had lately arisen. At the same time, though, it brought with it the seeds of yet greater difficulties. Specifically, the psychoanalytic theory was now bereft of that conflict between opposed forces by which psychological functioning had been formerly animated. The only conflict to be found was that between narcissistic, or ego-libido, and object-libido—a rather mild conflict at best, inasmuch as both were but interconvertible forms of the same, erotic, instinctual pressure. "This was clearly not the last word on the subject." Freud later observed, for biological considerations [!] seemed to make it impossible to remain content with assuming the existence of only a single class of instincts."[20]

(3) Freud spent several weeks of the following year, 1915, at his daughter's home in Hamburg. And it was here that he had occasion to observe a childish game in which his eldest grandson repeatedly engaged. He had no doubt observed similar childish games before. But at this particular time he happened to have before him those "biological considerations [which] seemed to make it impossible to remain content with . . . only a single class of instincts." As is well known, discontent of this sort often sharpens one's perceptions to an exceptionally keen edge. In any case, it was from this observation that he came several years later to write *Beyond the Pleasure Principle* (1920). Except for *The Ego and the Id,* which was to follow three years later, this was Freud's

last major theoretical work. It was here that he introduced the now-famous
hypothesis of a death instinct (*Todestrieb*).

Freud recounted arriving at the idea of a death instinct through the above-
mentioned observation of a child at play. He noticed that the child tended to
repeat activities which could not possibly be pleasurable to him. (We may
recall that Freud had a rather special conception of what constitutes "pleasure.")
In a more pronounced form, he noticed this same "compulsion to repeat" in
certain forms of adult behavior: the recurrent dreams of war neuoritcs in which
the original trauma is revived again and again, the repeated self-injuring
behavior of certain people, and the tendency of some patients under analysis
to act out unpleasant childhood experiences again and again. In all such cases,
Freud argued, this tendency to repeat unpleasant acts must be regarded as
operating independently of the pleasure principle.

Through an inference that remains something less than obvious, Freud
concluded that this compulsion to *repeat* must rest upon a more general
tendency of the organism to *restore* a prior state of affairs. From this, it was
then but a short step to the further conclusion that the ultimate aim of the
tendency is to restore a state of affairs which is prior even to life itself—
namely, abiosis, or "death." And so arose the much-debated conception of a
death instinct.

Freud's critics and apologists alike were quick to express uncertainty about
how the notion of a death instinct ever found its way into Freud's thoughts.
Even Ernest Jones, Freud's admiring biographer, spoke critically of the
conception, seeming almost to regard its publication as a sign of incipient
senility. Jones wrote: "[Freud] had, it is true, often admitted having a
speculative or even a phantastic side to his nature, one which he had for many
years strenuously checked. . . . Now he was surrendering the old control and
allowing his thoughts to soar to far distant regions."[21] There can be no doubt,
however, that Freud himself took the idea of a death instinct with utter
seriousness. It was not for him "speculative" or "phantastic," for he was quite
convinced that "modifications in the proportions of the fusion between the
['life' and 'death'] instincts have the most tangible results"[22] Indeed, he later
devoted an entire book, *Civilization and Its Discontents* (1930), to an elaboration
of the idea, undertaking to show that "the meaning of the evolution of
civilization . . . must present the struggle between Eros and Death, between
the instinct of life and the instinct of destruction."[23]

In light of Freud's underlying allegiance to the philosophy of physicalism,
his attraction to the idea of a death instinct is perhaps not so obscure as it
might otherwise seem. For it was with the introduction of the idea into
psychoanalytic theory that this allegiance came full circle. To an extent never
before possible within the theory, psychological functioning could now be seen
as the product of the conflict between attraction and repulsion, between the

"instinct [which seeks] to preserve living substance and to join it into ever larger units . . . [and the] contrary instinct . . . [which seeks] to dissolve those units and to bring them back to their primeval, inorganic state."[24] In truth, Freud's arrival at the idea of a death instinct was but the consummation of the task of physicalistic reduction which had been set for him so many years before: ". . . to assume new forces equal in dignity to the chemical-physical forces inherent in matter, reducible to the force of attraction and repulsion." As Freud himself observed in one of his last written works, "the analogy of our two basic instincts extends from the sphere of living things to the pair of opposing forces—attraction and repulsion—which rule in the inorganic world."[25]


## CONCLUDING REMARKS

In the preface to his last general work, the *Outline of Psychoanalysis* (1938), Freud issued a caveat which has since been echoed many times by his apologists:

> The teachings of psychoanalysis are based on an incalculable number of observations and experiences, and only someone who has repeated those observations on himself and on others is in a position to arrive at a judgment of his own upon it.[26]

The claim made by this pronouncement is highly exaggerated. It is certainly true that Freud's observations and experiences had some effect on how he worked out the theory's details. But that does not change the fact that his general theory—his overall vision of things—was in very large measure an extrapolation from *a priori* assumptions. Many of these assumptions are questionable, some are just plain wrong—and one does not need to stretch out on the analytic couch, or sit behind it, in order to make that judgment. It is also possible to judge that Freud's *interpretation* of his "incalculable number of observations and experiences" was very strongly influenced by these prior assumptions.

And yet, for all his entanglement with physicalistic first principles and paraphernalia, it must be admitted that Freud has greatly enriched our understanding of psychodynamics. Indeed, it was largely on his account that psychology became involved in questions of psychodynamics at all. It is even possible that he was able to make these contributions, not in spite of his theoretical entanglements, but because of them. For even principles that are questionable or just plain wrong can have the effect, at certain historical moments, of opening one's eyes to things that might not otherwise be seen—though that, of course, does not mean that everything one sees under such circumstances is really there, or that what one sees is all that there is. We will raise this question again in Chapter 14, within a more general context.

## NOTES

1. S. Freud, *The Interpretation of Dreams* (Second Part), in *The Standard Edition of the Complete Psychological Works of Sigmund Freud*, ed. and trans. J. Strachey, vol. V (1953), p. 511.
2. Ibid., p. 536.
3. Ibid., p. 537.
4. Ibid., p. 538.
5. Ibid., p. 586.
6. Ibid., p. 599.
7. Ibid.
8. Ibid., p. 566.
9. Ibid.
10. S. Freud, "Repression," in *Standard Edition*, vol. XIV (1957), p. 148.
11. Ibid., p. 147.
12. Freud, *Interpretation of Dreams*, p. 608.
13. Ibid., p. 615.
14. S. Freud, *The Ego and The Id*, in *Standard Edition*, vol. XIX (1961), p. 23.
15. Ibid., p. 25.
16. Ibid.
17. Ibid., p. 17.
18. See the Editor's note on translation in *Standard Edition*, vol. I (1966), pp. xxiv–xxvi.
19. S. Freud, "On Narcissism," in *Standard Edition*, vol. XIV (1957), pp. 73–74.
20. S. Freud, *An Autobiographical Study*, in *Standard Edition*, vol. XX (1959), p. 57.
21. E. Jones. *The Life and Work of Sigmund Freud*, vol. III (New York: Basic Books, 1957), p. 41.
22. S. Freud, *An Outline of Psycho-Analysis*, in *Standard Edition*, vol. XXIII (1964), p. 149.
23. S. Freud, *Civilization and Its Discontents*, in *Standard Edition*, vol. XXI (1961), p. 122.
24. Ibid., pp. 118–119.
25. S. Freud, *Outline of Psycho-Analysis*, p. 149.
26. Ibid., p. 144.

## FOR FURTHER READING

Biographical treatments of Freud's career exist in great number and varying quality. Of these the unquestionable best, though it tends to be something of a panegyric, is E. Jones, *The Life and Work of Sigmund Freud*, 3 vols. (New York: Basic Books, 1953–57). For more casual study, this work is also available in a one-volume abridgment by L. Trilling (New York: Basic Books, 1961).

Freud himself published two works of an autobiographical—or, at least, autohistorical—nature: *On the History of the Psycho-Analytic Movement*, in *Standard Edition*, vol. XIV (1957), and *An Autobiographical Study*, in *Standard Edition*, vol. XX (1959). The most complete edition of Freud's psychological writings is also the best edited and translated: J. Strachey, trans, and ed., *The Complete Psychological Works of Sigmund Freud*, 24 vols. (London: Hogarth, 1953 et seq.). For the student who may wish to follow the post-1900 evolution of Freud's thought at first hand, the following sequence of selections from the *Standard Edition* would be recommended: *The Interpretation of Dreams* (1900), vols. IV and V, 1953; "Instincts in their Vicissitudes," "The Unconscious," "A Metapsychological Supplement to the Theory of Dreams," and "Mourning and Melancholia" (1915), vol. XIV, 1957; *Introductory Lectures on Psycho-Analysis* (1915–17), vols. XV and XVI, 1963; *Beyond the Pleasure Principle* (1920), vol. XVIII, 1955; *The Ego and the Id* (1923), vol. XIX, 1961; "Inhibitions, Symptoms, and Anxiety" (1924), vol. XX, 1959; *Civilization and Its Discontents* (1930), vol. XXI, 1961; and *An Outline of Psycho-Analysis* (1938), vol. XXIII, 1964. Most of these works are available in other editions, and some have even been published in inexpensive paperback editions. In all such cases, the editions translated by James Strachey or Joan Riviere are to be preferred.

# Chapter 11
## Gestalt Theory:
## The New Physicalism

We are not in the position to derive the respective physiological and phenomenal characteristics [of psychological pro-
cesses] in individual cases; but the directions taken by such
processes show clearly enough that they involve *Gestalten* of
the same basic character as are found in physics.
> Wolfgang Köhler, *Die physischen Gestalten in*
> *Ruhe und im stationären Zustand* (1919)

The term Gestalt is a short name for a category of thought
comparable to other general categories like substance, causality, function. But Gestalt may be considered more than
simply an addition to preexisting conceptual principles, its
generality is so great that one may ask whether causality
itself or substance does not fall legitimately under it.
> Kurt Koffka, *Encyclopedia of the*
> *Social Sciences* (1931)

We now go back to the closing years of the nineteenth century to follow a
quite different path of psychological theorizing. In essence, the argument upon
which the psychological tradition of Helmholtz, Wundt, and the Wundtians
had been based ran as follows: If the nervous system operates in *this* fashion,
then psychological processes must take place in *that* fashion; moreover, we
know that the nervous system does operate in this fashion, for that is precisely
what is dictated by the physics of the situation. The founding of Gestalt

psychology, early in the second decade of the present century, amounted to an attack against this argument upon all fronts. First came a series of research publications in which certain psychological phenomena were reported to be at variance with the doctrines of Helmholtz, Wundt, and the others. Then, following immediately upon this assault, there came a sustained and elaborate attempt to explain these variant phenomena on the basis of a new model of the nervous system. Finally, though almost simultaneously with the second assault, there came a sophisticated attempt to find support for this new model of the nervous system from among the more recently evolved conceptions of physical theory. The result, some years later, was another full-blown psychological theory—shaped and guided by physical conceptions and extending itself to phenomena far beyond those with which it had formed its initial alliance.

*1890–1912*

The three principal founders of the Gestalt movement—Max Wertheimer (1880–1943), Wolfgang Köhler (1887–1967), and Kurt Koffka (1886–1941)—traced the lineage of their views to a paper published in 1890, the same year in which James' *Principles* appeared, by the Austrian philosopher Christian von Ehrenfels (1859–1932).[1] This paper, in turn, was a descendant of Ernst Mach's then recently published *Contributions to the Analysis of Sensations* (1886). We need not consider Mach's *Analysis* here in any detail; it is sufficient to say that it discussed the perception of "form" at length, and that it was this discussion that served to elicit Ehrenfels' reflections upon the same subject.

Ehrenfels took the matter up from where Mach had left it, though carrying it on in a rather different direction. Consider what is involved, he began, in the perception of a musical form, or melody. If we examine the process closely, and refrain from artificial analysis, it becomes quite clear that the perceptual "form-quality" occasioned by the melody is not simply the "sum" of its several tonal elements. On the contrary, it is a quality that transcends any particular set of such elements. This conclusion is amply warranted by two well-known musical facts: the first, that we can take the same tonal elements as are found in one melody and rearrange their order so as to produce an entirely different melody; the second, that we can take the same melody and construct it out of entirely different tonal elements. Thus, if the original melody is composed of the tonal sequence *egfa ggfeced,* this can easily be permuted into, say, *fefg adegceg.* The tonal elements are identical in the two cases, but the resulting melodies are quite different. Conversely, we may with equal ease take the melody given by the sequence *egfa ggfeced* and transpose it into a different key. In this case, the sensory elements of the two perceptions are entirely different, but their form-qualities are quite the same.

So it is, Ehrenfels went on to argue, within the other sensory modalities as well. In vision, for example, four black lines arranged in one manner may yield the form-quality of "squareness"; these same four lines, arranged otherwise, may yield an entirely different form-quality. Conversely, the same form-quality of "squareness" may be occasioned by any number of different sets of lines, provided that the members of each set are arranged in the proper fashion. In all such cases, he concluded, the perceptual form-quality (*Gestaltqualität*) is determined not so much by the sensory elements (*Fundamente*) themselves as by the structure or pattern of their interrelationships (*Grundlage*).

Ehrenfels' observations upon perceptual *Gestaltqualitäten* may seem in retrospect to be a little obvious, perhaps even banal. Surely it comes as no surprise to anyone that a perceived musical melody is determined by the melody of the music perceived. It comes as no surprise either that four lines do not a square make—unless they happen to be arranged approximately in the form of a square. Taken by themselves, then, Ehrenfels' observations may seem to have all the novelty of the assertion that a bag of plaster is not the same thing as a plaster statue.

What we must remember, though, is that Ehrenfels wrote in 1890, in the face of a widely accepted theory which held that perceptual form-qualities are not *perceptual* at all! Discrete, punctiform excitations of sensory receptors give rise to discrete, punctiform sensations, and it is these sensations, and they alone, that then serve as the building blocks for all complex perceptions. This, in brief, was the theory of perception promulgated by German physiological mechanism and its mentalistic handmaiden, the "New Psychology." By 1890, of course, the "New Psychology" was no longer quite so new, but it was still very much alive. So, too, was the physiological model from which it was in such large measure derived. Indeed, both of them survived in some quarters, fairly intact, until well into the present century.

One of the principal implications of the theory was this: A complex perception, it was held, is composed of punctiform sensations and nothing more. Accordingly, while one can perceive the individual lines which compose a square, he cannot perceive the form of the square itself. For though there may be visual sensations corresponding to the lines, and to their various parts, there can be none corresponding to the arrangement of these parts.

The proponents of the theory, of course, recognized that one manages to gain an "impression" of the square's form nonetheless. What they argued was that this impression is not so much a perception as an *apperception*—the result of a process of associative inference. Thus, the visual sensations pertaining to the lines of the square are associated with certain nonvisual sensations such, for example, as those derived from eye movements. And it is from these attendant sensations that one (unconsciously) infers the arrangement of the lines. Of course, as Helmholtz noted, the inference is characterized by perceptual immediacy, but, strictly speaking, it is not a perception. The same interpretation would have been applied to the "perception" of form within the other sensory modalities as well—though, alas, without the handy explanatory device of "eye movements."

In any case, let it be said that the orthodox theory of the day (ca. 1890) did not deny the existence of form-qualities in experience; what it did deny was that they are directly given in perception. Ehrenfels, on the contrary, was arguing that they *are* directly given, and he based the argument upon his observation that *Gestaltqualität* is more a function of *Grundlage* than of *Fundamente*. In order to convince the proponents of the orthodox theory, however, he would have had to show not only that *Gestaltqualität* is dependent upon *Grundlage* (which they already tacitly acknowledged), but also that it cannot be the result of associative inference. This he did not do, and that is why his observations failed to set fire to the psychological world when they fell hot from the press. At the very least, though, Ehrenfels supplied the basic conceptual armament with which later workers might take up the battle anew. His treatment of the matter did not go entirely without issue during the decades that followed, but it is still fair to say that little of consequence came of it until it was picked up, some twenty years later, by the Gestalt movement.

It was in 1912 that Max Wertheimer, then of Frankfurt, published a rather long paper under the title "Experimental Studies in the Visual Perception of Motion."[2] The title itself was somewhat misleading, for, in fact, the paper dealt only with a very special kind of perceived motion. This was, namely, "illusory" or "apparent" motion. Still, the title was by no means a careless oversight on Wertheimer's part; the point he wanted to make was that the perception of *apparent* motion depends upon quite the same conditions as does the perception of *objective* motion. Of course, not even the most dedicated Wundtian would have protested this point, save for one thing: In the course of his experimental studies, Wertheimer demonstrated that the conditions on which the perception of apparent motion depend are not at all as the orthodox perceptual theory of the day had described them.

So far as the orthodox theory was concerned, the perception of motion fell into the same class of events as did the perceived form-quality of a square. That is to say, it was held to be not a perception but an apperception, the result of an associative inference. Thus, one may see a moving object in several different places successively, but he cannot see the movement itself. How, indeed, could he, in view of the fact that there are no visual sensations corresponding to the movement? Rather, the theory held, what happens is this: One's observation of a moving object is accompanied by eye movements of a certain sort, and it is from these movements of the eyes that the movement of the object is inferred.

The same principles were invoked to account for the perception of apparent motion. Now, it is often imagined that Wertheimer discovered apparent motion, and that this discovery sent the orthodox theory into immediate retreat. On the contrary, *Bewegungstäuschungen*—illusions of motion—had been the subject of investigation, now and again, since the 1870s. If anything, their existence seemed to the proponents of the orthodox theory to provide a very strong confirmation of their views, for as it happened, all cases of apparent motion were seen to depend upon the very same stimulus conditions as did the perception of objective motion. Thus, in both apparent motion and objective motion, the *Bewegungseindruck* (impression of movement) depends upon the presentation of objective stimuli in several different locations successively. The only difference between the two is this: In the case of objective motion, the successive stimuli derive from a single object which actually *is* in motion, whereas in the case of apparent motion, they derive from several different objects which in fact are *not* in motion. At any rate, the reception of the successive stimuli is in both cases accompanied by eye movements, and it is from these latter movements that the movement of the external object is, accurately or inaccurately, inferred.

What Wertheimer did, among other things, was to show that the eye-movement hypothesis was not tenable in the case of apparent motion and thus, presumably, that it was ruled out in the case of objective motion as well. Let us begin by describing a representative instance of apparent motion, under laboratory conditions, and then go on to consider how Wertheimer went about delivering the final blow to this particular aspect of the orthodox theory.

Imagine that we have mounted on a black background two horizontal rods—of the same width and length, one above the other, and separated by a distance of 8 inches—which can be alternately illuminated at any rate desired. If now, we alternate the rods at a relatively slow rate (allowing, say, 250 milliseconds between each illumination), we shall see simply what is there— that is, two rods being alternately illuminated. If, on the other hand, we alternate the rods at a relatively fast rate (say, 20 milliseconds), we shall see something quite different—namely, two rods being illuminated continuously and simultaneously. Finally, though, if we allow the rate of alternation to fall between these two extremes (optimally, at about 60 milliseconds), what we shall see is movement; there will appear to be a single, continuously illuminated rod moving up and down, from one position to the other. Wertheimer systematically investigated several varieties of such apparent motion, though the one we have just described will suffice for purposes of illustration.

Wertheimer delivered the home thrust to the eye-movement hypothesis in three separate steps. First, he demonstrated that apparent motion could be produced even when the complete cycle of alternation did not exceed 100 milliseconds—a period of time that is less than the minimal reaction time for eye movements. Second, he demonstrated that the phenomenon could be

obtained even when the experimental subject was required to fixate rigidly a
definite point in the visual field—a requirement designed to preclude, or at
least to minimize, the possibility of eye movements. Finally, and most
conclusively, he showed that antagonistic apparent motions could be produced
simultaneously—a fact that would be compatible with the eye-movement
hypothesis only if the eyes were possessed of special and hitherto unsuspected
gymnastic abilities. (We may illustrate this last point by continuing the
example given above. Let us mount two additional rods above the ones that
we already have. This will give us four, which we may label, from top to
bottom, *a, b, c, d.* Imagine, now, that we illuminate these rods in the
following order of alternation: *a* and *d* simultaneously, followed by *b* and *c*
simultaneously, and so on. If the rods are thus alternately illuminated, and at
the proper rate, we shall have one apparent motion within the pair *a-b* and
another within the pair *c-d;* moreover, they will be motions in *opposite directions.*)

And so, Wertheimer concluded, the eye-movement theory of apparent
motion (and, thus, of perceived motion in general) cannot be upheld. Now,
one could, of course, reject the eye-movement theory specifically, but still hold
fast to the more general notions of "apperception" and "unconscious inference."
Wertheimer, however, elected to set another course entirely. If eye movements
do not suffice to account for impressions of motion, he reasoned, then these
impressions can scarcely be the result of associative inference; accordingly, they
must be genuine perceptions (directly given) rather than mere apperceptions.
And yet, as it happens, the orthodox model of the nervous system does not—
and cannot—allow for this fact; thus, he concluded, a new model of the
nervous system is required.

Toward the end of the paper, Wertheimer went on to sketch the outlines
of just such a new model. It was brief and incomplete, and it took a great
part of the orthodox theory entirely for granted; but even so, it contained one
departure from the orthodox theory which was to lead quite naturally to later
Gestalt notions about the nervous system. What properties must the nervous
system have, he asked in effect, in order for the phenomenon of apparent
motion to come about? To illustrate, consider again the case in which two
rods are alternately illuminated at the proper rate. Clearly, the light from the
upper rod is falling upon one part of the retina, while the light from the
lower rod is falling upon quite another part. Moreover, these two parts of the
retina are *separated* from each other. Now, it is also clear that the retinal
stimulation deriving from the upper rod is conducted to one place in the
brain, while that deriving from the lower rod is conducted to quite another
place. It is, of course, true that these two "places" are neighbors, but it is
still the case that they, too, are *separated* from one another, just as are the
affected portions of the retina to which they correspond. Here, then, is the
theoretical problem, for one does not *see* two separated rods, but rather a

single rod moving back and forth from one place to another. Such a perception can only come about, Wertheimer concluded, if excitation within the brain moves back and forth from one place to another in a corresponding fashion. This, he imagined, might take place through "a kind of physiological short circuit [*Kurzschluss*]."[3]

## GESTALTPSYCHOLOGIE: *FOUNDING AND FIRST PRINCIPLES*

Wertheimer's paper of 1912 has usually been portrayed as the proximal event by which the Gestalt movement was brought into existence. There is truth to this, but it is a truth that must be qualified. Those who read Wertheimer's paper at the time it was published were given little reason to suspect that in its wake would soon come a movement calling itself *Gestaltpsychologie*. In the opening pages of the paper, he had mentioned—in good Germanic scholarly fashion—every psychological and physiological theory of the day which might have had something to say about the perception of motion. There were about a dozen of these, and mixed in among them was an undistinguished reference to Ehrenfels' paper of 1890. Apart from this, though, there was scant mention of either Ehrenfels or perceptual *Gestaltqualitäten*. To be sure, Wertheimer's findings and interpretations were entirely congenial with what Ehrenfels had written some twenty years earlier, but if he saw the connection, he failed to make much of it. The truth of the matter is that the Gestalt movement, though surely by this time conceived, had not yet been visibly born.

The reason for this was that the basic working hypothesis of the movement—its major empirical generalization—had not yet been fully drawn. The orthodox theory held that stimulation of a sense organ gives rise, within the brain, to a mosaic pattern of discrete excitations. Wertheimer's "physiological short circuit," on the contrary, was intended to suggest that this is not the case at all. If we are to do justice to the phenomena of perceived motion, he argued, then we must assume that the various excitations within the brain become integrated into a kind of "physiological whole-process [*Gesamtprozess*]."[4] The implications of this view were perhaps not very obvious at the time, but in retrospect they are quite clear. If the various excitations within the brain are not discrete and punctiform, then the sensations arising from them cannot be discrete or punctiform either. Indeed, they cannot be "sensations" at all—at least, not in the sense in which the term had been used ever since Locke. It is still true, of course, that any given perception includes a number of distinguishable aspects, but these aspects can scarcely be spoken of as "sensations," since they are in every instance determined by the configuration, or "whole-form" (*Gesamtform*),[5] of the underlying neural process. The point to be made is this: If the state of excitation at a given place within the brain is influenced by the states of excitation of its neighbors, then it simply makes no sense to speak of "sensations" and "sensory elements"; for the doctrine of sensations requires that the sensory projection areas of the brain be influenced by nothing more than the respective sensory receptor units with which they are neurally connected.

Here, then, lying implicit within Wertheimer's view of the workings of the nervous system, was that basic working hypothesis of the Gestalt movement to which we alluded above. Some twenty years before, Ehrenfels had put forward the non-too-novel hypothesis that the form-quality of a perception is a function of the configurational properties of the stimulus. Now, following Wertheimer's empirical researches and theoretical reflections, the way was paved for a kindred hypothesis which proved to be very novel indeed: namely, that perception *as a whole* (including both its form-qualities *and* its "sensory elements") is a function of *Gestaltfaktoren*. It was with the emergence of this hypothesis into explicitness that Gestalt psychology was born. We cannot say with certainty just when this occurred, nor even to which of the three founders of the movement it may be best attributed. But it is quite clear, nonetheless, that the event followed almost immediately upon Wertheimer's paper of 1912. Thus, as early as 1913, Wolfgang Köhler published an important theoretical paper in which he took to task the orthodox doctrines of "sensory elements" and "unconscious inference."[6] By the time Köhler published his *physischen Gestalten* around 1920,[7] it may be said that the Gestalt movement was not only fullborn, but very nearly fullgrown as well.

One of the reasons the Gestalt movement gathered momentum so rapidly was that its major hypothesis proved to be immediately applicable to a great number and variety of perceptual phenomena with which psychologists were already familiar. Students of perception had known for years, for example, of the various geometrical illusions. None, though, had ever been able to arrive at a satisfactory explanation of them. The Gestalt psychologists, on the other hand, were able to explain them easily, convincingly, and almost without exception in terms of "configuration." Indeed, virtually all perceptual "illusions"—geometrical and otherwise, and including the various perceptual "constancies"—submitted in some degree to a configurational interpretation. It was with a perceptual illusion (Wertheimer's *Bewegungstäuschungen*) that the Gestalt movement began, and it was to perceptual illusions that a large portion of its effort continued to be directed thereafter. This, of course, stands to reason, for it is in the waters of perceptual illusion (i.e., of disparity between the external stimulus situation and the resulting perception) that the orthodox theory would have the hardest time staying afloat.

There were certain other, more recently discovered perceptual phenomena which also yielded readily to a configurational interpretation. A good example of this is found in a very thorough study of "The Modes of Appearance of Colors," published by David Katz in 1911.[8] Katz' study is usually described as a splendid example of the "phenomenological method." There was, however, a great deal more to it than this. Ever since the appearance of Newton's *Opticks* in the early eighteenth century, psychologists and physiologists had shown a great deal of interest in the perception of color. There were several reasons for this interest, of course, but not the least of them was that the perception of color seemed to comport very comfortably with the doctrine of punctiform, elementary sensations. Indeed, a perceived color was taken by many of the advocates of Locke's mental mechanism and Wundt's "New Psychology" to be an exemplary instance of an elementary sensation. There were certain phenomena, such as color contrast and color constancy, which did not fit into this scheme very well, but these, it was hoped, were merely exceptions that proved the rule. That rule was this: that the excitation of a given color receptor gives rise to a given color sensation, and further, that the excitation of the same receptor on another occasion gives rise to the *same* sensation.

What Katz did was to bring to light a number of color-perception phenomena which were clearly incompatible with the orthodox doctrine of sensations. He pointed out, for example, that any given hue can appear in any of three quite distinct "phenomenal modes." Thus, a given shade and intensity of blue can have quite a different appearance depending upon whether it is the color of an opaque object, a translucent object, or of the sky. In the first instance it is a "surface color" (two-dimensional and definitely localized), in the second a "volumic color" (three-dimensional), and in the third a "film color" (two-dimensional and indefinitely localized, such as in most color after-images and in the hues one sees when the eyes are illuminated by colored light through closed lids). Here, then, was a case in which the same individual color receptors were being excited by the same individual color stimuli, but yet in which the resulting overall perceptions were quite different. Moreover, the difference was clearly the result of configurational factors. Thus, as Katz observed, if one views a "surface color" out of context (as through a reduction screen), it immediately becomes a "film color"; in so doing, it loses both its definite spatial localization and its tendency to appear as the same hue (color constancy) under varying conditions of illumination. It may be readily understood how phenomena of this sort ended up in the "debit" columns of orthodox perceptual theory and in the "credit" columns of *Gestaltpsychologie.*

In any case, so it was that a great many perceptual phenomena seemed from the outset to bear witness to the truth of the configurational hypothesis. That hypothesis, put into other words, held that the properties of any perceptual *part* are determined, in some measure, by the properties of the *whole* of which it is a member. This is the point that Wertheimer wanted to make when he characterized the orthodox perceptual theory as a mere *sinnlose Und-Verbindung* (senseless additive combining). It is also the point he sought to make when he wrote in 1923:

> I look out of my window and see a house, some trees, the sky. On theoretical grounds I could say: There are 327 brightnesses and color-tones. But do I experience 327? No. Sky, house, trees, and the experiencing of the 327 items as such no one can realize. If in this odd reckoning we assume that 120 items pertain to the house, 90 to the trees, and 117 to the sky, it is nonetheless true that I have *this* "togetherness" and *this* "separateness," and not [mere aggregations of 120, 90, and 117 sensory elements].[9]

## GESTALTEN: *PERCEPTUAL, PHYSIOLOGICAL, AND PHYSICAL*

Perception does not always correspond exactly to its external stimulus. On the contrary, there is often discrepancy between the two; and this, it was held, is in every instance a product of configurational factors. But how or in what fashion is it a product of configurational factors? Gestalt psychology's attempt to answer this question was contained in what has since come to be known as the "law of *Prägnanz*." As an empirical generalization, what the law of *Prägnanz* held was this: Whenever a stimulus and a perception are discrepant, it will be found that the perception is more *prägnant* (terse, concise), *einfach* (simple), and *regelmässig* (regular, well-proportioned) than the stimulus; conversely, whenever a perception and a stimulus correspond exactly, it will be found that the stimulus is already as *prägnant, einfach,* and *regelmässig* as it could possibly be. This law of *Prägnanz* was also spoken of, at times, as the law of "good form."

A good illustration of the law of *Prägnanz* is to be found in Kurt Koffka's ingenious application of it to the perceptual illusion associated with the Necker cube.[10] The Necker cube is a two-dimensional line drawing of a cube with transparent sides and opaque edges. Almost anyone who looks at this two-dimensional drawing will readily agree that it has a three-dimensional appearance. Before the arrival of Gestalt theory, the explanation usually given for the Necker-cube illusion was an empiristic one, that is, it held the illusion to be the result of one's previous experience with genuine, three-dimensional cubes. Koffka, on the other hand, pointed out the following: Imagine that we take a three-dimensional wire-frame cube and rotate it through a variety of positions. Imagine, too, that for each of these positions of the cube we draw a two-dimensional projection. Each of these new line drawings, of course, will be but a variation upon the original Necker cube; they will be two-dimensional representations of a cube as seen from a number of perspectives. Now, as it happens, some of these two-dimensional projections will have a three-dimensional appearance, as did the original Necker cube; others, however, will not. Specifically, those drawings which are symmetrical in two dimensions retain the appearance of two dimensions; those which are asymmetrical in two dimensions assume the appearance of three dimensions. Further, the drawings of the latter group, though asymmetrical in two dimensions, become entirely symmetrical when projected into three dimensions. Thus, Koffka concluded, the drawings that give rise to two-dimensional perceptions are *prägnant, einfach,* and *regelmässig* already; the drawings that are not *prägnant, einfach,* and *regelmässig* give rise to perceptions that are so. In the first case, the stimulus and the perception correspond; in the second they are discrepant. In both, however, the law of *Prägnanz* is fulfilled.

Now, up to this point, the law of *Prägnanz* was an empirical generalization and nothing more, for though it described the conditions under which stimulus-perception discrepancy comes about, it did not go on to tell just how they serve to *bring* it about. Even granting, then, that the law of *Prägnanz* is descriptively accurate, we must still ask, How is it enforced? It should come as no surprise that Gestalt psychology sought to answer to this question in the workings of the central nervous system.

As we have noted, Gestalt perceptual theory was at its best in just those cases where the orthodox theory was at its worst—namely, in cases where there was a discrepancy between sensory "input" and perceptual "output." The reason why orthodox perceptual theory found cases of this sort difficult to deal with should by this time be fairly clear. In cases where there is a discrepancy between the initiatory sensory-receptor process and the resulting perception, we must assume one or the other of two things about the brain process that stands intermediate between them. We must assume either than the mediating brain process is on a par with the sensory input, but not with the perceptual output, or that it is on a par with the perceptual output, but not with the sensory input. The orthodox theory had, of course, embraced the first of these assumptions; as we have seen, it held the mediating brain process to correspond point-for-point with the initiatory sensory-receptor process. In consequence, it was obliged to regard the discrepant perceptual output as being not *perceptual* at all, but rather *ap*perceptual—the result of unconscious associative inference. (Of course, this associative inference was held to be the result of a brain process too, but it was of a different, parallel, nonperceptual brain process.)

Consider, now, what happens if we reject the first assumption and embrace instead the second. That is, in cases where there is a discrepancy between sensory input and perceptual output, consider the consequences of assuming that the mediating brain process is on a par with the perception, but not with the initiatory sensory-receptor process. The first and most obvious consequence is that the task of explaining the discrepancy of the perception becomes a task of a very different order. Indeed, there is now no need of *explaining* perception at all; all that need be said of it is that it is the *immediate* correlate and correspondent of the underlying brain process. This, of course, was a conclusion well suited to the Gestalt point of view, for it carried with it the suggestion that perception is, after all, directly given. Thus, it was with this second assumption and all its attendant implications that the Gestalt theory of the nervous system began. It was spoken of under the title "psychoneural isomorphism," and its status as an assumption was—at the outset, at least—freely admitted.

What often goes unrecognized about this Gestalt assumption of psychoneural isomorphism is that, in and of itself, it did not solve the problem of input-output discrepancy any better than the contrary assumption of orthodox theory. All it did was shift the burden of explanation from one shoulder to the other. Thus, the orthodox assumption held that the mediating brain process corresponds point-for-point with the sensory-receptor process; it had then to explain the discrepancy of the perception, but it did not have to explain the brain process any further than it already had. Conversely, the Gestalt assumption of psychoneural isomorphism required no further explanation of the perception, but it did require a further explanation of the brain process. Specifically, Gestalt theory had to go on to explain the supposed discrepancy between the brain process and its initiatory sensory-receptor process.

This, then, was the task, and the proponents of the Gestalt point of view set about it straightaway. As we have seen, orthodox theory took the brain to be a mere passive recipient of peripheral sensory excitation. Gestalt theory, of course, agreed that the brain is a *recipient* of peripheral excitation, but it went on to argue that it is not a mere *passive* recipient. On the contrary, it held, the role that the brain plays is an *active* one. It receives the peripheral excitation, to be sure, but it then goes on to transform this excitation in accordance with its own inherent dynamic properties. And it is precisely these, the inherent dynamic properties of the brain, that are responsible for any disparity that might exist among the sensory-receptor process, the intermediate brain process, and the resulting perception. Considering that the term "dynamic" is tossed about with such abandon these days, we shall do well to point out that within Gestalt theory it had a fairly precise and unequivocal meaning. Orthodox theory had held that the workings of the brain are determined principally by the brain's anatomical structure—that is, by the arrangement of its pathways and their various interconnections. Gestalt theory contended that these workings are determined also, and in large measure, by the distribution of *forces* within the brain—and this, moreover, in a fashion which is relatively independent of "pathways" and "interconnections." Here, of course, was what Wertheimer was already working toward in 1912 with his notion of a "physiological short circuit."

Let us grant that incoming sensory excitation is, as claimed, transformed in accordance with certain inherent dynamic properties of the brain. We must now ask, In just what fashion does this transformation take place? The answer that Gestalt theory offered was simple and direct: The transformation must be of precisely the sort required to produce the observed discrepancy between sensory input and perceptual output. Now, as it happens, all instances of such discrepancy may be subsumed under the empirical law of *Prägnanz;* that is, the perceptual output is in each case more *prägnant, einfach,* and *regelmässig* than the sensory input. Thus, since the mediating brain process and the perceptual output are isomorphic with each other, it must surely be that the brain process, too, is more *prägnant, einfach,* and *regelmässig* than the incoming sensory excitation. This, then, was the inferred nature of the transformation, and so it was that Gestalt theory's "inherent dynamic properties of the brain" amounted to nothing more nor less than a law of *Prägnanz* of the central nervous system. It all followed, of course, from the initial assumption of psychoneural isomorphism. Once that assumption is granted, one can do none other than conclude with Wertheimer: *"Denn was innen, das ist aussen."*

The argument, up to this point, is apt to appear rather circular. It begins by asserting that input-output discrepancy may be explained in terms of the mediating brain process, and then it goes on to infer the properties of this mediating brain process from input-output discrepancy. In truth, the argument *was* circular and would have remained so, but for one thing: the Gestalt theorists insisted that there are other considerations, independent of input-output discrepancy, which lead to quite the same inference concerning the properties of the central nervous system. These were considerations supplied by none other than that old, familiar guiding light of psychological theory—physics.

During the several decades preceding the birth of Gestalt psychology, the science of physics had been undergoing a rather large-scale theoretical overhaul. Up until this time, its major conceptions had been quite thoroughly and unmistakably *mechanistic;* now they were becoming less and less so. By way of illustration, let us consider again the physical theories of Galileo and Newton. As we have seen, the Galilean theory was entirely mechanistic; it held that all physical phenomena may be explained in terms of matter-in-motion and that one body can affect another only through direct contact or through a series of direct contacts. Newtonian theory retained this emphasis upon matter-in-motion, and so, to this extent, it too was mechanistic. At the same time, though, it sowed the seeds of an eventual revolution. These, of course, were the seeds contained in Newton's notion of "action at a distance" by way of attractive and repulsive *forces.* As we indicated earlier, this notion bid fair to give the doctrine of mechanism a rather severe theoretical cramp, for it suggested that distant bodies could affect one another *in vacuo*—that is, in the absence of any material medium which might transmit the effect through a series of "direct contacts." Newton was keenly aware of the difficulty, and it was as an attempt to resolve it that he put forward the felicitous conception of an "ether." This, we may recall, was an invention pure and simple. Mechanistic doctrine demanded that effects between distant bodies be transmitted by a dense material medium. The "ether" had one job and one only— to satisfy that demand.

This notion of an "ether" went fairly uncontested within physics until well into the nineteenth century, and so it was that mechanistic doctrine was enabled to survive even in the face of "forces" and "action at a distance." Nonetheless, it was an essentially defective conception, and toward the end of the century this began to be recognized. We cannot enter into the matter in detail here, so we shall say just this: As the nineteenth century drew to a close, the "ether" concept was beginning to fall upon increasingly hard times; as a result, physicists found themselves talking about "forces" which were propagated (in the absence of an "ether") through empty space. The situation was further complicated by the fact that physical "forces" were now known to be more numerous, complex, and important than even Newton had imagined.

Anyway, what finally came of it all was a line of reasoning that took somewhat the following form: If "forces" can be propagated through space without the assistance of a material medium, it must be that they themselves have spatial properties; specifically, they must have spatial *extension* and spatial *configuration*. Indeed, we ought no longer speak of "forces" at all, for what we are really dealing with are *fields of force*—motive agencies which are spatially extended and configured, and whose strength varies continuously from one part of the configuration to another. Take, for example, the familiar case of an iron magnet. If we place a sheet of paper over the magnet and then shake iron filings onto the top surface of the paper, we shall find that the filings become distributed on the paper in a characteristic pattern. The filings are not in contact with the magnet, but they are nonetheless affected by its extended and configured field of force. Magnetism, electricity, and light were the forces which seemed most clearly at the time to have such field properties. By the 1880s, there was good reason to believe that all three of these were but special cases of a single electromagnetic force. Indeed, there were even some who suspected that other varieties of force, or energy, might also be electromagnetic. All in all, then, physical field theory (as it came to be called) was just about ready to carry the day.

This characterization of a field of force as extended and configured should betray at once the relevance of physical field theory to Gestalt psychology. The brain is, after all, a physical system. As such, it is the locus of physical forces, of which at least some are apt to have field properties. Might it not be, then, that the configurational properties of forces within the brain will serve to explain the configurational properties of perception? If perception is isomorphic with brain activity, then the answer is clearly yes. Such was the line of reasoning pursued by Wolfgang Köhler in his very thorough and difficult work of about 1920, *Die physischen Gestalten in Ruhe und im stationären Zustand* (*Static and Stationary Physical Configurations*).

Köhler began his *physischen Gestalten* with the observation that psychology, being a young science, would do well to find parallels whenever it can between its own phenomena and those of the older, better established sciences. He then pointed out that such parallels already exist, waiting only to be noticed, in the realm of physics. Certain psychological processes have configurational properties; so also do certain physical processes which we may assume take place within the brain. The task, then, is simply to determine the extent to which these two types of configurational properties correspond. We are already familiar with the configurational properties of psychological processes, so let us proceed to consider those of physical processes.

Though Köhler's argument beyond this point was long and complex, it may be summarized fairly briefly. The processes associated with physical force fields, he observed, may exist in one or the other of two states: They may be either *stationary* (unchanging) or *dynamic* (changing). A stationary state will remain stationary until it is altered by some external force, whereupon it will become a dynamic process. On the other hand, a dynamic process will, if left to itself, eventually become a stationary one. Thus we may conclude that a dynamic process tends to *become* stationary, and that a stationary process tends to *remain* stationary.

What, now, is the difference between a stationary and a dynamic process, apart from the fact that one is changing and the other is not? It is simply this: A stationary process is one in which the several constituent forces have reached a state of equilibrium; a dynamic process is one in which the constituent forces are still in a state of *dis*equilibrium. Thus, speaking more broadly, we may say that an unbalanced configuration of forces tends to change in the direction of equilibrium; further, once it has achieved equilibrium it will change no more.

These, then, are the general properties of physical force fields. For all who have eyes to see it, the parallel with psychological phenomena should be perfectly plain. Let us assume, Köhler argued, that sensory excitation gives rise to a force-field process within the brain. If the several constituent forces are balanced at the outset, then the process will be and remain a stationary one and the resulting perception will correspond exactly to the sensory input. Contrariwise, if the constituent forces are *un*balanced, the process will change so as to achieve a state of equilibrium, and the resulting perception will be discrepant with sensory input. In the latter case two kinds of changes take place, and each is entirely parallel with the other: First, the constituent forces of the brain process have achieved a state of greater equilibrium; second, the resulting perception is more *prägnant, einfach,* and *regelmässig* than the initiatory sensory-receptor process. Surely we are not stretching things too far if we conclude that the perceptual tendency toward *Prägnanz* is but the phenomenal counterpart of the tendency of force fields within the brain to achieve equilibrium.

Köhler's treatment of physical and psychological *Gestalten* naturally left a great many details to be worked out. As he noted, even though we may understand the generalities of the relationship between the physical and the psychological, we are still "not in the position to derive the respective physiological and phenomenal characteristics [of psychological processes] in individual cases." Nevertheless, he went on to observe, "the directions taken by such processes show clearly enough that they involve *Gestalten* of the same basic character as are found in physics." [11] And so it is that the ultimate explanation of perceptual phenomena is to be found among the principles of physical field theory.


### THE FURTHER REACHES

Gestalt psychology began as a theory of perception, but it did not long remain within that confine. Indeed, its authors began almost immediately to enlarge it into a theory of psychology in general. A good illustration of this attempt to expand the theory is found in Kurt Koffka's *Principles of Gestalt Psychology,* published in 1935. Understandably, Koffka began with several chapters devoted to perception, principally visual perception. He then went on, though, to devote about an equal number of chapters to such diverse matters as "reflexes," the "ego," "adjusted behavior," "attitudes," "emotions," the "will," "memory," "learning," and even "society and personality." Similar attempts to expand the theory were made by Wetheimer, Köhler, and others. We cannot examine these in detail here, so let us instead try to convey something of their rationale and general form.

The rationale of the expansion ran somewhat as follows: Perception is a function of configurational factors, and the basal reason for this is that the activity of the brain, on which perception depends, is itself a function of configurational factors. Now, it is clear that psychological processes in general are, like perception, dependent upon the activity of the brain; and so, to this extent, psychological processes in general must be functions of configurational factors. From this we may conclude that *all* psychological processes, perceptual and otherwise, will be found to fall under something akin to the law of *Prägnanz.*

What this rationale came down to in practice was an attempt to portray each and every psychological phenomenon as the result of a dynamic process whereby forces are brought into balance. Here is one example from Koffka's *Principles:*

> Think of yourselves as basking in the sun on a mountain meadow or on a beach, completely relaxed and at peace with the world. You are doing nothing, and your environment is not much more than a soft cloak that envelops you and gives you rest and shelter. And now suddenly you hear a scream, "Help! Help!" How different you feel and how different your environment becomes. Let us describe the two situations in field terms. At first your field was, to all intents and purposes, homogeneous, and you were in equilibrium with it. No action, no tension. As a matter of fact, in such condition even the differentiation of the Ego and its environment tends to become blurred: I am part of the landscape, the landscape is part of me. And then, when the shrill and pregnant sound pierces the lulling stillness, everything is changed. Whereas all directions were dynamically equal before, now there is one direction that stands out, one direction into which you are being pulled. This direction is charged with force, the environment seems to contract, it is as though a groove had formed in a plain surface and you were being forced down that groove. At the same time there takes place a sharp differentiation between your Ego and the voice, and a high degree of tension arises in the whole field.[12]

The "shrill and pregnant sound" has cast things into disequilibrium. This disequilibrium has its source in the "behavioral environment" and its reflection in the "phenomenal field." Its locus, however, is in the brain, and it is there that a dynamic process will be established, which will persist until equilibrium is once again established. The resulting behavior (e.g., running off toward the source of the sound) is the product of this dynamic process; its aim is to alter the "behavioral environment" so as to make it less a source of disequilibrium.

The above example does not get us very far into motivation, cognition, learning, or any other of the farther reaches of psychology into which Gestalt theory sought to penetrate. It does, however, convey something of the manner in which the attempt was made. In any case, the attempt rested throughout upon quite the same principles as sustained the Gestalt theory of perception: "force," "field," "balance," "equilibrium," *"Prägnanz,"* and the like. Indeed there was even an attempt made to extract from these principles certain ethical considerations. This, though, should come as no surprise, for the results of the psychological enterprise can scarcely be innocent of ethical implications.

### THE NEW PHYSICALISM

It has often been said that Gestalt psychology differs from other major psychological theories, such as those of psychoanalysis and behaviorism, in that it is not mechanistic. Whether this is true depends upon how we define our terms. As applied to psychological theory, the term "mechanistic" can have one or the other of three quite separate meanings. First, it can mean that the psychological theory in question has been in part derived from mechanistic physical assumptions. Psychoanalysis would fall under this heading in large measure, behaviorism somewhat less so. Gestalt theory, of course, would not fall under it at all. Second, it can mean that the psychological theory in question inclines toward atomism. Behaviorism, with its tendency to analyze behavior into its elementary constituents, would of course be an example of this kind of mechanism, as would psychoanalysis and every other psychological theory that we have mentioned, with the sole exception of Gestalt theory. Finally, the term "mechanism" can refer to what William James described as "automation theory," the central assertion of which is simply that consciousness is causally irrelevant to behavior. Now it is true that Gestalt psychology was not mechanistic in either of the first two senses of the term. In this third sense, however, it most surely was. This is not to suggest that the Gestalt psychologists were so naïve as to deny the existence of consciousness, but it does mean that they, along with their psychoanalytic and behavioristic colleagues, denied its causal efficacy. They held that consciousness is nothing other than the isomorphic "phenomenal counterpart" of the underlying brain activity—which, though not "mechanical," is nonetheless entirely *automatic!*

To appreciate this point, we have only to recall that Gestalt psychology was, after all, a *physicalistic* psychology. To be sure, its principal concern was with the phenomena of psychology, but the conceptions by which it sought to understand these phenomena were imported, virtually unaltered, from the realm of physics. In this, of course, Gestalt psychology has much company, for we have seen time and again how psychological theories, ever since the time of Descartes and Hobbes, have tended to incorporate physicalistic assumptions. There is, however, one very important difference. All such theories prior to Gestalt were guided by assumptions which came principally from Galilean or Newtonian physical theory. Gestalt theory was the first to be guided by assumptions deriving from physical *field theory.*

## NOTES

1.  C. Ehrenfels, "Ueber Gestaltqualitäten," *Vierteljahrschrift für wissenschaftliche Philosophie* (1890).

2.  M. Wertheimer, "Experimentelle Studien über das Sehen von Bewegung," in *Drei Abhandlungen zur Gestalttheorie* (Erlangen: Verlag der philosophischen Akademie, 1925).

3.  Ibid., p. 88.

4.  Ibid., p. 92.

5.  Ibid.

6. W. Köhler, "Ueber unbemerkte Empfindungen and Urteiltäuschungen," *Zeitschrift für Psychologie*, 66 (1913).

7. W. Köhler, *Die physischen Gestalten in Ruhe und im stationären Zustand* (Erlangen: Verlag der philosophischen Akademie, 1924).

8. D. Katz, "Die Erscheinungsweisen der Farben und ihre Beeinflussung durch die individuelle Erfahrung," *Zeitschrift für Psychologie*, 7 (1911).

9. M. Wertheimer, "Untersuchungen zur Lehre von der Gestalt," *Psychologische Forschung*, 4 (1923).

10. K. Koffka, "Some Problems of Space Perception," in *Psychologies of 1930*, ed. C. Murchison (Worcester, Mass.: Clark University Press, 1930), and K. Koffka, *Principles of Gestalt Psychology* (New York: Harcourt, Brace, 1935), pp. 159 ff.

11. Köhler, *physischen Gestalten*, p. 259.

12. Koffka, *Principles of Gestalt Psychology*, p. 43.

## FOR FURTHER READING

Valuable background material for the matters discussed in this chapter is to be found in S. Toulmin and J. Goodfield, *The Architecture of Matter* (New York: Harper & Row, 1962), and in Chapters 6 and 9 of W. James, *The Principles of Psychology* (New York: Holt, 1890).

The student who might wish to inquire into Gestalt theory at greater length would be advised to begin with the following works: M. Henle, ed., *Documents of Gestalt Psychology* (Berkeley: University of California Press, 1961); K. Koffka, *Principles of Gestalt Psychology* (New York: Harcourt, Brace, 1935); W. Köhler, *The Place of Value in a World of Facts* (New York: Liveright, 1938); W. Köhler, *Dynamics in Psychology* (New York: Liveright, 1940); and M. Wertheimer, *Productive Thinking* (New York: Harper, 1945).

Unfortunately, there is no full English translation of Köhler's *physischen Gestalten.* There is, however, a condensed translation in W. D. Ellis, *A Source Book of Gesltat Psychology* (New York: Harcourt, Brace, 1938).

Good alternative accounts of Gestalt theory are to be found in E. G. Boring, *A History of Experimental Psychology* (New York: Appleton-Century-Crofts, 1950); G. W. Hartmann, *Gestalt Psychology: A Survey of Facts and Principles* (New York: Ronald, 1935); G. Murphy, *Historical Introduction to Modern Psychology* (New York: Harcourt, Brace, and World, 1949); and R. I. Watson, *The Great Psychologists from Aristotle to Freud* (Philadelphia: Lippincott, 1978).

A theoretical scheme closely associated with Gestalt psychology is the "field theory" of Kurt Lewin. It has never really expanded into a full-blown theoretical movement, nor does it bid fair to do so. Indeed, it is not so much a theory as a prolegomenon to a theory. The interested student may be referred to the principal works of K. Lewin: *A Dynamic Theory of Personality* (New York: McGraw-Hill, 1935); *Principles of Topological Psychology* (New York: McGraw-Hill, 1936) and *Field Theory in Social Science* (New York: Harper, 1951).

Chapter 12
# Behaviorism I: The Advent of the Behaviorists

[The concept of behaviorism], when rightly understood, goes far in breaking down the fiction that there is any such thing as mental life.

John B. Watson, *Behaviorism* (1924)

In the preface to his famous *Psychology from the Standpoint of a Behaviorist* (1919), John B. Watson warned his reader right at the outset that he would find "no discussion of consciousness and no reference to such terms as sensation, perception, attention, will, image and the like." For the truth is, he went on to assert, "I have found that I can get along without them both in carrying out investigations and in presenting psychology as a system to my students." And fortunate it was that Watson *could* get along without these terms, for as he added in the next sentence, "I frankly do not know what they mean, nor do I believe that anyone else can use them consistently."[1]

Of course, many years have passed since Watson's *Standpoint* of 1919, and in that time behavioristic theory has changed a very great deal indeed. But there is still this one guiding principle, article of faith, or call it what you will, which has been with the behavioristic movement throughout. It is that an adequate understanding of *behavior* can be achieved without reference to *consciousness*. And this, of course, is simply another way of saying that consciousness is irrelevant to behavior. The several varieties of behavioristic theory that have evolved over the years may be looked upon as but different ways of fitting this same initial assumption onto the actual phenomena of behavior. Our task in this chapter and the next will be to examine just how, and with what difficulties and successes, this "fitting" has been carried out.

## BEHAVIORISM AND THE REFLEX MODEL OF BEHAVIOR

In view of behaviorism's guiding assumption, it will surely come as no surprise that the movement has always had a certain penchant for the notion of the "reflex." For here, indeed is a conception that satisfies the behaviorist assumption *prima facie:* it refers to a form of behavior which is ostensibly "automatic" and "involuntary," and thus independent of consciousness. And so, as is only reasonable in light of the movement's principal aim, a persistent strategy of behaviorism has been to expand the notion of the reflex into a full-blown theory of behavior in general. For this reason, let us pause here and review the development of reflex theory up to this point.

As we have seen, the reflex model of behavior was first explicitly proposed by Descartes toward the middle of the seventeenth century. From the perspective of the present, of course, this early Cartesian version seems a crude affair at best. But in the seventeenth century it was an entirely plausible version, for it was built upon what were then two quite plausible assumptions: the first, that brute animals do not think; the second, that the nervous system operates like a partially closed hydraulic apparatus.

Descartes' assumption that animals do not think has endured in some quarters even up to the present. In the course of time, however, his second assumption, pertaining to the activity of the nervous system, was recognized to be false. The brain, it was discovered, is not just a jug with animal spirits sloshing around in it; quite the contrary, it is composed of some rather substantial tissue whose particles are clearly incapable of dashing about from pillar to post, or from sense organ to muscle. Thus, the neurological scheme that brought the Cartesian reflex model into existence eventually became lost in the wash of history. Curiously enough, though, the Cartesian reflex model *itself* survived and even flourished. The principal reason for this was that the theory of neural activity that succeeded the Cartesian scheme differed from it only in details; in its general outlines, it remained quite the same. We refer here to the model of neural activity that came into being between 1750 and 1850, and endured until fairly recently. The Cartesian scheme was based upon the view of the nervous system as an hydraulic apparatus; the newer scheme achieved the same effect by regarding the entire nervous system as an electrical *conductor* and the brain as a kind of electrical *switchboard* between afferent and efferent pathways. Both schemes began with peripheral excitation and ended—innately, invariably, and automatically—in peripheral action.

It was this latter, more neurologically sophisticated version of the model that lay at the heart of what William James wrote about in 1890 under the heading "automation theory." And it was James who saw the limitations of the theory—both in its 1890 version and in its original Cartesian form—as clearly as anyone. "The dilemma in regard to the nervous system," he observed, is just this:

> We may construct one which will react infallibly and certainly, but it will then be capable of reacting to very few changes in the environment—it will fail to be adapted to all the rest. We may, on the other hand, construct a nervous system potentially adapted to respond to an infinite variety of minute features in the situation; but its fallibility will be as great as its elaboration.[2]

A man like James, of course, could not fail to be impressed with the fact that invariable behavior would be *adaptive* only in an invariable environment.

Involving as it did the notions of "function" and "adaptation," James' criticism of the reflex model could scarcely have been made prior to the Darwinian theory of evolution. At any time from 1650 onward, though, it would have been possible to describe the same limitation of the model in other words. Thus, the reflex model (ca. 1650–1890) could account quite readily for the observed *regularities* of stimulus-response relationships, but it could not begin to handle their observed *ir*regularities. Why, for example, does a given stimulus sometimes *terminate* in one action, sometimes in another, and sometimes in no action at all? Or conversely, why does a given action sometimes *result* from one stimulus, sometimes from another, and sometimes from no stimulus at all? The problem, in brief, was to reconcile the observed *changeability* of behavior with the *un*changeable reflexive connections that were presumed to underlie it. As early as the 1860s, the Russian physiologist Sechenov attempted to deal with the problem—or part of it, at least—by means of an elaborate theory of cerebral inhibition. For the most part, though, it was a problem not fairly grappled with, nor even very clearly recognized, until almost the beginning of the present century.

This, then, was the approximate state of reflex theory as the nineteenth century was drawing to a close: Its conjectured neurological substratum had become more sophisticated, but its limitations were as great as ever. As we shall see later, there were certain researches, soon to be initiated, whose effect would be to render these limitations less constricting. For the moment, though, we may leave the reflex model where it stood around 1890 and proceed to witness the birth of behaviorism proper.

## *JOHN B. WATSON AND THE BIRTH OF BEHAVIORISM*

Behaviorism, of course, did not spring freshborn from the head of John B. Watson (1878–1958) in the second or third decades of the twentieth century;

the theoretical stuff of which it was made was already quite extant long before Watson drew his first reflexive breath. Watson's contribution lay not in creating behaviorism, for no single person did this, but rather in giving it a name, infusing it with a tough, scrappy, polemical spirit, and propagating it with an almost evangelical zeal. In short, he was not so much the first behaviorist as the first *promoter* of behaviorism. This, however, is not to deny that Watson's efforts had a very great influence upon the modern course of the behaviorist movement.

In his *Behaviorism* of 1924, Watson wrote:

> Possibly the best way to bring out the contrast between the old psychology and the new is to say that all schools of psychology except that of behaviorism claim that "consciousness" is the subject matter of psychology. Behaviorism, on the contrary, holds that the subject matter of human psychology is the behavior or activities of the human being. Behaviorism [moreover] claims that "consciousness" is neither a definable nor a usable concept; that it is merely another word for the "soul" of more ancient times. The old psychology is thus dominated by a kind of subtle religious philosophy.[3]

A few pages later in the same volume he further observed:

> By 1912 the behaviorists reached the conclusion that they could no longer be content to work with intangibles and unapproachables. They decided either to give up psychology or else to make it a natural science. . . . [And so] in his first efforts to get uniformity in subject matter and in methods the behaviorist began his own formulation of the problem of psychology by sweeping aside all medieval conceptions. He dropped from his scientific vocabulary all subjective terms such as sensation, perception, image, desire, purpose, and even thinking and emotion as they were subjectively defined.[4]

And so it was that Watson arrived at what he spoke of as "the behaviorist's platform":

> The behaviorist asks: Why don't we make what we can *observe* the real field of psychology? Let us limit ourselves to things that can be observed, and formulate laws concerning only these things. Now what can we observe? Well, we can observe behavior—what the organism does or says. And let me make this fundamental point at once: that saying is doing—that is, behaving. Speaking overtly or to ourselves (thinking) is just as objective a type of behavior as baseball.[5]

The reader is probably familiar with Watson's famous assertion that "so-called thinking" is nothing more nor less than minute "sub-vocal" contractions of the muscles involved in the production of speech. Watson was aware that the evidence for this view was not entirely overwhelming—indeed, that it was "largely theoretical." As he admitted on several occasions, the reason he put it forward was not that it was demanded by the evidence, which it was not, but rather that it was the "one theory so far advanced which explains thought in terms of natural science." [6]

As we noted earlier, automaton theory around 1890 regarded thinking—mental life in general—as the epiphenomenal correlate of events in the central nervous system. We may at this point wonder why Watson was unwilling to accept this easy and straightforward materialist solution to the mind-body problem. The answer is to be found in a crucial section of his early volume, *Behaviorism: An Introduction to Comparative Psychology* (1914). "If thoughts go on in terms of centrally aroused sensations," he observed, then "we should have to admit that there is a serious limitation on the side of *method* in behaviorism." And this is so because a purely behavioristic method could not even begin to give "anything like a complete record of your 'mental content or of the totality of conscious processes.' " [7]

The behaviorist, then, if he is to remain true to his platform,

> must content himself with this reflection: "I care not what goes on in [a subject's] so-called mind; the important thing is that, given the stimulation . . . it must produce [a] response, or else modify responses which have been already initiated. This is the all-important thing, and I will be content with it." I.e., he contents himself with observing the initial object (stimulation) and the end object (the reaction). [8]

If Watson had left the matter simply at this, he would have found himself in somewhat the same position as the would-be radio engineer who contents himself with observing the sound that goes into the microphone (stimulation) and the sound that comes out of the receiver (the reaction). He would be able to say that the two sounds are not unrelated to each other, but he would have scant chance of finding employment.

Watson apparently foresaw the corner that he was painting himself into, for as he noted in a moment of unaccustomed humility:

> Possibly the old saying, "half a loaf is better than no bread at all," expresses the attitude the behaviorist ought to take; and yet we dislike to admit anything which may be construed as an admission of even partial defeat. . . . [And so] it seems wisest, even at the cost of exposing the weakness of our position, to attack rather than to remain upon the defensive. [9]

In short, Watson recognized that the existence of central thought processes would mean that the use of behavioral observation alone could secure only half the psychological loaf. And rather than be content with half a loaf, yet not willing to buy the other half, Watson contended that the half he had—the behavioral half—happened to be the *whole* loaf. Thus, he could not help but see "so-called thinking" as simply another kind of overt behavior—subtle, perhaps, but in principle nonetheless observable from the outside.

Thus, psychology from the standpoint of Watson's behaviorism was to be concerned *solely* with the relationships between externally observable stimuli and externally observable responses. And of such relationships, the simplest and most regular case was that of the *reflex*. Accordingly, Watson pinned his early theoretical hopes for behaviorism upon classical reflex theory. Earlier we observed that the problem of the classical reflex model of behavior had always been to reconcile the observed *changeability* of behavior with the *un*changeable reflexive connections that were presumed to underlie it. Watson was keenly sensitive to this problem and directed a great portion of his efforts to its solution. This we shall see in a moment.

Watson's earlier theoretical principles were virtually indistinguishable from those of automaton theory around 1890. Thus, the unit of behavior is the *reflex*. An organized array of reflexes is an *instinct* if the organization is innate, and a *habit* if the organization is acquired. A habit, then, is simply an *acquired* instinct; an instinct, simply an *innate* habit. Both are but organized chains of reflexes. Thus:

> Instinct and habit differ so far as concerns the origin of the pattern . . . and the order . . . of the unfolding of the elements composing that pattern. In instinct both pattern and order are inherited: in habit both are acquired. [And so] we do not hesitate to define habit as we do instinct—as a complex system of reflexes which function in a serial order when the organism is confronted by certain stimuli, provided we add the clause which marks off habit from instinct, viz., that in habit the order and pattern are acquired during the life of the individual animal. After habits are perfected they function in all particulars as do instincts.[10]

For Watson, then, the problem of classical reflex theory resolved itself into the task of accounting for the acquisition of "habits." This, of course, had also been one of the chief preoccupations of his late countryman William James, whose writings on the subject Watson had certainly read. Watson's own theorizings about habit came in two stages.

### The Principle of Frequency

His initial approach to the problem arose in part from a rather curious, or at least unusual, neurological hypothesis. The conventional view was that habit formation was the result of some sort of "neural plasticity." Thus, it was held, a habit, which is only an acquired stimulus-response relationship, comes about through the formation of new connections within the nervous system between afferent and efferent pathways. Watson, on the other hand, argued that there is no such thing as "neural plasticity." As he asserted in his *Behaviorism* of 1914,

> When a stimulus arises in a receptor there is just as orderly a progression of events then as later when the habit is formed, viz., the stimulus is carried off along preformed and definite arcs to the effectors in the order in which the arcs offer the least resistance to the passage of the current. This order may vary with variations in the sum of intra- and extra-organic stimulation. But there is no formation of new pathways.[11]

Watson saw quite clearly that this hypothesis of "neural rigidity" raised a very difficult question: If no new connections can be made within the nervous system, how then can we explain the fact that new relationships between stimulus and response *can* be formed? His answer to the question was inadequate but nonetheless ingenious.

The first step in attacking the problem was to overhaul the conception of the "reflex." Up to this point in the history of psychology, the term "reflex" had usually been taken to denote a kind of ironclad relationship between *one* particular stimulus and *one* particular response. Watson, on the other hand, considered that the reflexive relationship might be a much looser one, which obtains between a stimulus (or complex of stimuli) and *several* possible responses. Thus a given stimulus might give rise (reflexively) to response *a* at one time, to response *b* at another, and to response *c* at yet another. Just which of these responses happens to be called forth by the stimulus on a given occasion is an entirely random matter, depending only upon the "condition of tension in the conductors" at the time.[12]

With this comparatively simple modification of the reflex concept, Watson now had the makings of a rather full-blown and thoroughly behavioristic theory of "habit fixation." Consider, for example, the behavior of a cat in a puzzle box (a box in which the cat is confined, but which can be opened through the pulling of a certain string, lever, or the like). The particular stimulus situation will reflexively evoke certain responses from the cat, and the order of these responses will be random, depending only upon the "condition of tension in the conductors." Now, if one of these random, reflexive responses happens to be the "correct" one (i.e., the one that will open the box), the cat will immediately be confronted by a *new* stimulus situation, whereupon the former series of responses will end and a new series will commence. In all cases, the initial series of responses will be *interrupted* by the "successful" response; and learning, as we know, consists in nothing more nor less than the *elimination* of *unsuccessful* responses. Thus, Watson argued, we may see how the fixation of a response in "habit" may be explained entirely in terms of the *frequency* with which it has been produced.

This may seem a rather complex point, but it was really quite simple. Indeed, it was based on nothing more recondite than the "general theory of probability," from which we know

> that in any chance temporal arrangement of events the probabilities are equal that any one of them will precede or will follow any other, and that in a large number of such chance arrangements of the same events any given event will precede each of the others in just half of the arrangements and will follow in the other half. But if now each temporal series is interrupted at the occurrence of the given event and the occurrence of all that follow is prevented, the given event will occur twice as often as any other.[13]

And this difference alone, Watson argued, is sufficient to explain why it is that "successful" responses are fixated in habit while unsuccessful ones are "dropped out."

Thus, Watson held that the "principle of frequency" was by itself sufficient to account for all habit formation, which is to say, for all behavior that is not instinctive. (In truth, Watson also proposed at this stage a "principle of recency," but since he did not develop it, we need not consider it in detail.) That this "frequency" explanation of learning was entirely consistent with his behavioristic program may readily be seen, for its main effect was to keep psychological attention focused on a point *outside* the organism, or at least at its periphery. Frequency, after all, is the property of a response; it has nothing whatever to do with "so-called consciousness." Indeed, it has nothing to do even with the nervous system, for, as we have seen, "there is no formation of new pathways." Learning is simply the elimination of useless movements.

> and when the useless movements are eliminated the correct movements arise serially [on account of their greater frequency] without any chaining or linking in any material sense (bonds, connections, etc.). . . . Stated in other terms, we find no necessity for speaking of "associations." The "association" is given in heredity—the act by which the result is obtained is "associated" with the stimulus in the first place.[14]

The reader will perhaps perceive this last argument to be a little frail—as indeed it is, for it still leaves unanswered the question of *why*. Why, that is, does the sheer frequency of a response cause that response to become fixated in habit? Earlier theories of habit had also attempted to account for things in terms of frequency, but they had usually done so only on the basis of some sort of presumed neural modification. Watson was unwilling to admit of neural modification, and so he left the question hanging.

### The Conditioned Reflex

The previous discussion describes the theoretical career only of the "early" Watson. The "later" Watson—a less systematic but far more evangelical Watson—replaced the principle of frequency at one fell swoop with the Pavlovian notion of "conditioned reflexes."

Early in the century the Russian physiologist Ivan Pavlov (1849–1936) had reported his researches into what Watson first spoke of as "stimulus substitution." The Pavlovian paradigm is a familiar one, but we may repeat it here nonetheless.

Meat powder placed in a dog's mouth will cause the dog to salivate. The meat powder is in this case a reflexive stimulus, the salivation a reflexive response—the causal relationship between them is innate, invariable, and "automatic." What Pavlov discovered was that a neutral stimulus, say the sounding of a bell, could be *made* to evoke the response of salivation by being paired repeatedly with the presentation of the initial stimulus for that response, the meat powder. Now the relationship between meat powder and salivation is an *unconditional* one—that is, its effectiveness does not depend upon any prior conditions, save that the dog must be alive and intact. The relationship between bell and salivation is on the other hand a *conditional* one—the bell is an effective stimulus for salivation *only if* it has been previously paired with the *un*conditioned stimulus for salivation, the meat powder.

To appreciate the broader theoretical significance of Pavlov's discovery, we must at this point retrace our steps a bit. As we have noted several times, the enduring problem of classical reflex theory was to reconcile the observed *changeability* of behavior with the *un*changeable reflexive connections that were supposed to underlie it. At the heart of this problem lay the traditional conviction that reflexive connections were necessarily *innate*. The importance of Pavlov's discovery—as he himself perceived immediately—was that it served to make plausible the hypothesis that reflexes could also be (under certain special conditions) *acquired*. We say "hypothesis" here, for this is precisely what it was. No one had ever doubted that a dog would salivate at the sight of food or the sound of a dinner bell. Pavlov's argument was that these stimulus-response connections, though acquired, are *reflexive* in character nonetheless. The argument was based upon two considerations: the first, that the "conditioned stimulus" acquires the ability to evoke the "conditioned response" only through having been paired with the *"un*conditioned stimulus" for that response; the second, that the "conditioned response" and the "unconditioned response" are in fact the *same* response.

Thus, Pavlov's "conditional reflexes" had far-reaching theoretical implications—but only if they were interpreted in a certain way. If they were seen as being truly *reflexes*, then their effect would be to make the reflex model of behavior a far more powerful theoretical instrument. Now Pavlov, as we have said, perceived this point immediately; Watson took a little longer. In his 1914 volume *Behaviorism,* he mentioned Pavlov's method only briefly and rather in passing. He seemed to find the notion of conditioned reflexes interesting, but of no great theoretical or practical importance. It properly belongs, he observed, "among physiological methods." Its principal use is as a method "to determine the efficiency of animals' receptors," and even here "it has nothing like the general range of usefulness" of other methods used for that purpose.

Watson took up the question of conditioned reflexes at greater length in a paper of 1916 and again in his *Standpoint* of 1919. Up to this point, though, he still saw Pavlov's method principally as a useful technique for determining differential sensitivity and the like in cases where the investigator could not obtain verbal reports from his subjects. It was apparently not until Watson learned that human *emotional responses* could be "conditioned" by means of Pavlov's method that he waxed at all enthusiastic about conditioned reflexes; but when he waxed, he waxed very enthusiastic indeed.

Every student of psychology is familiar with the case of Albert, an infant of eleven months in whom Watson induced a conditioned fear response. At the beginning of the experiment, Watson reported, "Albert feared nothing under the sun except loud sounds (and removal of support). Everything coming within 12 inches of him was reached for and manipulated. This was true of animals, persons, and things." What Watson determined to do was "to take Albert and attempt to condition fear to a white rat by showing him the rat and as soon as he reached for it and touched it to strike a heavy steel bar behind him." The experiment, of course, succeeded entirely; Albert developed a conditioned fear response to rats and, through generalization, to other white furry animals and objects.

Watson's experiment with Albert was reported in 1921; following this, he took Albert's conditioned fear as the paradigm for all acquired emotional responses. As he observed in connection with the case of Albert,

> This is as convincing a case of a completely conditioned fear response as could have been theoretically pictured. . . . We thus see how easily such conditioned fears may grow up in the home. A child that has gone to bed for years without a light with no fears may, through the loud slamming of doors or through a sudden loud clap of thunder, become conditioned to [fear] darkness. . . . We can thus see further how it is that the sight of a nurse that constrains the movements of the youngster or dresses it badly may cause the infant to go into a rage, or how the momentary glimpse of a maiden's bonnet may produce the emotional reactions of love in her swain.[15]

Watson was so impressed with the conditioned reflex that in time he came to see it as the foundation not only of acquired emotional responses but of acquired behavior in general. Naturally, at the same time he abandoned his "principle of frequency." Following his adoption of the conditioned reflex as *the* fundamental principle of "habit formation," Watson no longer asserted with such confidence that "there is no formation of new pathways" in the nervous system. Still, he remained chary of all attempts at neurophysiological explanation. We may imagine that this was for the same reason as suggested earlier: If the nervous system were admitted to be anything other than a mere passive conductor, then it must also be admitted that a purely behavioristic method of inquiry is inadequate. Watson, of course, had no quarrel with neurophysiology as such; what he did abhor was the possibility that "so-called consciousness" might be slipped in through the back door of "so-called central processes."

## THE ADVENT OF THE BEHAVIORISTS

In attempting to understand any large theoretical movement in psychology, a distinction must be drawn between general aims and specific tactics. Watson's specific theoretical tactics were soon recognized by behaviorists and nonbehaviorists alike to be frail and contrived. Rather, what endured of Watson's behaviorism were its general aims. These aims fall into two categories.

The first aim of behaviorism, which we have already touched upon, was a theoretical or ideological one: to demonstrate that behavior, which formerly had been thought to be only half the psychological loaf, was in fact the whole loaf. Otherwise said, it was to show that behavior could be adequately understood without reference to consciousness, mental life, or the like. We have already seen Watson's specific tactics for fulfilling this aim, and in the next chapter we shall consider yet others.

The second aim of behaviorism was a practical or technological one. In his *Standpoint* of 1919, Watson asserted that one of the principal goals of "our psychological study" is to formulate "laws and principles whereby man's actions can be controlled by organized society."[16] And continued affirmations of this goal are evident throughout the remainder of his writings. Certainly, one of Watson's chief reasons for rejecting the "old psychology" was that, so far as he could see, no practical good had ever come of it. This practical or technological inclination doubtless accounts for much of the appeal of a strictly stimulus-response psychology, just as it accounted for much of the appeal of eighteenth-century environmentalism. A strictly stimulus-response psychology holds that behavior is determined, in some fairly simple fashion, by environmental conditions; accordingly, it promises that systematic alterations of environmental conditions can exert systematic *control* over behavior.

Watson, indeed, was so fully persuaded of behaviorism's technological promise that he saw it as "a foundation for all future experimental ethics." In the closing paragraph of his *Behaviorism* of 1924, he wrote:

I think behaviorism does lay a foundation for saner living. . . . I wish I had time more fully to describe this, to picture to you the kind of rich and wonderful individual we should make of every healthy child if only we could let it shape itself properly and then provide for it a universe in which it could exercise that organization—a universe unshackled by legendary folk lore of happenings thousands of years ago; unhampered by disgraceful political history; free of foolish customs and conventions which have no significance in themselves, yet which hem the individual in like taut steel bands. . . . For the universe will change if you bring up your children, not in the freedom of the libertine, but in behavioristic freedom—a freedom which we cannot even picture in words, so little do we know of it.[17]

In the introductory chapter of the same volume, Watson asked the rhetorical question, "Does this behavioristic approach leave anything out of psychology?" In the course of time, it was a question to be asked by a great many others as well.

## NOTES

1. J. B. Watson, *Psychology from the Standpoint of a Behaviorist* (Philadelphia: Lippincott, 1919), p. viii.
2. W. James, *The Principles of Psychology* (New York: Holt, 1890), vol. I, p. 140.
3. J. B. Watson, *Behaviorism* (New York: Norton, 1924), p. 3.
4. Ibid., p. 6.
5. Ibid.
6. Ibid., p. 191.
7. J. B. Watson, *Behavior: An Introduction to Comparative Psychology* (New York: Holt, 1914), pp. 16–17.
8. Ibid., p. 17.
9. Ibid.
10. Ibid., pp. 184–185.
11. Ibid., p. 259.
12. Ibid., p. 260.
13. Ibid., p. 263.
14. Ibid., p. 260.
15. J. B. Watson and R. R. Watson, "Studies in Infant Psychology," *Scientific Monthly*, 13 (1921).
16. Watson, *Psychology*, p. 2.
17. Watson, *Behaviorism*, pp. 247–248.

## FOR FURTHER READING

A good background for the matters discussed in this chapter is to be found in Chapters 4 and 5 of W. James, *The Principles of Psychology* (New York: Holt, 1890).

For a good and thorough historical account of the reflex concept up through about 1930, see F. Fearing, *Reflex Action: A Study in the History of Physiological Psychology* (Baltimore: Williams and Wilkins, 1930; and Cambridge, Massachusetts: M.I.T. Press, 1970).

The student who might wish to study Watson and the earlier behaviorism at greater length would be advised to begin with the following sequence: *Behavior: An Introduction to Comparative Psychology* (New York: Holt, 1914); *Psychology from the Standpoint of a Behaviorist* (Philadelphia: Lippincott, 1919); and *Behaviorism* (New York: Norton, 1924). One might also wish to read Watson's curious autobiographical statement in C. Murchison, ed., *A History of Psychology in Autobiography*, vol. III (Worcester, Mass.: Clark University Press, 1936).

# Chapter 13
# Behaviorism II:
# The Full Flowering

One aid to the attainment of behavioral objectivity is to think in terms of subhuman organisms. . . . A device much employed by the author [however] has proved itself to be a far more effective prophylaxis. This is to regard, from time to time, the behaving organism as a completely self-maintaining robot, constructed of materials as unlike ourselves as may be. . . . It is a wholesome and revealing exercise.

Clark L. Hull, *Principles of Behavior* (1943)

It was in the 1930 and 1940s that behavioristic theory erupted into what now seems to have been its full flower. The person principally responsible for this efflorescence was an engineer turned psychologist, Clark L. Hull (1884–1952). It is not often in any field that a true theoretical genius comes along; of the very few to whom psychology can lay claim, Hull must surely rank among the foremost. Hull had an understanding of the logic of theory construction unmatched by any other psychological theorist whom we have yet mentioned. This, joined with an uncommon ability for conceptual analysis and synthesis, made him the greatest and most consequential behavioristic theorist yet to have appeared. This, of course, is not to say that Hull was infallible, nor even that his theory comes anywhere near to the truth of things. But, as behavioristic theory goes, his is far and away the best that has been produced. Later behavioristic theories may be found to depart from Hull's on a few specific points, but none so far has differed fundamentally.

211

In 1937 Hull published a remarkable little paper under the title "Mind, Mechanism, and Adaptive Behavior."[1] He made three points, and we may examine each in some detail.

(1) The behavior of both human and other animals tends to be *adaptive* in the Darwinian sense of the term, that is, it tends to be directed toward the preservation of the individual and the propagation of the species. And it is this seeming direction, this ostensible *purpose,* that has made it "customary to attribute [adaptive behavior] to the action of a special agent or substance called 'mind.' " Hull asserted, in short, that mind is simply an *inference* drawn from the ostensible purposefulness of adaptive behavior.

(2) From this, he then went on to assert that "the controversy regarding adaptive behavior is theoretical, not factual." The *fact* of adaptive behavior is there, whether we draw the mentalistic inference or not. If the inference adds nothing to our understanding of the fact, then we have no particular need of it. Further, if there is another inference that will explain the fact better, then we are obliged as scientists to abandon the first in favor of the second.

(3) Hull's final point was that, indeed, there *is* another view that will explain the fact better than the mentalistic view. This, namely, is "the physical or mechanistic view of the nature of adaptive behavior." The remainder of "Mind, Mechanism, and Adaptive Behavior" was then taken up with Hull's attempt to sketch the outlines of his own version of this view. He followed these outlines, with some modification and much elaboration, throughout the rest of his theoretical career.

Before we go on to consider Hull's "physical or mechanistic view" in detail, a word is in order about what he took as its model. He had set for himself the task of explaining ostensibly purposeful behavior in terms of nonpurposeful, "automatic," or "mechanical" principles. And, with this as the goal, what then would be better than to follow the successful example of an earlier attempt to explain seeming purpose in nonpurposeful terms? This earlier attempt was, namely, the Darwinian theory of organic evolution. Darwin was confronted with the question, How is it, save by design of the Creator, that organisms are so well adapted to their environments? He answered it with the conceptions of "variability" and "natural selection." Analogously, Hull faced the question, How is it, save through purposeful mentality, that the *behavior* of organisms is so well adapted to the environment? As we shall see presently, Hull's answer was much the same as Darwin's.


## REFLEXES AND "INNATE BEHAVIOR TENDENCIES": REVISION OF THE REFLEX CONCEPT

Clearly, one way of explaining adaptive behavior in nonpurposeful terms would be by way of Pavlovian reflex theory. This, indeed, is precisely what Watson, before Hull, had tried to do. The argument would run something like this:' Reflexive responses are, on the whole, adaptive vis-à-vis the stimuli which elicit them. The reflexive contraction of the pupil of the eye to intense light, for example, is an adaptive response vis-à-vis the stimulus; it ensures that the light-sensitive receptors of the eye will not be damaged by excessivly intense stimulation. Further, the contraction of the pupil in response to a (neutral) stimulus which happens to be recurrently associated with intense light will be adaptive for the same reason; it will decrease the chances of damage to the light-sensitive receptors. Thus, reflexes are adaptive, and so also are conditioned reflexes. From this point on, the theoretical task would be that of showing that adaptive reflexes and conditioned reflexes suffice to account for adaptive behavior in general.

Now, as we have noted, the Pavlovian model of behavior admitted of acquired reflexes, and for this reason it was a vast improvement upon classical, Cartesian reflex theory. Still—and this point cannot be emphasized too strongly—it suffered from certain *inherent* limitations. Specifically, it implied that any conditioned response must at some time have been the unconditioned response for an unconditioned stimulus. Accordingly, an organism's *theoretically possible* behavior repertory was still limited to the terminal members of innate, unconditioned stimulus-response relationships.

This, of course, is the problem with any reflex theory—one gets out of it only what one puts in. Thus, with *n un*conditioned stimulus-response relationships, we could perhaps have an indefinite number of *conditioned* stimulus-response relationships, but still only *n* different response *possibilities*.

Conversely, if we wish to get more out of reflex theory, then we must begin by putting more in. And yet, simply to increase the number of unconditioned reflexive connections would be a mere backsliding into undisciplined nativism. This, then, was the task: to increase the organism's potential behavior repertory, in a manner consistent with reflex theory, but without increasing the number of unconditioned reflexive connections. The task was among the first to which Hull addressed himself.

When Watson first formulated his "principle of frequency," he found it necessary to consider that a reflexive (i.e., innate) stimulus-response relationship might be a fairly loose one between a given stimulus and several possible responses. It is not certain that Hull took this idea directly from Watson, but in any case he found it necessary to revise the concept of reflex in very much the same way as did Watson. In his *Principles of Behavior* of 1943 he observed:

> It may once have been supposed . . . that innate or reflex behavior is [based upon] a rigid and unvarying neural connection between a single reception discharge and the contraction of a particular muscle or muscle group. Whatever may have been the views held in the past, the facts of molar behavior, as well as the general dynamics of behavioral adaption, now make it very clear not only that inherited behavior tendencies (sUr) are not strictly uniform and

invariable, but that rigidly uniform reflex behavior would not be nearly so effective in terms of survival in a highly variable and unpredictable environment as would a behavior tendency. By this expression is meant behavior which will vary over a certain range, the frequency of occurrence of that segment of the range most likely to be adaptive being greatest, and the frequency at those segments of the range least likely to be adaptive being, upon the whole, correspondingly rare. Thus in the expression sUr, $R$ represents not a single act but a considerable range of more or less alternative reaction potentialities.[2]

And so, according to Hull, a stimulus may *tend* innately to evoke not just one response, as would be the case with a simple reflex, but rather a whole *range* of responses. The simple reflex is only the limiting case, the most rigid and invariable, of "innate behavior tendencies"; the more numerous of such tendencies, and the more important as well, are those which are less rigid and invariable. The key concept here is that of *tendency,* or *probability.* In the case of a simple reflex, for example, we may say that, given the stimulus, the probability of the response approximates unity. There will be other stimuli, however, for which the (innate) probability of a given response is less than unity. It is in these latter cases that the stimulus may be associated with a *range* of "innate behavior tendencies"; further, the several responses within this range may each have *different* probabilities of occurring. These two conditions— innate behavior tendencies and differential probabilities—are built into the organism as a result of evolution. They are what constitute the organism's "unlearned receptor-effector organization."

As we shall see presently, this revision of the reflex concept went a very long way toward freeing reflex theory from its former rigidity.

### RESPONSE-CONTINGENT REINFORCEMENT

There is one point at which Hull's revision of the reflex concept squares quite nicely with the facts. It is that, except for the limiting case of simple reflexes, unlearned behavior is, in fact, variable. Thus, in response to a given stimulus, the newly born human infant will produce a variety of behaviors. If he is too cold, for example (or too warm, or hungry, or wet), he may cry, scream, or thrash about. He may do other things as well, though these are the most frequently observed, which is to say, the most probable.

Now, for any given stimulus, some of these varied behaviors may prove to be adaptive; others may prove not to be. And, in the course of time and experience, those behaviors which are adaptive tend to be retained, while those which are not adaptive tend to be dropped away. This is a fact to be observed in both human and animal ontogenesis.

We have used the lofty word "ontogenesis" in the preceding paragraph for a particular reason, for, as it happens, Hull's theoretical task at this point may be profitably compared with the task that Darwin faced, almost a century before, in attempting to account for phylogenesis. We may recall that Darwin's first tactic in framing the theory of organic evolution was to emphasize the fact of intraspecial variation. Following this, all that remained was to conceive of a plausible mechanism whereby some of these variations might be retained while others are dropped away. Darwin's answer, of course, was *natural selection*. It is not difficult to see that Hull faced a similar problem. He began by emphasizing variability within the individual organism's unlearned receptor-effector organization; there then remained the task of conceiving of some ontogenetic counterpart of Darwin's natural selection. We take the conception that he nominated to fill this role so much for granted today that we are apt not to appreciate how deeply it is imbedded in Hullian theory.

Before examining the matter in detail, however, let us do a little backtracking. We saw earlier that Watson at different points in his career put forward two quite different theories of learning. The first was submitted under his "principle of frequency"; its exemplary case was a cat's learning to escape from a puzzle box. The second was his adoption of Pavlovian conditioned-reflex theory; its exemplary case was an infant's conditioned fear response. These two theories of Watson's serve to underscore the fact that, by 1920 or so, two fairly distinct types of "habit formation" were recognized. The first of these was what is usually spoken of as "trial-and-error learning." The second, of course, was Pavlov's "conditioned reflex."

### Trial-and-Error Learning

Psychological interest in trial-and-error learning dates from the publication in 1898 of a monograph by Edward L. Thorndike (1874–1949) entitled "Animal Intelligence: An Experimental Study of the Associative Processes in Animals." Thorndike's basic method was to place animals (mainly cats) in puzzle boxes, such as described in the preceding chapter, and then to observe their behavior. The general features of such behavior that he took to be the most significant were the following.

(1) A cat placed in a puzzle box will at first scratch and paw around in a random, aimless, unsystematic fashion. In so doing, however, it will eventually scratch or paw the string or lever that effects the opening of the box. The next time the cat is placed in the box, it will take less time to perform the correct act while at the same time it will perform fewer incorrect acts. Further decrease in time and errors is then to be found with each succeeding trial in the box until the correct act is learned to perfection. Thus, Thorndike concluded, learning in this case is a gradual process whereby correct responses are "stamped in" and incorrect responses are "stamped out."

(2) Thorndike further observed that the initial behavior of all but two of his cats "was practically the same. When put into the box [they] would show evident signs of discomfort and of an impulse to escape from confinement." There were two cats, however, who behaved quite differently from these. (One was "an old cat," the other "an uncommonly sluggish cat.") "They did not struggle vigorously or continually. On some occasions they did not even struggle at all." For these cats, "it was therefore necessary to let them out of some box a few times, feeding them each time. After they thus associated climbing out of the box with getting food, they [would] try to get out whenever put in."

This may have the appearance of a single observation, but it is in fact two observations: (a) that, in order to learn a correct response, animals must first *perform* that response; (b) that they are apt not to perform that response, or any other, unless they are *motivated*. From these two observations, Thorndike inferred that it was precisely this motivation that is responsible for the subsequent "stamping in" of the correct response. Thus:

> In either case, whether the impulse to struggle be due to an instinctive reaction to confinement or to an association, it is likely to succeed in letting the cat out of the box. The cat that is clawing all over the box in her impulsive struggle will probably claw the string or loop button so as to open the door. And gradually all the . . . nonsuccessful [acts] will be stamped out and the particular . . . successful act will be stamped in by the resulting pleasure, until, after many trials, the cat will, when put in the box, immediately claw the button or loop in a definite way.[3]

(3) Finally, Thorndike observed that in some cases of learned puzzle-box behavior "there is no congruity . . . between the act and the result." Thus, if an animal happened to be performing a certain act at the time the box was opened, this act would tend to be "stamped in" whether it was relevant to opening the box or not. There was one chick, for example, who "was thus freed whenever he pecked at his feathers to dress them. He formed the association, and would whirl his head around and poke it into the feathers as soon as dropped in the box." From observations of this sort, Thorndike concluded that trial-and-error learning is a purely automatic process depending only on the *contiguity* of act and result.

### Conditioned Reflexes

Pavlov's theory of conditioned reflexes was simplicity itself. All it required was that a neutral stimulus be paired repeatedly with the stimulus member of an "unconditional" stimulus-response relationship. If this were done, then eventually the neutral stimulus (presented alone) would come to give rise to the response member of that relationship. In all of this, there was no trial, no error, no "stamping in," no "stamping out"; there was just (according to Pavlov) the automatic modification of neural pathways between sense organs and effectors.

Pavlov had observed two secondary phenomena in the course of his researches, but he did not perceive how these might be turned to great theoretical advantage. Hull, as we shall see in a moment, did.

(1) Once a conditioned stimulus-response relationship has been established, Pavlov reported, the ability of the conditioned stimulus to call forth the conditioned response decreases with each occasion on which it is presented. Eventually, it ceases to give rise to the response at all. Thus, a dog who has been conditioned to salivate at the sound of a bell with salivate less and less as the bell is repeatedly rung. At length, it will stop salivating altogether. Pavlov spoke of this process as experimental *extinction*.

(2) If the unconditioned stimulus is now presented again with the conditioned stimulus, however, this will have the effect of reversing the course of extinction. Thus (to continue with the example given above), if the dog has almost ceased to salivate at the sound of the bell, the representation of meat powder (the unconditioned stimulus) in company with the bell will serve to restrengthen the bell's ability to evoke salivation. Pavlov spoke of this process as experimental *reinforcement*.

### The Natural Selection of Responses

In "Mind, Mechanism, and Adaptive Behavior," Hull asserted that "Pavlov's conditioned reactions and the stimulus-response 'bonds' resulting from Thorndike's so-called 'law of effect' are in reality special cases of the operation of a single set of principles." For in both cases, he argued, what we have is a stimulus-response bond which is strengthened by a certain state of affairs and weakened by the absence of such a state. Thus, the correct responses of Thorndike's cats are "stamped in" by success, while their incorrect responses are "stamped out" by lack of success. Similarly, the conditioned reflexes of Pavlov's dogs are "reinforced" by the unconditioned stimulus and "extinguished" by the absence of the unconditioned stimulus. In both cases, it is the consequences (or temporal correlates) of the response that determine whether the stimulus-response bond will be strengthened or weakened. Accordingly, we may say that the principle underlying both kinds of learning is that of *response-contingent reinforcement*. This, then, was Hull's ontogenetic version of the principle of natural selection. (Actually, Hull did not push the argument quite this far; if he had, he would have seen that the "reinforcement" of Pavlovian conditioning is not really response-contingent at all.)

*Why is reinforcement reinforcing?* Thorndike had suggested that successful responses tend to be "stamped in" by the pleasant sensations engendered by their consequences. Naturally, no behaviorist worthy of the title could accept an explanation couched in terms of "pleasant sensations." And yet, Hull conceded, Thorndike's suggestion is not entirely off the mark, for it so happens that those things which are reinforcing are also those which conduce to the well-being of the organism. Thus, for a hungry cat, food will serve as reinforcement; for a female rat in heat, sexual activity will serve as reinforcement, and so on. In all such cases, what we have is a need, or *drive state,* which is fairly abruptly "satisfied" (i.e., reduced in intensity) as a consequence of (or in temporal proximity to) a response. The drive state is the initial stimulus for the response; the reduction of the drive state is the effective "reinforcing state of affairs." A response which leads to drive reduction is an adaptive response, and thus it is, through response-contingent reinforcement, that adaptive responses survive while nonadaptive responses perish.

*What does reinforcement reinforce?* What drive reduction serves to reinforce, or strengthen, is the *likelihood* that the adaptive response will be produced again under similar drive-stimulus conditions. In this sense, it may be said that what reinforcement reinforces is the "bond" between drive-stimulus and response. Hull was convinced that the reinforcement of such a bond corresponds to some sort of underlying neural modification, but he was chary of speculating upon its precise details. In any case, he quite clearly perceived that a mechanism such as response-contingent reinforcement, whereby adaptive responses are retained and nonadaptive ones dropped out, would itself be a distinctly adaptive characteristic in the larger, evolutionary sense. As he observed in *Principles of Behavior:* "An organism will hardly survive unless the state of organismic need and the state of the environment in its relation to the organism are somehow jointly and simultaneously brought to bear upon the movement-producing mechanism of the organism."[4]

With "innate behavior tendencies" and "response-contingent reinforcement" behind us, we may now attempt to sketch the broader outlines of Hull's theory.

### LEARNING AND UNLEARNING

Let us begin with only three conceptions and see what we can make of them. The first two of these we have already mentioned; they are "innate behavior tendencies" and "response-contingent reinforcement." The third is what Hull spoke of as "habit strength," by which he meant the strength of the underlying "bond" between stimulus and response.

Imagine, now, a very simple organism which has only a single need (say, for food of a certain sort) and which is thus capable of only a single drive state. Let us also imagine that this organism's drive state, when activated, innately evokes four responses, $R_1$, $R_2$, $R_3$, $R_4$, which initially have equal probabilities of occurring.

If, now, the organism is deprived of food, so as to arouse its single drive state, it will begin producing its four responses. Further, since the responses have equal probabilities of occurring, they will be produced randomly (depending, among other things, upon random variations within the nervous system).

Imagine yet further, now, that when $R_3$ is produced, it is immediately followed by the presentation of food and subsequent drive reduction. The effect of this drive reduction will be to increase the habit strength of $R_3$, that is to say, it will reinforce the *bond* between the drive stimulus and $R_3$. And so the next time the drive state is aroused, the probability of $R_3$ will be greater. If, at that time, $R_3$ is again associated with drive reduction, then its habit strength will be even further increased, and so on, with progressively smaller increases for each subsequent reinforcement, up to a point where further increase of habit strength is physiologically impossible. (These last two specifications were required to render the concept of habit strength consistent with the familiar learning-curve phenomena of simple animal learning.)

The theory so far may seem a simple one. In truth, though, it is not simple at all, for already it has some rather complex implications. Consider, for example, the following: Up to the point of first reinforcement, $R_3$ has a probability of 0.25 (as have $R_1$, $R_2$, and $R_4$). After first reinforcement, on the other hand, its probability will be greater than 0.25, and from this it follows that the respective probabilities of its competitors $R_1$, $R_2$, and $R_4$ will be less than 0.25. The point has two important implications: (a) A decrease in the probability of a response does not require a decrease in the habit strength of that response; on the contrary, it can be effected simply by increasing the probability of a *competing* response. (b) Habit strength does not mean the same thing as "probability of response."

Presently we shall see how Hull built up the first of these implications into a full-blown and quite novel theory of unlearning, or extinction. For the moment, though, let us consider only the second. If the habit strength of a response is "an increasing function of the number of reinforcements," then clearly it cannot be identical with the probability of that response, for there are many instances in which the probability of a response is *not* an "increasing function of the number of reinforcements." Hull's strategy at this point was twofold: First, he drew a sharp distinction between habit strength (i.e., the strength of the underlying bond) and "reaction potential" (the actual tendency of a response); second, he attempted by means of several additional conceptions to account for the quantitative disparity between reaction potential and habit strength.

Most advanced students of psychology are familiar with Hull's formula

$$sE_R = D \times V_1 \times K \times sH_R$$

where $sE_R$ = reaction potential, $D$ = the magnitude of the *drive* to which the response has become bonded, $V_1$ = stimulus intensity dynamism, $K$ = incentive motivation, and $sH_R$ = habit strength. (We shall not pause here to define "stimulus intensity dynamism" or "incentive motivation," since both conceptions were rather obscure and neither played any further role in the theory. Drive, of course, was central to the entire theory, though by this point it scarcely needs definition.) The new conceptions here are $D$, $V_1$, and $K$; their theoretical function was to fill in the gap so to speak, between reaction potential and habit strength. Whether or not they filled the gap successfully, we need not here determine; suffice it to show how the attempt was made. By way of illustration, let us collapse the above formula into the form

$$sE_R = D \times sH_R$$

What this expression implies is that reaction potential is determined by the *product* of *drive* and *habit strength*. Thus, it is entirely possible for habit strength to remain constant while reaction potential varies in accordance with variations in drive. If any disparity remains, this could then be removed (in principle, at least) by the interpolation of yet other "components of reaction potential," such as $V_1$, $K$, and the like. Filling in the gaps in this fashion is, of course, a common procedure in quantitative theory construction.

Here, then, in essence, is Hull's theory of learning. We may reduce it to two points: The habit strength of a response is a function of the number of times the response has been reinforced (i.e., associated with drive reduction); the reaction potential of a response (its actual tendency) is a function of habit strength, but it is a function of other things as well, particularly of drive. If these two points seem rather too simple to account for the complexities of behavior, we need only remember that Newton attempted with some success to explain the complexities of physical phenomena by way of three fairly simple laws of motion.

We have so far examined how a response gets learned; let us now consider how it gets unlearned. Empirically, what happens is this: If a learned response is repeatedly produced in the absence of reinforcement, if will progressively diminish and at length cease altogether. It is then said to be *extinguished*. The theoretical question is, *Why* is it extinguished? Within the confines of Hull's theory as presented so far, there are only two possible answers to the question.

The first would be that a nonreinforced response has upon habit strength an effect converse to that of a reinforced response, that is, that it serves to decrease habit strength by a certain amount. Without going into the matter in detail, let us simply state that Hull recognized the existence of several phenomena (spontaneous recovery, savings, and the like) with which this interpretation of habit strength would have been incompatible.

The remaining possibility is to say that a nonreinforced response does not decrease habit strength. And yet, if a nonreinforced response does not decrease habit strength, then surely nothing else does either. We must therefore assume that habit strength, once formed, endures throughout the life of the organism. This may not be the precise line of reasoning by which Hull arrived at the conclusion, but he arrived at it nonetheless: Habit strength, he asserted, *does not decrease.*

Now, if habit strength does not decrease, and if drive and the other components of reaction potential are held constant, it follows that reaction potential itself will not decrease. Accordingly, the only way in which a response can be extinguished is for another, incompatible response to acquire a greater reaction potential. This, in brief, was Hull's theory of unlearning. In point of fact, it was simply his initial theory of learning made over by the introduction of a new concept.

Let us assume, Hull suggested, that the effort involved in the production of a response generates a drive state which tends to inhibit the production of that response in the future. Assume also that this negative drive state, which we may call *reactive inhibition,* decays with the passage of time. Finally, let us assume that reactive inhibition can accumulate if responses are produced in sufficiently close succession. From these three assumptions, in conjunction with the general theory of learning, we may now draw the following inferences.

(1) A response is reinforced if it leads to a reduction of the drive which produced it. If the drive is reduced, then the response is less likely to occur again in the near future. Therefore, the reactive inhibition generated by a reinforced response will probably have decayed before the response is produced again by a renewal of its drive state. Accordingly, reactive inhibition will not accumulate under conditions of reinforcement.

(2) A nonreinforced response, on the other hand, is *not* associated with drive reduction; accordingly, the response probably will be produced again in the near future, before the first quantity of reactive inhibition has fully decayed. Thus, under conditions of nonreinforcement, reactive inhibition will tend to accumulate into appreciable amounts. At length, this accumulated reactive inhibition will be sufficiently great to inhibit the nonreinforced response. The response will thereupon cease and reactive inhibition will no longer accumulate; indeed, it will begin again to diminish through decay.

(3) Now, as we have noted, this accumulated reactive inhibition is, in

effect, a *drive state;* accordingly, the cessation of the nonreinforced response is, in effect, a response to this drive state. It is a response, moreover, which is associated with the reduction of its drive state, and so, it is a response which is reinforced. In short, the organism is reinforced for *not responding!* (We may speak of this response of not responding as an "inhibitory response.") Given further reinforcement of the inhibitory response, its habit strength will increase in the same manner as that of any other reinforced response. (We may speak of the habit strength of the inhibitory response as "conditioned inhibition.") This conditioned inhibition is a component of the reaction potential of the inhibitory response. (We may speak of this negative reaction potential as "inhibitory potential.")

(4) As we noted earlier, habit strength (conditioned inhibition) is only one component of reaction potential (inhibitory potential). Another, equally important, component is drive, and we may now ask just what is the drive-stimulus to which the inhibitory response becomes bonded. It is not difficult to see that the conditioned inhibitory response, in order to be an effective agent for extinction, must be bonded not just to the drive-stimulus of reactive inhibition, but also to the original drive-stimulus—that is, the drive-stimulus to which the original response is bonded. For only thus can the reaction potentials of the original response and of the inhibitory response be truly incompatible. (According to Hull, the establishment of a stimulus-response bond through reinforcement does not require that the stimulus and the response be bonded at the outset. It requires only that they both occur in temporal proximity, in the presence of drive reduction. Clearly, this relationship between (a) the original drive-stimulus, (b) the inhibitory response, and (c) the reduction of reactive inhibition is to be found in the case that we have just described.)

And this, Hull argued, is precisely what unlearning, or extinction, consists of. It is a process whereby two incompatible responses (the original response and the inhibitory response) become bonded to the same (the original) drive-stimulus. Thus, when the drive is aroused, it gives rise to two incompatible reaction potentials. When the habit strength of the inhibitory response exceeds that of the original response, then the reaction potential (inhibitory potential) of the former will prevail, and the original response will be, in effect, extinguished.

The concept of conditioned inhibition has the distinct advantage of portraying *un*learning, or extinction, as simply a special case of *learning.* For this reason, Hull's use of it might seem at first blush to be a perfectly reasonable theoretical step. In point of fact, though, "conditioned inhibition" was far and away the most problem-laden conception in the whole of Hull's theory. By way of example, let us recall two points that were made earlier: (a) In the process of extinction, the original response and the inhibitory response became bonded to the same drive-stimulus; accordingly, their respective reaction potentials can differ only if their respective habit strengths differ. (b)

One of the required theoretical properties of habit strength is that it reaches a limit beyond which it cannot be increased by further reinforcement. Consider, now, in the light of these two points, the case of an original response whose habit strength has already reached its limit; clearly, it could be extinguished only if the habit strength (conditioned inhibition) of the inhibitory response exceeds it. From this, we are obliged to conclude that habit strength in the form of conditioned inhibition reaches higher limits than do the regular forms of habit strength; otherwise, the extinction of an original response at its maximal value of habit strength would be theoretically impossible.

This required property of conditioned inhibition is neither an absurdity nor a contradiction. It is simply a contrivance, an assumption whose sole reason for existing is that it is required for the conciliation of other assumptions. This is but one example of several such contrivances and conceptual difficulties to which Hull's notion of conditioned inhibition led. Some of these he was aware of, some apparently not, but in any case he recognized that "the theory of the origin of [conditioned inhibition] must be regarded with somewhat more than the usual amount of distrust."[5] What he did not recognize is that distrust of conditioned inhibition is tantamount to distrust of the entire theory. Theoretical conceptions have a way of stacking up on one another. In Hull's case, it all begins with the notion of response-contingent reinforcement. In order to account for learning in terms of reinforcement, he had to invoke the concept of habit strength; and then, in order to explain unlearning in a manner compatible with the concept of habit strength, he had to invoke the concept of "conditioned inhibition." Thus, he could not abandon "conditioned inhibition" without at the same time abandoning "habit strength" and the principle of response-contingent reinforcement. On the other hand, he probably could not have revised "conditioned inhibition" without causing the theory to seem more contrived than it did already.

## SUBSIDIARY CONCEPTIONS

We have so far considered the major conceptions, along with their principal interrelationships, of Hull's general theory of learning. We may now examine some subsidiary, or special-purpose, conceptions. With one exception, these conceptions all take the form of mopping-up operations—that is, they were designed to enable the general theory of learning to account for certain specific phenomena of learning.

### Secondary Motivation

A rat is naturally adverse to having an electric current passed through its body. Indeed, electric shock induces a full-blown drive state in the rat, the goal of which is to terminate the shock, and the reduction of which serves to reinforce the associated response. And so, at length, a response which terminates the shock will be learned in the same fashion as any other reinforced response. If, now, we precede the electric shock on each occasion with a flashing light, we shall discover that the rat comes eventually to respond to the light as though it were the shock—that is, it produces the learned escape response in consequence of the light, prior to the onset of the shock.

This phenomenon, often spoken of in the language of common sense as "anticipation" or "expectation," is of course not limited to the behavior of rats. It is a very common phenomenon, indeed, and very important as well. Hull's task was to explain the rat's ostensible *inference* ("If light comes, can shock be far behind?") in the noncognitive terms of his general theory. It was to this end that he invoked the principle of "secondary motivation," the formal statement of which was as follows:

> When neutral stimuli are repeatedly and consistently associated with the evocation of a primary or secondary drive and this drive stimulus undergoes an abrupt diminution, the hitherto neutral stimuli acquire the capacity to bring about the drive stimuli . . . which thereby become the condition . . . of a secondary drive or motivation.[6]

Thus, with respect to the example given above, the principle of "secondary motivation" would suggest that the light (a "neutral stimulus") eventually "acquires the capacity to bring about" the drive state (let us call it "aversion") which is initially occasioned only by the electric shock.

It is plain to see, of course, that this statement of "secondary motivation" is not so much an explanation as a description, for it still leaves unanswered the questions of why and how. Hull sought to answer the questions by arguing that the principle of secondary motivation follows directly from the principle of response-contingent reinforcement. His reasoning was as follows: Electric shock may be regarded as a *stimulus;* the aversive drive state may be regarded as a *response* to that stimulus. Now, the flashing light is also a *stimulus;* further, since it occurs in close association with the electric shock, it also occurs in close association with the aversive drive state. And this close association between a stimulus (flashing light) and a response (aversive drive state) is all that is required for the establishment, through drive reduction and reinforcement, of a stimulus-response bond.

### Secondary Reinforcement

Imagine that a hungry rat is given food each time it pushes a certain lever. The food in this case will lead to drive reduction, and so the response of pushing the lever will be reinforced. Imagine further, now, that each time the lever is pushed it makes a clicking sound. It may be empirically demonstrated that this clicking sound will have a "reinforcing effect." Thus, if the food is no longer presented when the bar is pressed, the response will be more resistant to extinction if the click is heard than if it is not heard. Further, the click alone will serve (within limits) as a reinforcing agent in the learning of some new response.

Here, too, of course, is a phenomenon that is not restricted to the behavior of rats. Like secondary motivation, it is a phenomenon which common sense would be inclined to regard as the outcome of some sort of cognitive or inferential process ("If the click comes, can food be far behind?"). The task that Hull faced was entirely analogous to that of secondary motivation, and so he invoked the equally analogous principle of "secondary reinforcement":

> A stimulus which occurs repeatedly and consistently in close conjunction with a reinforcing state of affairs . . . will itself acquire the power of acting as a reinforcing agent.[7]

In his earlier writings, Hull considered the possibility that the principle of secondary reinforcement might be quite distinct from that of primary reinforcement. Later, though, he argued that it follows directly from primary reinforcement, in much the same way as does secondary motivation. His reasoning at this point was obscure, and we shall not attempt to reconstruct it.

### Goal Gradient and Behavior Chaining

Although the precise theoretical status of secondary reinforcement remained something of a mystery, Hull nonetheless made it do yeoman's service. Adaptive behavior, he observed, does not ordinarily consist of a single, discrete response; rather, it must usually take the form of an integrated series, or chain, of responses. Take, for example, the case of a hungry rat who must run to the end of a rather complex maze to find food. When it gets to the end of the maze, it finds the food, eats it, and thus its final response (the one that occurs "in close association with drive reduction") is reinforced. But what of the rat's earlier responses in the sequence, the ones that may be separated from drive reduction by a considerable period of time? How is it that they, too, get learned?

On the basis of experiments concerned with delayed reinforcement, Hull concluded that primary reinforcement extends (in progressively smaller amounts) only to those responses that occur within a period of about thirty seconds preceding drive reduction. Beyond this point, he argued, the job of chaining responses together must be handled by secondary reinforcement. This would be accomplished in the following manner: The maze at any given point presents to the rat a variety of stimuli. Those stimuli at the end of the maze become secondary reinforcers, inasmuch as they are closely associated with (primary) reinforcement; this means that they reinforce the responses immediately preceding them. Moreover, stimuli at the next earlier stage of the maze become secondary reinforcers also, for they too are now closely associated with reinforcement (albeit, secondary reinforcement). And so on, back through the maze. In effect, then, secondary reinforcement spreads backward through the maze, and thus it is that responses get chained together. Hull spoke of this combined, sequential effect of primary and secondary reinforcement as "goal gradient."

### Consciousness, Cognition, and "Pure-Stimulus Act"

"But what of consciousness," Hull asked toward the end of his "Mind, Mechanism, and Adaptive Behavior." And it was a question to which he returned ever and again. He shared with Watson the fundamental behaviorist assumption that consciousness, cognition, and other such lapses into "anthropomorphic subjectivism" could not be of any great theoretical (or ontological!) significance. Unlike Watson, however, he was not so naïve or postured as to suggest that consciousness is simply some sort of subtle, peripheral response, such as subvocal speech. The consequence of this dilemma was that Hull undertook to make a place for consciousness within the borders of his theory as it already stood—a small place where its existence would be recognized, but where it would stir up no trouble of any consequence.

If consciousness is a purely central, or implicit, phenomenon, then clearly it may play two roles: On the one hand, it may be a *response* to some external stimulus; on the other, it may serve as the *stimulus* to some external response. This, as Hull observed, would be of "peculiar significance":

> [For] it does not itself produce any change in the external world; neither does the act itself bring the organism any nearer to the food. What the act does is to produce the goal stimuli which evoke responses by the organism that tend to lead it to food, a mate, or whatever the goal or terminus of the action sequence at the time may be. In short, its function is strictly that of producing a critically useful stimulus in biological problem solution, i.e., it is a *pure-stimulus act*.[8]

The thing of "peculiar significance" here is this: in treating consciousness as a special case of stimulus-response relationships, Hull could now go on to argue that it is subject to the same principles of habit formation as are any other stimulus-response relationships. He could, in short, accept consciousness, cognition, and the like, as legitimate psychological data, without compromising his fundamental behavioristic assumptions.

### B. F. SKINNER AND THE HEART OF BEHAVIORISM

After Hull, the leadership of the behavioristic movement passed to B. F. Skinner, whose theoretical approach is more difficult to describe because it is far less explicit. Indeed, Skinner himself might object to being mentioned in this connection at all, for he has insisted all along that he is not really in the theory business. His avowed aim has been to focus solely on the observable relationships between environment and behavior, and to have no traffic with inferences and theoretical constructions. And he has held to this aim unwaveringly, even to the extent of disallowing those constructions so dear to the Hullian heart: "drive," "drive reduction," and "stimulus-response bond." To anyone steeped in these Hullian conceptions, the punctilious Skinnerian avoidance of them must have seemed a kind of willful blindness. The proponents of the Skinnerian view would scrupulously avoid speaking, for example, of a hunger drive and drive reduction—and yet, before beginning a laboratory experiment, they would restrict their experimental animals' food supply in order to get them down to only 75 or 80 percent of their *ad lib.* body weight; they would use pigeons, which, being birds, have a high metabolic rate and are thus almost always ready to eat; and by a remarkable coincidence they would note that pigeon food tended to be an effective reinforcer under these circumstances. Similarly, they would rule stimulus-response bonds out of court—and yet they did not scruple to describe "discriminative stimuli" that are antecedent to the response and become somehow an "occasion" for it as a result of reinforcement.

At any rate, it is true that we cannot speak of Skinnerian theory in the same way that we can speak of Hullian theory. Almost anything one might say of Skinnerian "theory" would be only a variation on the following theme: If a behavior is associated with reinforcement, it will have an increased probability of recurring in the future under similar environmental conditions; "reinforcement," in turn, is to be defined strictly empirically as "an event that increases the probability of the behavior recurring in the future under similar environmental conditions"; beyond this, it is idle to theorize and speculate; the proper task is to investigate the *facts* of the matter in the greatest possible detail. And it must certainly be admitted that Skinner and his followers have assiduously practiced what they preach, at least in the matter of detailed investigation of the facts. Their approach has achieved great success as an experimental science and, lately, as a technology; and in the process it has given us much valuable insight into the ability of environmental "reinforcement contingencies" to "shape" behavior. Moreover, it has all been achieved with the barest minimum of explicit theoretical elaboration of the Hullian type.

All of this, however, does not mean that Skinner has avoided theory, but only that he has avoided a certain kind of theory. He has stayed away from the retail end of the business, so to speak, in order to do a flourishing wholesale business. In case this imagery is too abstruse, let us put the matter plainly: although Skinner has had no interest in framing a theory of specifics and details, he has been very vigorously involved in promulgating a grand, sweeping, all-encompassing view of what organisms (including people, of course) are really all about. In this respect he is akin to Watson, who was also chiefly involved in the wholesale end of the business. Hull, on the other hand, had been active in both ends, although his wholesale theorizings did not reach nearly so wide an audience as Watson's or Skinner's. Hull's behaviorism has often been called "rat psychology," and there is truth in this derision, to be sure. But to see this truth and none other would be to miss the point entirely. Hull's retail theory was not simply an interpretation of how hungry rats learn to push levers and run mazes; it was intended as a paradigm of psychological functioning in general. Similarly, Skinner's "pigeon psychology" does not derive from a simple interest in seeing how many clever things an essentially witless creature can be trained to perform. Hull, Skinner, and Watson, too, were all playing for much higher stakes. It was nothing less than to turn psychological thinking upside down—or as Skinner prefers putting it, "inside out."

This is the very heart of the behavioristic movement in all of its phases. For all its success as experimental science and technology, for all the empirical riches it has produced, it is still in very large measure what William James described as "philosophic faith, bred . . . from an aesthetic demand." It is, moreover, at its core the same philosophic faith that James was criticizing when he used the phrase in 1890, namely, mechanism-automatism. The aesthetic demand that underlay the late nineteenth-century version of this philosophic faith seems to have been that things should be neat, orderly, and thoroughly grounded in palpable material reality. For the modern behavioristic version, two other conditions appear to have been added: that things should also be predictable and controllable. It is certainly for these reasons that behaviorism has tended to steer clear of the possibility that there might be complex, active processes going on *inside* the organism. For while such processes might still be grounded in palpable material reality (a complex, active central nervous system), they would be a can of worms with respect to the demand that things be neat, orderly, predictable, and controllable.

The tendency is especially obvious in the current behaviorism of Skinner, whose rejection of active internal processes has been even more thoroughgoing than Watson's. Watson had at least admitted the possibility of "centrally aroused" mental processes; and his rejection of the possibility was quite deliberate, on the grounds that if it were true there would be a "serious limitation on the side of *method* in behaviorism." Hull had also admitted the possibility of central processes, so long as they could be tamely herded into his corral of "pure stimulus acts." Skinner, on the other hand, has rejected them utterly. He of course admits that there is a nervous system "inside the skin" and that thoughts and feelings occur in connection with it. What he most vigorously denies is that there is anything in all this that would seriously complicate the quest for neatness, predictability, and control. Here, for example, is his view of consciousness in relation to the nervous system. The assumptions, even the words, would have been quite at home in the late nineteenth-century strongholds of mechanism-automatism.

> After all, what are the anatomy and physiology of the inner eye? So far as we know, self-observation must be confined to the three nervous systems [previously described]—an interoceptive nervous system going to the viscera, a proprioceptive nervous system going to the skeletal frame, and an exteroceptive [external sense organ] system bringing a person mainly into contact with the world around him. . . . All that a person comes to know about himself with their help is just more stimuli and responses. He does not make contact with that vast nervous system that mediates his behavior. He does not because he has no nerves going to the right places.[9]

And what of that vast nervous system that mediates behavior? Here Skinner distinguishes between the "real nervous system" and the "conceptual nervous system." Not to put too fine a point on it, the conceptual nervous system is what the nervous system has been falsely conceived to be by those who would regard it as active and integrative (these include even some misguided neurophysiologists). The real nervous system is the one which, when its details are finally worked out by physiologists, will be seen to be entirely consistent with the view that the true sources of behavior are not to be found inside the skin, much less in the "depths of mind or personality," but rather in "genetic history, environmental history, and the present setting—all of which lie outside."[10] If this is not an act of philosophic faith, one hardly knows what is.

## NOTES

1. C. L. Hull, "Mind, Mechanism, and Adaptive Behavior," *Psychological Review,* 44 (1937).
2. C. L. Hull, *Principles of Behavior: An Introduction to Behavior Theory* (New York: Appleton-Century-Crofts, 1943), p. 58.
3. E. L. Thorndike, "Animal Intelligence: An Experimental Study of the Associative Processes in Animals," *Psychological Review* (Series of Monograph Supplements), 2 (1898), p. 13.
4. Hull, *Principles of Behavior,* p. 18.
5. Ibid., p. 298.
6. C. L. Hull, *A Behavior System* (New Haven: Yale University Press, 1952), p. 6.
7. Ibid.
8. Ibid.,p. 151.
9. B. F. Skinner, *About Behaviorism* (New York: Alfred A. Knopf, 1974), p. 216.
10. Ibid., p. 225.

## FOR FURTHER READING

For the student who might wish to follow Hull's theorizings at length, the following sequence would be recommended: "Knowledge and Purpose as Habit Mechanisms," *Psychological Review*, 37 (1930); "Mind, Mechanism, and Adaptive Behavior," *Psychological Review*, 44 (1937); *Principles of Behavior: An Introduction to Behavior Theory* (New York: Appleton-Century-Crofts, 1943); *Essentials of Behavior* (New Haven: Yale University Press, 1951); and *A Behavior System* (New Haven: Yale University Press, 1952).

Also recommended is Hull's autobiographical statement in E. G. Boring, H. S. Langfell, H. Werner, R. M. Yerkes, eds., *A History of Psychology in Autobiography*, vol. IV (Worcester, Mass.: Clark University Press, 1952).

Of the attempt to apply Hullian principles to broader psychological issues, the following volumes are the best examples by far: J. Dollard, L. W. Doob, N. E. Miller, O. H. Mowrer, and R. R. Sears, *Frustration and Aggression* (New Haven: Yale University Press, 1939); N. E. Miller and J. Dollard, *Social Learning and Imitation* (New Haven: Yale University Press, 1941); and J. Dollard and N. E. Miller, *Personality and Psychotherapy* (New York: McGraw-Hill, 1950).

B. F. Skinner's book-length works include: *The Behavior of Organisms: An Experimental Analysis* (New York: Appleton-Century-Crofts, 1938); a utopian novel, *Walden Two* (New York: Macmillan, 1948); *Science and Human Behavior* (New York: Macmillan, 1953); *Verbal Behavior* (New York: Appleton-Century-Crofts, 1957); *Schedules of Reinforcement* (New York: Appleton-Century-Crofts, 1957); *The Technology of Teaching* (New York: Appleton-Century-Crofts, 1968); *Contingencies of Reinforcement: A Theoretical Analysis* (New York: Appleton-Century-Crofts, 1969); *Beyond Freedom and Dignity* (New York: Alfred A. Knopf, 1971); *Cumulative Record* (New York: Appleton-Century-Crofts, 1959, 1961, 1972); and *About Behaviorism* (New York: Alfred A. Knopf, 1974). Of these, *Walden Two* and *Beyond Freedom and Dignity* are the books that reached the widest popular audience. G. S. Reynolds presents a crisp, concise summary of the technical side of the Skinnerian approach in his *Primer of Operant Conditioning* (Glenview, Illinois: Scott, Foresman and Co., 1968).

# Chapter 14
# Epilogue: Ideals and Over-Beliefs

Such, then, are the views regarding *psyche* that have come down to us and the grounds on which they are held.

Aristotle, *De Anima*

The most interesting and valuable things about a man are his ideals and over-beliefs. The same is true of nations and historic epochs; and the excesses of which the particular individuals and epochs are guilty are compensated in the total, and become profitable to mankind in the long run.

William James, Preface to *The Will to Believe and Other Essays in Popular Philosophy* (1897)

Our preceding description of behaviorism as a philosophic faith does not distinguish it from any of the other psychological theorizings that we have examined. Certainly psychoanalytic theory has a large component of philosophic faith; so does Gestalt theory; and so, indeed, do all the other psychological "schools" and "isms." The same is true of a great many theorizings that have appeared in the biological and physical sciences as well. Every science has had its grand visions—its ideals and over-beliefs, going beyond what is compelled by the facts—of what its subject matter is really all about. We could probably not get rid of this visionary tendency in psychology even if we tried, and that is just as well, for we would surely be throwing out the baby with the bath if we did so.

Still, there is a bath that needs to be thrown out, or at least clearly recognized; and that is what we must now turn to examine. One of its chief sources is the fact that these visions are, after all, a kind of *faith* that the truth of things will turn out to be pretty much what one believes it to be in the first place. Whether we call them visionary over-beliefs, theoretical first-principles, or simply points of view, these visions of what the subject matter is really all about are not just tentative, dispassionate hypotheses that one is willing to abandon at a moment's notice. They are objects of commitment, and the great risk is that we will cling to them come what may, exaggerating some truths, ignoring others, and overall becoming so entangled in the psychological vision as to distort, or be blinded to, important parts of psychological reality. It is a very delicate balance. On the one hand there is value in pursuing one's vision as far as it can be taken, in order to see where it will lead. But the ledge is narrow and strewn with pitfalls. There are two kinds of pitfalls, in particular, to which psychological theorizing has shown itself to be especially susceptible.

## THEORETICAL JUGGERNAUTS

Here is a dynamism that seems to be inherent in theorizing of almost any sort. Once assumptions are made, they tend to run like snowballs down a hill, gathering mass and momentum as they go. A large part of the dynamism is explained by a single word—logic. If one begins by assuming that A and B are true, one might then be led by the logic of the case to assume that C and D are true also. Then, in order to reconcile C and D with a certain range of facts, the further assumptions E, F, and G might also have to be added. These, in turn, might lead by logic to H, I, and J, which then need to be reconciled with some other range of facts through the introduction of yet further assumptions. And so on down the line. The result can be an elaborate tissue of explanations, no single one of which was required by the facts, or even suggested by them, apart from the web of assumptions in which the theory's author was entangled.

The process is especially obvious in those cases where the initial assumption is patently untrue. Here is a famous example from the early history of physics, which shows one aspect of this first pitfall in sharp relief. Medieval physicists believed (following Aristotle) that an inanimate object could be in motion only insofar as it was impelled by an external motive force, that is, only insofar as its motion was both initiated and *sustained* by an external "mover." Up to a point the theory made perfectly good sense; ox carts, for example, do not move without oxen. But beyond that point it quickly ran afoul of the facts. Take, for example, the case of an arrow shot from a bow. According to the theory, the arrow should move only so long as it is impelled by its external mover, the bowstring; the moment it loses contact with the bowstring it should stop dead in its tracks and fall straight to the ground. Much to the theory's embarrassment, however, arrows—even medieval arrows—perversely refused to comply with the expectation; they kept right on going!

Faced with this embarrassing discrepancy between fact and theory—between what *should* be and what *is*—medieval physics had only two possible courses open to it: accommodate the theory to the fact or the fact to the theory. And because the medieval world was so deeply committed to the theory (by reason of its venerable origins and its connection with the Aristotelian proof of the existence of God as "Unmoved Mover"), only the second of these was really a live possibility. The task was not an easy one, but medieval physics was fully equal to it. Behold: The arrow, as it is moved along by the bowstring, displaces the air from each new position that it comes to occupy. Conversely, when it vacates a position, it leaves a vacuum in its wake. Nature of course abhors a vacuum (*vide* Aristotle), and so it happens that air keeps rushing in to fill the spaces successively vacated by the arrow. It is this continuous turbulent rush of air behind the arrow that takes up where the bowstring leaves off, impelling the arrow along until it finds its mark. Q.E.D.

The explanation was a bald contrivance whose only reason for being was that it was required in order to square the facts with the theory. Certainly it would not have been suggested by the facts alone, independently of the theory. Indeed, it had its own problems with the facts. It would have had to predict, for example, that a ribbon tied to the arrow's tail would be pushed forward from its point of attachment; whereas it would in fact trail along behind. Medieval physicists would have been well aware of this perverse noncompliance of the ribbon—but undoubtedly they had an explanation for that too! For such is the agility of the human mind in clinging to its theories, faiths, and prejudices, come what may.

It is less easy in psychology to find initial assumptions that are patently untrue—or, at least, that we can all agree are patently untrue. Here is one that comes fairly close. The early tradition of mental mechanism began by assuming that all of "our knowledge and ideas" derive *wholly* from sensory experience. It did this, not because the assumption was demanded by the facts, but because it wanted to toss overboard all of the philosophical and theological baggage that had come with the contrary doctrine of innate ideas. Like the medieval theory of motion, this "empiricist" assumption worked just fine up to a point, namely, so long as it was dealing with immediate perception and specific memory, and did not look too closely into either. But what of abstract ideas, imagination, visualization, reasoning, and other such knowledges and ideas that cannot readily be traced to particular sensory experiences? *Voila!* It must be that all experience is composed of simple, atomic units, and that these units then serve as building blocks for the associative fabrication of the mind's more complex phenomena. A later generation of mental mechanists accepted this contrivance of simple mental units as a first-principle, combined it with some assumptions about the nervous system, and came up with the further *ad hoc* contrivances of "local signs" and "unconscious inference" to explain how it is that we can perceive spatial relationships in the absence of any particular simple sensations corresponding to these relationships.

But even when the initial assumptions are not patently untrue, the theoretical snowball effect can still be discerned readily enough. Take, for example the first principle shared by all versions of automaton theory, to the effect that consciousness is causally irrelevant to behavior. It is neither obviously true nor obviously untrue, neither required by the facts nor compellingly contradicted by them; and it is not likely to be definitely proved or disproved for a long time to come, if ever. Nevertheless, let the assumption once be made and down the hill it rolls, picking up further assumptions along the way. Watson: "so-called thinking" is just subvocal speech. Hull: consciousness is a pure-stimulus act, a mere passive link in the chain of stimulus-response connections. Skinner: much of what we call consciousness is just "verbal behavior"; and for all the rest, it is "just more stimuli and responses." Freud: consciousness is not a producer of action, but only a "gateway" to it, a merely passive "sense-organ for the perception of psychical qualities." Gestalt: consciousness is just the passive, isomorphic, phenomenal counterpart of underlying neural processes. The common thrust of all these second-stage assumptions is that the only real actor in the drama, once the effects of bodily states and environment are taken into account, is the nervous system. Or perhaps this assumption came first and was then followed by the assumption concerning the causal irrelevancy of consciousness. In either case, assumptions about the nature of the nervous system also get mixed into it sooner or later: that it is basically a reflexive apparatus; a great commutative switchboard of stimulus-response connections; a field-volume conductor tending toward equilibrium of forces; a quasihydraulic apparatus whose primary process is to discharge excitation as expeditiously as possible; or a vast unknown "inside the skin," whose details, when finally they are worked out, will show that operant conditioning explains everything after all. Down and down they roll, growing ever larger: habit strength; reinforcement; secondary reinforcement; behavior chaining; primary and secondary processes; displacement; *Prägnanz;* on and on.

The situation is of course more complicated than this brief description might have it seem. For one thing, the assumptions that underlie psychological theorizings do not usually make their appearance in such nice, neat, logical sequence. More often they come as a package, the snowball having already rolled in the author's mind before words are set to paper. For another, they do not often come dressed as assumptions, but rather as facts, self-evident truths, or "the only reasonable hypothesis." But the general point still holds. Assumptions do not stand passively by—they lead to consequences, which lead to other consequences, and so on down the line. Once Freud assumed, for example, that the "psychical apparatus" is basically a reflexive apparatus, whose principal aim is to maintain or achieve quiescence by discharging excitation, he could hardly avoid drawing the distinction between "primary" and "secondary" processes; for the "secondary process" of "storing energy" was then required in order to square the initial assumption with the plain fact that many human phenomena seem to be the result of something other than reflexive discharge. And once he assumed that stimulation is pain, and its absence pleasure, he was well on his way to discovering that beyond this pleasure principle lay the "death instinct." Here, indeed, was a conceptual juggernaut of the first rank. A young boy repeatedly performed an act of childish play. And since it involved stimulation rather than quiescence, it could not possibly be pleasurable for him. Ergo it was something else, a compulsion to *repeat*, based on a deeper tendency to *restore* the greatest quiescence of all, nonlivingness, abiosis, death. The comparable example from the behavioristic side is Hull's "conditioned inhibition." The die was cast the moment he assumed that learning is a matter of stimulus-response bonds strengthened by "reinforcement." Phenomena such as spontaneous recovery and savings required the further assumption that these bonds, once strengthened, remain so. Mix these two assumptions together, fold in the phenomena of extinction for leavening, and the only possible outcome is conditioned inhibition or something very much like it.

Although Freud's "death instinct" and Hull's "conditioned inhibition" both referred to facts, neither would have been suggested by the facts alone, apart from the prior assumptions. It would probably be a healthy strategy to suspect that all psychological explanatory conceptions possess this characteristic in some degree. There is a commonly expressed view that holds the development of a science to consist in the slow but steady accumulation of facts and in the equally slow but steady progression of explanatory conceptions to which these facts give rise. Thus we find quite a few psychological theorists contending, as did Freud, that their theoretical notions evolved "as a direct expression of experience . . . [by] hypotheses which were designed [only] to facilitate the handling of the material." But alas, in psychology as elsewhere, the claim is often much exaggerated. Explanatory conceptions rarely if every come into being solely as "expressions of experience." This is not to suggest that their genesis is entirely unrelated to experience, but it does mean that these conceptions bring with them, almost always, an entourage of extraempirical assumptions.

And here lies the great danger, for in the course of time the distinction between fact and hypothesis begins to blur, and things that are properly assumptions are taken to be parts of the discipline's factual subject matter. William James wrote of such assumptions that once they have "established themselves (as they have a way of doing in our very descriptions of phenomenal facts) it is almost impossible to get rid of them afterwards or to make anyone see that they are not essential features of the subject." This is exactly what had happened with the doctrine of simple sensations, which was the particular assumption that James had in mind when he wrote this passage. By the time the Wundtians took over the doctrine in the late nineteenth century, it had long since ceased to be an assumption or hypothesis, and had become simply a *fact*. Well, not really a fact, but so taken for granted as one that it was difficult for anyone steeped in the tradition to see that it was not.

A prime contemporary example would be the concept of reinforcement. In whichever clothing this concept might come dressed—Hullian or Skinnerian—its principal aim is to explain the process of learning in one way and to avoid explaining it in another. Specifically, it aims to explain the learning process solely in terms of environment and behavior (for Hull add drive, stimulus-response bonds, and habit strength) and to avoid explaining it in terms of such behavioristic anathemas as mental processes, intelligence, insight, and the like. Up to a point the reinforcement concept works quite well, and certainly it has led to some interesting discoveries. But for all that, it is still a theoretical construction, an hypothesis, an extra-empirical vision of what the subject matter is really all about. It is of course perfectly legitimate to adopt and pursue such a vision, so long as it is clearly held in view that this is what one is doing. What has happened, however, is that with each passing decade the extra-empirical status of reinforcement has grown less clear, so that nowadays even those who do not accept the full scheme of behaviorism tend to take the "fact" or reinforcement entirely for granted. Some might follow Hull and consider that what is getting "reinforced" is a stimulus-response bond. Others, following Skinner's lead, might substitute response probability for Hull's stimulus-response bond. In either case the assumption, when taken as a fact, brings with it a tendency to see some aspects of the phenomena as fundamental, others as secondary or derivative, and still others as just illusory pseudophenomena. The risk pertains to assumptions in general, but especially to those that get sanctified as essential features of the subject: they will work as lenses that selectively magnify some aspects of the subject matter, sometimes larger than life, while diminishing others, sometimes to the vanishing point.

A part of the problem is that the names by which our theoretical conceptions are known get incorporated into our language; and then, when these words are used to describe phenomena, they tend to bring with them, at least tacitly, the whole web of presuppositions in which they are entangled. A description cast in terms of reinforcement, for example, does not just describe the facts; it divides them up in its own particular way, stretching here, trimming there, and overall tailoring the phenomena to fit the preconceived pattern. Thus, the A that a student receives on an exam is a "positive reinforcer" by which she will be "conditioned" to "emit" similar studying behavior prior to the next exam. (When the instructor says "There will be an exam next Tuesday," that is a "discriminative stimulus" for the emission of conditioned studying behavior.) The D that a second student receives is a "negative reinforcer"; and if this student subsequently mends his ways and studies harder for the next exam, instead of partying, it is because the partying behavior has been subjected to "aversive conditioning." If, on the other hand, he keeps right on partying, it is because the discriminative stimuli that cue the partying behavior, and the reinforcers that sustain it, are too strong; or perhaps because the D was too weak a negative reinforcer.

Anyone who has spent much time among psychologists has heard descriptions of this sort uttered in all sincerity, and with little apparent recognition of the considerable presuppositional baggage that they carry with them. Such a person will also have heard descriptions couched in other theoretical languages, and the same point can be made for these as well. Consider how very much is being assumed, for example, when one describes fantasy as "primary-process thinking" and logical inference as "secondary-process thinking"; or when something is described as an instance of repression, "displacement," or "sublimation." Certainly it is possible to use these terms without affirming the whole corpus of Freudian theory—but they come trailing clouds of assumptions nonetheless.

Once again, it is a question of striking a balance. It would be naïve to suppose that our dealings with psychological reality could ever be pure and unsullied by presupposition. Nor would we want it so, for presupposition is the inescapable accompaniment of hypothesis, vision, and imagination. The risk lies not in the mere having of guiding assumptions, but in becoming entangled in them. The second pitfall is a special case of such entanglement, for which psychological theorizing in almost all its forms has shown a particular partiality.

## THE GREAT GOLDEN TRUTH SYNDROME

In the closing chapter of one of his latest books, B. F. Skinner notes that his behavioristic approach is "especially vulnerable to the charge of simplification because it is hard to believe that a fairly simple principle [contingencies of reinforcement] can have vast consequences in our lives." The statement itself is something of a simplification, for what the critics have found difficult to believe is not that a simple principle can have *vast* consequences, but that it can have *all* consequences. And this, after all, is what Skinner is really claiming—not that contingencies of reinforcement explain a lot, but that they explain just about *everything!* Can contingencies of reinforcement "really be the roots of wars, say, or—at the other extreme—of art, music, and literature," as Skinner claims? For that matter, can they really be the roots of B. F. Skinner? Undoubtedly they are *among* the roots, but is it not just a bit of an exaggeration to say that they are *the* roots? Skinner, of course, is not the only one who has fallen into this pit. Exaggeration and oversimplification are the inevitable results of trying to explain the whole, complex, hurley-burley array of psychological phenomena by means of one or a few fairly simple principles.

This, however, is only the shallowest part of the pit. The great temptation, to which so many psychological theorizings have succumbed, is to proclaim (in effect) something like this: Here it is, the Great Golden Truth, the grand unifying principle; and everything we can know, everything we need to know, is either contained therein or derivable therefrom. Such an extravagant claim can fuel the enthusiasm of both leaders and followers, and it can make for some exciting, perhaps useful controversy along the way. But it can also be an impediment of the most severe kind. For what it is saying is: These are the limits; there is nothing beyond them. It was the custom of medieval mapmakers to draw in the Atlantic coasts of Europe and Africa, and then to the west of these to inscribe the words *Ne Plus Ultra*—"Beyond this point there is nothing." But of course there *was* something beyond that point; and if the history of science and exploration shows anything at all, it is that there is likely to be *something* beyond almost any point that we might have the temerity to declare a boundary. There is surely no reason to suppose that this lesson is any less applicable in psychology than in, say, physics or astronomy. In all likelihood it is more applicable, since our maps in psychology are far sketchier than anything physics or astronomy have seen for several hundred years. Perhaps this is because the psychological landscape is more varied and complex. Whatever the reason, it is a presumption of the highest order to suppose that there is nothing beyond the current horizon. It is exactly what James had in mind when he cautioned against a "premature closing of our accounts with reality."

Freud, Watson, Hull, Skinner, the Gestaltists, and before them the mental mechanists, the Physiological mechanists, the Wundtians—all had their Great Goden Truths. In each case there was a certain grain of truth, some principle or set of principles that made perfectly good sense up to a point. For the behaviorists, it was that environmental contingencies can affect the likelihood of certain kinds of behavior being performed; for Gestalt, that perception is a function of the configurational properties of the stimulus; and for Freud, that sexuality can be a powerful human drive, that there are dynamic processes going on beneath the surface of consciousness, and so on. So, too, for the earlier schemes of mental and physiological mechanism: the former with its focus on the processes of association, the latter in making the point that bodily mechanisms alone (*sans* "mind") can account for at least a certain portion of psychological phenomena. In each case, however, what happened was that the grain of truth, which served quite well in limited application, was inflated into a kind of cosmic principle. In mellower moments, each would have admitted that the scheme was incomplete, that details needed to be worked out, loose ends tied off, and so forth. But each also proclaimed that their scheme made closest contact with the basic truth of things, and thus that everything known or potentially knowable was included within its purview.

## STRIKING THE BALANCE

These, then, are the major risks of psychological theorizing. We now come to the question of what can be done about them. One obvious answer would be to point out that the surest way to avoid the risks of an activity is to avoid the activity itself. In the present case, however, that would not be a solution, but only a different kind of problem. For one thing, it is exceedingly unlikely that we really could avoid theorizing—and any pretense that we were doing so, when we were not, would only exacerbate the problems. But even if it were possible, it would be like avoiding the risks of falling by never letting our feet leave the ground: there would certainly be security in this, but only at the price of never climbing very high or seeing very far.

We cannot have it both ways. Either we have our visions and risk the problems, or we forego the visions and turn psychology into something bland, tepid, and probably inconsequential. Without its visionary over-beliefs, psychology would be only a collection of mute facts and pedestrian generalizations, perhaps also of some more or less marketable technical skills. It might be the very epitome of "science" in some narrow, idealized, positivistic sense of the term; but for all that, it would probably never find or do anything very interesting, except by accident, because it would have no synoptic vision, no mountains to climb, and no sense of momentous issues hanging in the balance. Try to imagine what a sterile affair psychology would be today without the visionary enthusiasms of those twentieth-century figures whom we have mentioned in this book, plus those of a great many others whom we have not mentioned: Jung, Fromm, Mowrer, Maslow, Piaget, Rogers, Murphy, Murray, Allport, to name only a few. Certainly it is possible to become carried away by our visions into entanglement, exaggeration, and all the rest. The risk that we run without them, however, is not to be carried anywhere at all.

So how shall we strike the balance? Our best hope, it seems to me, is to cultivate our theoretical visions as fully as possible, while at the same time making them run the most rigorous gauntlet of critical skepticism. If the lessons of psychology's history are to be trusted, this gauntlet is especially called for by those theorizings that might seem at first blush to be "obvious," "required by the facts," or "the only reasonable hypothesis," as they are the least likely to inspire skepticism spontaneously. It is easy enough to be critical and skeptical of theorizings that do not appeal to one's own sense of what the truth of things really is. The trick is to bring the same attitude to bear on those that do appeal. Yet this is where it is most needed, because it is here that flawed assumptions are most likely to go unexamined and, so, to take root, flourish, and spread out in all directions. William James put it all quite succinctly a century ago. The only way to prevent our theoretical visions from running away with us, he advised, is to "scrutinize them beforehand and make them give an articulate account of themselves before letting them pass." It is no mere intellectual exercise, but a matter of the utmost practical importance. For the truth is that there *are* mountains to climb in psychology—and momentous issues *do* hang in the balance.

# Index